Christian Marriage
A Sacrament of Love

A Christian Perspective on Marriage, Love, and Human Sexuality

Ronald J. Wilkins
Mary E. Gryczka

Religious Education Division
Wm. C. Brown Company Publishers
Dubuque, Iowa

Nihil Obstat
   Rev. Richard L. Schaefer

Imprimatur
   ✠Most Rev. Daniel W. Kucera, O.S.B.
   Archbishop of Dubuque
   June 21, 1985

The Nihil Obstat and the Imprimatur are official declarations that a book or a pamphlet is free of doctrinal or moral error. No implication is contained therein that those who have granted the Nihil Obstat or Imprimatur agree with the contents, opinions, or statements expressed.

Book Team

Publisher—Ernest T. Nedder
Editorial Director—Sandra J. Hirstein
Production Editor—Mary Jo Graham
Art Director—Janet K. Helms
Photo Research—Karla McCarey

Scripture Sources

Good News Bible: The Bible in Today's English Version. Old Testament: © American Bible Society, 1976. New Testament: © American Bible Society, 1966, 1971, 1976. Maps © United Bible Societies, 1976.

The New American Bible, copyright © 1970 by Benziger, Inc.

The Jerusalem Bible, copyright © 1966, 1967, and 1968 by Darton, Longman & Todd LTD and Doubleday & Company, Inc.

Photo Credits

Michael Carpenter—2, 10 right, 197
Bob Coyle—cover, vi, 75, 92
Louis Cremonie—40 right, 156, 194
Mimi Forsyth—40 left, 72, 90, 100
Frank Harrison—190
Brent Jones—8, 48
Carolyn McKeone—9, 10 left, 49, 71, 74, 78, 108, 111, 112, 122, 126, 132, 137, 141, 142, 144, 147, 149, 161, 165, 166, 184, 193, 199
Jim Shaffer—6, 13, 15 left, 15 right, 16, 24 left, 24 right, 27, 29 right, 30, 38, 43, 47, 50, 54, 57, 58, 61, 64, 77, 81, 86, 94, 104, 107, 115, 125, 128, 131, 138, 151, 153, 168, 171, 172, 177, 180, 201, 208, 214
David Strickler—29 left, 82, 143
United Press International—195
Jim Whitmer—18, 53, 99, 117, 162, 212, 215

ISBN 0–697–02071–1

10 9 8 7 6 5 4 3 2

Contents

On Being an Adult Catholic

The people of our time are more and more convinced that the human person's dignity and vocation demand that they should discover, by the light of their own intelligence, the values innate in their nature, that they should ceaselessly develop these values and realize them in their lives, in order to achieve an ever greater development.

— Sacred Congregation for the Doctrine of the Faith, December 29, 1975

A unique aspect of the Christian religion is belief in the interrelatedness between God's self-revelation and people's created destiny. Christians believe that God has revealed through the Bible that people are created to share God's life and that they (Christians) should share that belief with others.

The Old Testament is filled with examples of people being "called" by God to play important roles in His plans for creation. Abraham was called from his native land, Ur, an ancient city at the eastern end of what is now Iraq, to Canaan, roughly, modern Palestine. He was called to be "the Father of the Jewish people," and it is to him that Judaism traces its origins (Genesis 12–25). Noah is pictured in the Old Testament being called by God to save the human race from the great flood (Genesis 7–9) and Joseph, one of Jacob's sons, was called by God to save the Jewish people and the Egyptians from starvation (Genesis 37–48). The most famous call in the Old Testament is the call of Moses to lead the Jewish people out of slavery in Egypt and to bring them into the Promised Land (Exodus 2–20). All of the Old Testament prophets were called by God to fulfill a special mission in the religious history of ancient Israel. In all of these events, and in all other cases of people being "called" by God to do His will in Jewish history, it is important to note that God uses people to carry out His plans. The "chosen people" have a religious mission in life.

This theme is also carried forth in the New Testament. There Jesus is sent by God to save people from a nondivine existence to share God's life forever (John 14:23). The apostles were called by Jesus (Matthew 4:18–22, 9:9, 10:1–5) and sent to "make disciples of all nations" (Matthew 28:16–20). St. Paul was called by God to be an apostle (Acts 9) and Stephen and the other deacons were called to fulfill a special social ministry in the first days of the Church (Acts 6).

This consciousness of being selected and having a mission to bring the message of Jesus to others is at the heart of what being a Christian is. This being called and the responding to the call is "the Christian vocation." All Catholics are called to this mission. It comes with being baptized. It is affirmed in the Sacrament of Confirmation and becomes a reality at the beginning of adolescence. It is usually during middle and late adolescence that young men and young women become more aware that they are called "to be Christ" to their world. Most young Catholics do not realize that all Christians are called to be Christ to their world—not just priests and nuns.

This consciousness of being selected and having a mission to bring the message of Jesus to others is at the heart of what being a Christian is. This being called and the responding to the call is "the Christian vocation."

Responding to the Call during Adulthood

It is when Catholics enter adulthood that they are able to more fully carry out the call to bring the message of Jesus to their wider world (Matthew 28:20). It is there that they can have the greatest influence. It is in what they do and say that they can influence the political, economic, and cultural world in which they live.

Mothers and fathers, for example, influence the way their families grow and develop. They have a special "family vocation" to raise their children religiously—introducing them to Catholic ways when they are young and training them as they grow into adolescence. They have, as we say, an obligation to pass on their religious heritage to their children and give them the opportunity to live it.

Vocation: strong impulse to follow a particular career.

In their social and business world, adult Catholics are called on to influence the people among whom they live and work. They are called to help develop in society and in the political, economic, and financial world of their job, their city, and their nation a religious consciousness based upon their conviction of the Fatherhood of God and the common humanity of all people. "You are the salt of the earth," Jesus said to his followers. "You are the light of the world," he continued. ". . . your light must shine before people so that they may see goodness in your acts and give praise to your heavenly Father" (Matthew 5:13–15). Adult Catholics are called on to live their lives in response to the Christian principles they say they believe in. "The fact is," says St. Paul, "that whether you eat or drink—whatever you do—you should do all for the glory of God" (1 Corinthians 10:31).

> *"What specifically characterizes the laity is their secular nature. . . . The laity, by their special vocation, seek the kingdom of God by engaging in temporal affairs and by ordering them to the plan of God. . . . The laity are called in a special way to make the church present and operative in those places and circumstances where only through them can it become the salt of the earth."*
>
> —*Vacitan Council II*
> Constitution on the Church

Special Vocations among Adult Catholics

Some adult Catholics respond to their Christian vocation by choosing to live lives of special dedication to God in what is known as "the religious life." They give particular witness to the Christian vocation of religious service by the special kind of life they live. They pledge themselves by vows or solemn promises to the special work of the religious group to which they belong. They direct whatever economic prosperity may be theirs to the work of their religious community, and they give up marriage in order to devote their entire lives to the work of the religious group.

Women "religious" are often called "sisters" because they live together in community as sisters, or else "nuns". . . from "nonna," the female form of the Latin word "nunnus" which means "monk." They give special witness to their Catholic vocation by the kind of lives they lead as nurses, teachers, scientists, doctors, missioners, lawyers, day-care-center workers, and so forth. They bring a special religious dedication and witness to the world in which they live and work. Some women "religious" live together as cloistered nuns and choose to live lives dedicated almost exclusively to prayer and worship, rather than to social involvement in the wider world. They remain within their convents, removed from the active world around them. They give constant witness to the "God-ness" of creation. Their lives are a witness to others that there is a dimension of life beyond the activity in the world of economic and political gain.

Men who choose the special Catholic vocation as "religious," taking vows of poverty, chastity, and obedience, may be either priests or "brothers." They, too, live in and with a community dedicated to special social or religious service. If they are priests, they are ordained to be special ministers of the liturgy. If they are "brothers," they are not ordained. Like the sisters or nuns, men religious dedicate their lives to special social service or to lives of prayer and worship. In the first case, they live in a "religious house." In the second, they live in a "monastery."

Some Catholic men are called to the special religious vocation of the Catholic Church called "the priesthood." They are called to be the "Eucharistic ministers" of the people. They devote their lives to building up, sanctifying, and pastoring the Body of Christ by proclaiming the Good News of Jesus Christ, through personal witness, missionary work, catechesis (teaching), celebrating the sacraments, and serving the spiritual and other needs of the people. They are "ordained" for this role. That is, they are chosen by the community—through the bishop of the diocese—they are trained, and, through the Sacrament of Holy Orders, they are given special privileges and powers reserved for the special ministry of the priesthood. They are highly visible witnesses of the Catholic Church's role as a worshipping community devoted to the work of Jesus in the world of people.

All Catholics are called to be witnesses to the coming of Jesus and to spread his message. Some are called to do so as "lay" persons, some as "religious," some as priests. By far, the greater number are called to do so as married people. It is to them that this book is devoted. It attempts to give a Catholic perspective to the human drama of married life and to help Catholic married couples and their children understand their role as Catholics in their family life.

Introduction

There are many ways to interpret and explain marriage, human love, and sex. *Christian Marriage: A Sacrament of Love* presents a Catholic interpretation. Starting from the same basic premises about marriage, love, and human sexuality that most people acknowledge (that human love is unique; that sexual expressions of love are enjoyable and urgent; that marriage is the expression of a special relationship between a man and a woman), Catholics interpret love, sex, and marriage from a religious standpoint. They believe that each one of these realities individually and all together flow from the dynamics of God's creative acts and design and that they have a religious meaning, purpose, and goal. *Christian Marriage: A Sacrament of Love* is written for young people in search of an understanding of the Catholic Church's interpretation of the meaning of love, sex, and marriage in the life of a Christian.

Understanding sex, love, and marriage, however, goes beyond merely acquiring information. It includes meaning, sensitivity, and reverence. Without meaning, love, sex, and marriage are sterile. Without sensitivity, they are selfish. Without reverence, they are exploitive. *Christian Marriage: A Sacrament of Love* brings the dimensions of meaning, sensitivity, and reverence as they are understood by the Catholic community to its discussions of sex, love, and marriage.

To achieve its goal, *Christian Marriage: A Sacrament of Love* discusses what sex is for Christians, what sexual feelings are and what they mean, what the sexual natures of men and women are—the complementarity of men and women as they live out their lives in shared relationships—and what marriage is for Catholic Christians.

Christian Marriage: A Sacrament of Love is also written for young men and women beginning the search for their own sexual identity. It assumes that they have long since become familiar with sexual facts and are in search of the meaning of sex in their lives. It is hoped that through a thorough, prayerful study of the Christian meaning of sex, love, and marriage afforded by this book, they will arrive at a better understanding of themselves and others as sexual beings, of the meaning of sex in their own lives, and of the sacredness of Christian marriage. If they do, they will embark on a road of human happiness, comfortable with themselves as men or women, at ease with others as men or as women, and confident in God, the Source of their human sexuality.

The authors gratefully acknowledge the advice, assistance, and encouragement of Anita Hocker, Director of Health Education, Sarasota (Florida) County Schools. She provided the authors with results of her research in the areas of sex education and the needs of high school students, and provided valuable insights and materials on parenting and on abused children and abused spouses. They also acknowledge, with gratitude, the help and encouragement they received from their spouses; from Sister Gloria Hillman, O.P., Director of Religious Education, St. Thomas More Church, Sarasota, Florida; and from the many parents, students, and friends who cooperated in the writing of this book. Without their immense help, this book could not have been written.

Mary Gryczka
Ron Wilkins
May 1985

Part 1

Marriage: A Sacrament of Love

The family is the first and fundamental school of social living. As a community of love, it finds in self-giving the law that guides it and makes it grow. The self-giving that inspires the love of husband and wife for each other is the model and norm for the self-giving that must be practiced in the relationships between brothers and sisters and the different generations living together in the family.

— Pope John Paul II

Chapter 1

CHRISTIAN MARRIAGE

Marriage: Totally Committed Love

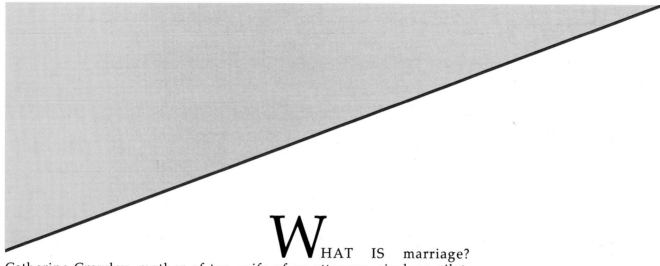

W HAT IS marriage? Catherine Crowley, mother of ten, wife of an attorney, airplane pilot, teacher, and president of the Glenview, Illinois, Park Board says, "It's love and caring, happiness and sorrow, privacy and sharing. It's fidelity and honor and patience and compassion. It's frustration and quiet contentment. It's idealism and realism. It's almost what the romanticists say it is and never what the pessimists say. It's giving and receiving, sacrifice, and self-control, growing and learning, understanding and acceptance. It's housework and dishes and diapers. It's money worries and sickness, disagreements and conflicts, hurts and squabbling children. It's babies and pets, and in-laws and relatives. It's great joy and bitter disappointment. It's being with the ones you love. It's loving and being loved. It's the greatest thing that can happen to you, if you let it. It's whatever I put into it. For me, my marriage, my husband, and my children are my life."

1. How does Mrs. Crowley describe her marriage—theoretically or from what she experienced? Which do you think is the best way to understand marriage?
2. From your own experience, how is marriage generally pictured in the movies and on TV? Do you know of any exceptions? Can you name examples of both kinds—the typical and the exception?
3. What do you think marriage is?
4. Why do people get married?
5. What do most people expect from marriage? Some time in the next couple of days, separately, ask boys and girls you know what they expect from marriage. Report your findings to the class.
6. Ask your parents about their expectations in marriage. Try to find out what they felt and expected when they were young and thinking of marriage and what their expectations are at the present time.

What Is Marriage?

Men and women living together in an arrangement society calls marriage is natural. It is an obvious fact that women bear children fathered by males. It is also obvious that children need care, nurturing, and training for the first years of their lives. Society has learned that the best arrangement for this care, nurturing, and training is in the living arrangement it calls marriage. This living arrangement is so important that

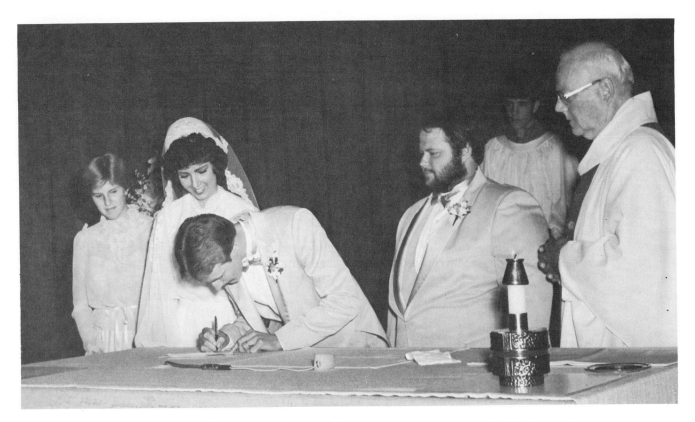

Before 1950, most American women were housewives raising, on the average, four children. In 1984, over 42 percent of the workforce in America was made up of women. By the year 2000, it is estimated that a majority of job holders in America will be women.

society protects it from harm by law and provides the means whereby it can be reasonably successful. Every human society in every age since the beginning of the human race has had such an arrangement.

Although marriage in today's developed societies is far different from marriage in previous stages of human civilization, its purpose is still the same. Two people come together to form a family unit in society. In primitive societies, having children insured the survival of the group. Because infant mortality was high, women had to have many babies. Caring for them was a full-time job. As civilization developed, having many children not only insured the survival of the group, it also provided the many workers required for developing economies. Raising these children remained, for most women, a full-time job, as a general rule.

In today's developed societies, living in marriage has changed. Improved health services have lowered the infant mortality rate. Having many children is no longer necessary for the survival of these societies. In addition, technology has freed developed societies from the need for many workers to sustain their economies. These realities have freed women from the need to bear many children and have changed their primary role from childbearing to a broader role in the total development of their societies. Besides having babies, women in today's developed societies pursue careers, engage in a wide variety of leisure-time activities, provide a great number of specialized social services, and contribute substantially to the economic, political, and cultural development of their societies.

Because of these changes, men and women in developed countries do not get married just to have children. They marry, generally, because they love each other. They are drawn to each other, first, because they are especially attracted to each other physically. One or the other, or both, see something in the other that gets their attention. Then, if everything progresses normally, love begins to blossom. This is followed by a strong desire for physical union. Soon, a deeper, more personal love develops, and a desire for total union follows.

When this stage is acknowledged by both parties, marriage usually follows. This is totally committed love. The couple acknowledges publicly, in some form of public ceremony, that they are committed to each other exclusively. From that point on, growth into mature love should follow.

True married love is that special devotion, respect, tenderness, and care we give to someone because of our strong, positive feelings of love for that special someone. Married love is knowing. It is understanding. It is trust. It is safe and secure. It is open. It is sacrificing. It is life-giving.

Because it is, it calls people to a special lifestyle we call marriage. *Marriage, then, is a way of living which best fosters that special love, which best promotes the marriage and enables it to grow and develop unthreatened by the limitations which could destroy it.* Marriage is a personal covenant we make with another person. It is a social institution which protects that covenant. And, for Catholics, it is a sacrament.

> Marriage is love that begins as excitement and matures into peace. It is a blend of respect for freedom and awe at the mystery of another person.

Marriage: A Personal Covenant

When a man and a woman decide to marry (as distinct from simply living together), they begin a special relationship that is unlike any other kind of relationship either one has with any other human being. It is a covenant relationship. That is, it is a relationship in which each party individually and both together promise and publicly declare total commitment to each other alone and adopt a way of life which expresses this special relationship. This way of life is called marriage. It is understood in this way by both parties and by the society which accepts and protects it.

The best reason for entering a marriage relationship is, of course, true love. If two persons enter a marriage relationship based on love for each other—and they continue to grow in this love—their marriage will be an adventure in living which is at once personally fulfilling, happy, productive, and successful.

If, however, they enter a marriage relationship for other reasons, and do not develop some kind of a love relationship involving concern for each other, their marriage will be less happy, less fulfilling, less productive, and less successful than if they do. This is one of the reasons why many marriages are not successful, or are at least not as happy as they might be. People enter into this unique way of life for reasons other than love, or they fail to grow in love together, or they expect too much of marriage, or too little.

The key to success in modern marriage, then, is love—the love that two people have for each other which causes them to want to live together, to share all they have and are, and to become one. All other human relationships are, for the most part, tentative, tenuous, and partial. Friends come and go, business associates are often just that and no more. Even relatives are often only names or faces in a picture, and children, even in the happiest of family situations, eventually seek their own way.

The marriage relationship, however, is so special that two people pledge themselves with a solemn promise to each other which they, and society, intend and understand to be special, particular, and lasting.

Married love is knowing. It is understanding. It is trust. It is safe and secure. It is open. It is sacrificing. It is life-giving.

Covenant Relationship: A relationship in which each party individually and both together promise and publicly declare total commitment to each other alone and adopt a way of life which expresses this special relationship.

Romantic love: Idealized love; infatuation.

Persons may live together, cohabit for a longer or shorter time, share interests, or goods, or bodies, but until they choose, mutually, to pledge each to the other with all they are and have forever (at least in firm intent), they do not have a marriage relationship. It may look like a marriage relationship, but if anything is held back, if anything is tentative, on trial, or part-time, it is not what people generally understand as a marriage relationship.

When a person marries, he or she enters a new phase of his or her personal history. Before marriage, this personal history may have been self-centered; now it must be in a radical new way other-centered. Neither one's life will ever again be the same, for though marriage has some of the same characteristics as friendship (and indeed, husband and wife should be good friends!), its essence is much more intimate, more personal, more far-reaching and comprehensive than any other kind of friendship. In marriage, one no longer free-lances; life, work, ambitions, and desires must always include the other. What was his or hers is now theirs; what was singular is now dual; what was without specific limits is now limited by the special personal intimate relationship which marriage implies.

Before marriage, a person's interest is focused outside the home; after marriage, it is home-centered. Before marriage, activity centers around "number one"; once marriage is contracted, life revolves around two people. Before marriage, one person plans, saves, experiences; after marriage, two persons plan, experience, and share. Before marriage, privacy and self-interest are the hallmarks of a maturing young adult; after marriage, privacy is stripped away and mutual interests motivate to achievement. Before marriage, a person thinks of self; after marriage a person must include "the other."

Married love is different from romantic love. Romantic love by its nature cools. Married love grows and develops. Romantic love, of course, can grow into married love, but it does not necessarily do so.

For a marriage to succeed, or at least to be reasonably successful, there must be respect for the individuality, dignity, and freedom of one's marriage partner. There must be control of selfish concerns, curbing of impatience, anger, self-indulgence, and self-pity. A successful marriage demands restraint, respect, courtesy, and a willingness to suffer interference with ego-demanding drives. It requires the self-discipline necessary to put the real good of the marriage partner before the desired good of self. It demands flexibility of character and patience, an expression of joy, and a willingness to serve that is undreamed of in the unmarried state.

Because marriage implies a relationship which is intimate, very personal, extremely mutual, and tremendously constant, it requires maturity, growth in love, and constancy in practice.

If the real relationship between two married people is not as ideal as this description, both should realize that it may not be because such a relationship is too high for human nature. It may be because their own maturity has not yet evolved to the level to which human nature at its fullest calls them.

A successful marriage demands restraint, respect, courtesy, and a willingness to suffer interference with ego-demanding drives.

Communication in Marriage

In a way, marriage is simple because, if you like a person well enough to share yourself completely, you throw in your lot with that person. Yet marriage in practice is difficult. The intimacy of the relationship, the complete exposure of self to another, and the defenseless position in which you put yourself exposes you to the risks inherent in any delicate situation.

The unique relationship pledged in the personal covenant each makes with the other in marriage is a covenant of love. Marital love is communication—the communication of self to self. Unlike other relationships, marriage involves an intimate self-revelation which embodies

the *entire* self: body, mind, and spirit. It requires a stripping away of the
ego-defenses built up over a period of years and demands making oneself
knowable.

It is for this reason that a husband and wife must realize that in marriage, especially, communication is a two-way street. *Not only do we show
ourselves by our own actions, but we show ourselves by how we receive another's
actions.* In other words, communication does not consist only in speaking.
It also involves listening—receiving messages from another and responding to the *meaning* of what is said or conveyed. It is understanding,
or trying to understand, the depth and mystery of another's person, and
of another's personal freedom.

In a situation, for example, in which one or the other spouse works
in a particularly stressful job, or has an especially difficult day, the other
must understand that a short temper, a moment of impatience, a sharp
word, or the desire for quiet is not due to a lack of love. It is probably
due to mental exhaustion or some frustration experienced at work, in
traffic, or in the neighborhood. Married love understands the cause for
the outburst or the manifestation of frustration and quietly accepts it for
what it is.

Likewise, a man, home from a hard day's work, must understand
that if his wife has been bound to the house all day, she may want to eat
out, or go to a meeting, or tell him about her day. It is not that she dislikes
her home, or does not enjoy his company alone, or does not respect his
need for quiet. She just wants to get away, to operate in a field of adults,
to do something besides dishes and housework, meals and picking up,
and the thousand and one other things that might, from time to time,
drive a woman who is at home all day up a wall.

Everyone experiences frustration and disappointment, feelings of impatience and lack of control, sorrow, and pain, and hurt. And everyone needs support, understanding, and tender, loving care. A man and wife feel they can get what they need from one another in marriage. Having had to curb disappointment or anger, or impatience in the threatening world of work or business, a spouse can let down his or her guard, vent frustration, speak of disappointment, or relax in the quiet of home without worrying about the effects. Nowhere can a person find the security he or she needs better than in the company of a loved spouse.

It is because of these things that marriage is basically a matter of communication. In marriage, we tell, by the way we do things, the kind of person we are. We tell the other person the kind of person we are, not in the heroic acts of life or in occasional recitals of love, but in the little, everyday things we do: how we speak, what we say, how we eat, how we dress, how we keep ourselves clean, what we do to assist our partner, and the thousand and one other things we do in daily life to show ourselves to our marriage partner. In marriage, as in no other life situation, we are what we do because in marriage we play no roles. We communicate our person, our self as we are, our values, and our esteem and respect for the other person.

It is upon each person's capacity to communicate—to give and receive the other—that marriage relationships depend. This communication, rooted in the body, is, nevertheless, more than the body. It is spirit. It is the person who gets married; it is not simply sex organs. It is in the total relationship of the two persons that marriage is fulfilled, in communion.

This relationship is not enslavement. It does not mean burying one's personal ambitions, suppressing one's needs and desires, or destroying one's personality. It means the free giving of oneself to another in love and the receiving of another in love.

> Nowhere is body language so important as in marriage. Every word, gesture, tone, facial expression, and body response conveys a special meaning interpreted in light of the total commitment made in marriage.

---

1. What is marriage?
2. Describe ways in which living in marriage has changed in today's society.
3. What is the key to success in modern marriage?
4. Name several ingredients for a successful marriage.
5. Why is communication important in a marriage?
6. In the next day or two, ask your parent(s) what they think is the key to a successful marriage.

Marriage: A Social Institution

The complex physical and psychological forces which bring a man and a woman to the decision to share their lives also leads them to live together in a lifestyle which enables them to share each other completely and in a unique way. They form a new social unit called a family.

Society, in general, recognizes the uniqueness of this sharing and lifestyle and provides the conditions in society which preserve and protect it from whatever dangers could threaten it. *This is the reason for civil laws concerning marriage.*

Recognizing the selfishness and sinfulness of some of its members and the blindness of others, society tries to protect individuals in marriage from exploitation, deception, and the undue pressures of persons seeking to influence, in some way, the free choice of individuals in marriage. It also seeks to protect society itself from the dangers that would threaten society if marriage as a social unit is threatened. It is for both of these reasons that marriage vows or promises are exchanged in public. They are a public affirmation that the two persons have freely chosen to form a new unit in society. When this is done, society gives the weight of its corporate protection to the new family unit, and the new family unit is entitled to the protection of society.

Over and above this, when a man and a woman decide to set up their own family situation, they create a stable environment for children of their own and provide them with the best conditions in which to grow as human beings.

A child does not receive the maximum protection of society or the psychological assurance of parental love outside the family situation.[1] Compare, for example, the effect on the individuals and on society of a child conceived and born out of wedlock with that of a child conceived and born into a stable family situation.

Outside of the atmosphere of security offered by a married couple, a fetus becomes an object of fear, of deprivation, and, in many cases, of rejection or hatred. Pregnancy outside of wedlock is often a shock and sets up a whole series of events detrimental to the pregnant woman and the child. It changes her entire life before she is ready and triggers a chain of problems, the least of which are frustration, shame, and fear.

For the man who has contributed to the woman's pregnancy (unless he is completely without feeling), there is anxiety, a feeling of helplessness, and fear for the future. The parents of both suffer, and society must provide all kinds of services to compensate for the lack of family structure. As for the child, what is his or her future?

Within a stable family structure, however, a child can be conceived in joy and pride. In such families, the mother is transformed. Her life is focused on the child in her womb. The father becomes proud, more concerned, tender, and industrious. Society welcomes the child, and the parents of the couple become "proud grandparents." The child is assured, insofar as this is possible, of growth in a warm, friendly, loving atmosphere.

When Children Come

With the arrival of children, the family community broadens its scope and purpose. The husband and wife come to love each other more in both themselves and in the children. From the self-centered view of the premarriage situation, and the couple-centered view of early marriage, the man and woman now become family-centered, and much of the structure of society functions to make the family community experience meaningful.

In addition to the supportive role which society plays in making it possible for two people to share their lives completely in the lifestyle we call marriage, and the role it plays in making it possible for children to

---

1. The single-parent family which, though not ideal, may provide a stable family situation to which the child can relate and in which he or she can feel secure.

grow to maturity in an atmosphere of love, marriage as a social institution provides the best conditions for the family itself to develop as a constructive unit in society.

Despite the limitations which militate against a healthy family atmosphere (discord instead of harmony, for example), the family situation makes it possible for people to function as members of society in ways that are not usually possible outside of the family situation. Within the family unit, there is meant to be a feeling of unity, cohesiveness, security, and support that is both naturally and psychologically stronger than outside of it. Within the family situation there is a feeling of trust, an interchange of leadership roles, a common direction, similarity of philosophy, and agreement on goals and values that are missing in other societal units.

Within the family unit, all members can share equally in the natural and psychological effects of being a family: emotional support, encouragement, loyalty, a feeling of having roots, and common effort to meet the psychological and physical needs of all the members. Within the family situation, children can hope to be provided with the physical, emotional, and psychological supports that are not found in other units in society. Husbands and wives experience acceptance, love, and emotional support that can be provided by no other unit in society. Within the family unit, the members experience a sense of belonging, of having ties that adversity and time cannot destroy, and a feeling of being rooted in a past that carries hope for the future.

All other societal institutions have a tentative, experimental nature. They are created by people to meet the needs of society as it faces the challenges of progress. The family, however, is the permanent unit of society. It is based on biological, psychological, and sociological imperatives that are inherent in what it means to be human.

The family as a societal institution arises out of the personal covenant which a man and a woman make when they pledge to each other their entire person. Its creative and cohesive force is love—that special love which a man and a woman experience when they are so drawn to each other that they wish to be together "in sickness and in health, for richer or poorer, till death do us part."

Marriage: A Sacrament

For Catholics, marriage is not only a personal covenant with its own integrity and a social institution arising out of the nature of this personal covenant. It is also a Catholic sacrament. A sacrament is an official act which signifies God's special action in the life of the person or persons receiving the sacrament.

Sacrament: An official act of Catholic worship which signifies God's special action in the life of the person or persons receiving the sacrament.

It is a sacrament for Catholics, not just because it was declared such by the Church or because it is witnessed by a priest. It is a sacrament because of what it is for Catholics: *a way of life in which God is present in a special way in the lives of the two baptized persons joined with Christ in a union of love.*

As you know, Catholics believe that God lives in them and acts through them in a special way because of their baptism. They also believe that God acts in them and through them in a particular way in each of the sacraments. Marriage is a sacrament for Catholics because God acts in them and for them in a particular way in their married lives, enabling them to live their married lives as witnesses of His saving actions in Christ.

"Marriage is a recalling, a making present and a prophetic anticipation of the covenant history," says Pope John Paul II. "In marriage two people embark on an adventure which inserts them into salvation history. They *recall* the grace-filled marvels of God; they *make present* to their children and the world the demands of a forgiving and a redeeming love; they *bear witness* to the hope of a future encounter with Christ."

The Sacrament of Matrimony, therefore, because it is a way of life and not simply an isolated action, is not just in the ceremony, in the pledge, in whatever rituals accompany the ceremony. It is in the entire life of the married persons. *For Catholics, God is not acting in the lives of the married persons only when they pledge each to the other in the ceremony. He is acting in their whole lives.*

The fact that marriage is a sacrament for Catholics does not mean that two Catholics entering into marriage are "more married" than two persons who are not Catholics. The essence of marriage is the personal covenant between the man and the woman. They marry each other. They are not married by a priest, or a minister, or a rabbi, or a judge, or a justice of the peace. They are united in marriage by their mutual pledge of faithful love.

The civil or religious representative present at a wedding acts only as an official witness in the name of society (and the Church). So married Catholics are not more married than those who are not Catholics; they

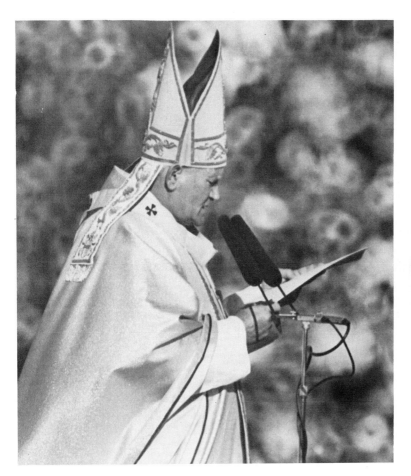
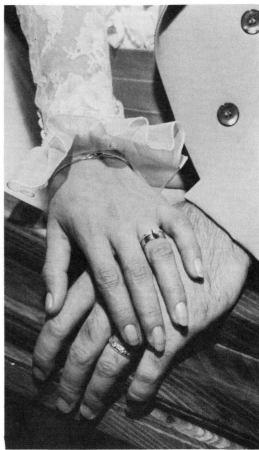

are *sacredly married in a special way.* Their marriage has a *Christian* meaning. It is a sacred action in which God is present with His special grace (called "sacramental grace"), offering His special assistance to the married persons to help them live their married lives in a Christian way.

It is for this reason that the Catholic Church, through its consecrated ministers, the bishops, tries to guide Catholic Christians in their married lives. The norms and guidelines—laws, regulations, rituals, ceremonies, theological interpretations, and the like—are designed to help make Catholic marriages a realization of the Christian meaning of marriage. They are intended as norms and guides to help a man and a woman contemplating marriage or living in marriage achieve the goal they have in entering marriage as Christians.

Unfortunately, many people in and out of the Church community do not understand the role of the Church in the Catholic interpretation of human sexuality and marriage. Granted that there are many voices singing different tunes and laws can outlive their historical origins and be changed. Be that as it may, the constant endeavor of the Church has been to Christianize truly human experiences.

Like Christ, the Church's attitude toward sex and marriage is not rigid, but it is firm. It is based upon Christ's demonstrated understanding of and concern for the dignity of the human person, the mystery of human existence, the equality of men and women, the nature of sexuality, and the need for interpersonal relationships based upon the giving and receiving of love. *For the Church, marriage is a sacred way of life. Whatever promotes its sacredness is encouraged; whatever attacks it is opposed.*

The essence of marriage is the personal covenant between a man and a woman. They marry each other, united by their mutual pledge of faithful love.

The Church's View of Marriage and You

The Catholic Church is not against love, sex, marriage, and the joys and pleasures of human relationships. The goals of the Catholic Church and the goals of humanity are the same—they both want people to be happy and fulfilled. The only difference between the two is that the Catholic Church, while listening to the voice of human experience and the findings of modern psychology, listens also to the voice of Christ as it comes to the Church. In doing so, it attempts to illumine the human experience of life in all its aspects with its understanding of the meaning of Jesus for all people.

The Church's view of marriage is expressed by St. Paul, for instance, who gives us some of the mind of Christ concerning the religious meaning of the human experience of marriage. In writing to the first Ephesian Christians, he said:

> "Husbands, love your wives just as Christ loved the Church and gave his life for it. He did this to dedicate the Church to God by his word after making it clean by washing it in water, in order to present the Church to himself in all its beauty—pure and faultless, without spot or wrinkle or any other imperfection. Men ought to love their wives just as they love their own bodies. A man who loves his wife loves himself. (No one ever hates his own body. Instead he feeds it and takes care of it, just as Christ does the Church; for we are members of his body.) As the Scripture says, 'For this reason a man will leave his father and mother and unite with his wife, and the two will become one.' There is a deep secret truth revealed in this Scripture, which I understand as applying to Christ and the Church. But it also applies to you: every husband must love his wife as himself, and every wife must respect her husband."
>
> —Ephesians 5:25–33

16

As you approach the period of your life when your decisions are becoming more and more independent and self-directed, you need to determine the role that religion will play in your decision-making. Your Church presents a view of sex, sexuality, and marriage that will help you express your sexuality in a Christian way. Through your baptism, God has called you to live your life as a Catholic Christian. He asks you to reflect in your life now the Catholic community's view of sex and sexuality, and in the future, the Catholic view of marriage.

Other people your age live out their way of thinking about these things. In order to live out your Catholic way of thinking, you will need to utilize the best human views and the best Christian views of sex, sexuality, and marriage and incorporate them into the Catholic value system which guides your choices.

---

1. Why are there civil laws regarding marriage?
2. Describe how a family benefits from having marriage as a social institution.
3. Why is marriage a sacrament for Catholics?
4. How does Pope John Paul II describe marriage?
5. Why does the Catholic Church try to guide Catholic Christians in their married lives?

Married Love

As has been noted, the thing that most often brings a man and a woman together in marriage is love. Admitting that there are other reasons for marrying and many reasons why married people remain married to each other even though they may no longer be in love (the children, money, religious affiliation, social necessity, and so forth), love binds married people together in all successful marriages, keeps the couple faithful to each other, and makes such marriages "work."

The word *love* is used to describe or define many kinds of attachments, relationships, associations, and feelings. In use, it can range from a broad, all-inclusive noun, as in "God is love" (I John 4:8) to a limiting adjective, as in "puppy love.' Married love refers to that special feeling that exists between a man and a woman who have learned, in marriage, to truly love each other.

The best way to distinguish true married love from other kinds of love is to compare it to other kinds of love. Although it has all the ingredients of other kinds of love, married love is more than any of them. It is physical, emotional, social, and spiritual. It is romantic, mature, and sexual. It combines all of the attributes the ancient Greeks used to define various kinds of love: *storge, philia, eros,* and *agape.*

For the Greeks, *storge* meant a strong, natural affection found among family members who love and respect each other. It is a nurturing and protecting love. It is a tolerant and accepting love. It is not restrictive or binding, or narrow. It is a love that is felt and given because of the natural binding relationship between two related persons. Married love is like that.

Married love: That special feeling that exists between a man and a woman who have learned, in marriage, to truly love each other.

Married Love

VIKTOR FRANKL, a world renowned psychiatrist, wrote the following about an experience he had when he escaped from an infamous prison camp for European Jews during World War II.[2] It says all there is to be said about love, sex, and marriage:

As we [my friend and I] stumbled on for miles, slipping on icy spots, supporting each other time and again, dragging one another up and onward nothing was said, but we both knew: each of us was thinking of his wife. Occasionally, I looked at the sky, where the stars were fading and the pink light of the morning was beginning to spread behind a dark bank of clouds. But my mind clung to my wife's image, imagining it with an uncanny acuteness. I heard her answering me, saw her smile, her frank and encouraging look. Real or not, her look was then more luminous than the sun which was beginning to rise.

A thought transfixed me: for the first time in my life I saw the truth as it is set into song by so many poets, proclaimed as the final wisdom by so many thinkers. The truth—that love is the ultimate and the highest goal to which man can aspire. Then I grasped the meaning of the greatest secret that human thought and belief have to impart: The salvation of man is through love and in love. *I understood how a man who has nothing left in this world still may know bliss, be it only for a brief moment, in the contemplation of his beloved.*

In a position of utter desolation, when man cannot express himself in a positive action, when his only achievement may consist in enduring his sufferings in the right way—an honorable way—in such a position man can, through loving contemplation of the image he carries of his beloved, achieve fulfillment.

2. Excerpted from *Man's Search for Meaning* by Viktor L. Frankl. Copyright © 1962 by Viktor Frankl.

The Greeks used the word *philia* to describe the special kind of love, affection, and attachment that is found in good friends. It is a word used to signify, also, a kind of universal, or all-encompassing love—a love that extends to all human beings, for example, because they are human and worthy of love. It is interesting to note that the English word *philanthropy*, meaning an active giving to promote human welfare, is rooted in the word *philia*, as is the name of the city of brotherly love in Pennsylvania called Philadelphia. Married love is like that. Happily married couples are good friends. They like each other and want to be in each other's company.

The Greek word *eros* describes a physical, sexual kind of love. It is used to describe the human passion aroused by a sexually exciting object. The words *erotic* and *erogenous* come from that Greek word. The first word means capable of arousing sexual feelings and the other means sexually sensitive. True married love is erotic because husbands and wives in love are sexually exciting to each other and express this erotic love in their desires, arousal, words, and actions. Married people in love want each other physically. When they do, and they come together in love, they express the deepest and most sacred union and communion known to human beings.

Erotic: Capable of arousing sexual feelings.

Erogenous: Sexually sensitive.

The Greek word *agape* means a special kind of self-giving love. It describes a love that gives without the thought of, or need for, a return of love. It is a generous outpouring of self toward another regardless of how a person feels about the other or how the other person feels about the one giving the love of agape. It is an unselfish love given to others in service even though the object of such love neither merits nor returns love.

Married love is like that. It extends beyond the love of kinship, the love of friends, and the expressions of sexual attachment. It is a deep, abiding love encompassing the entire person of the loved one. It is the kind of love that weathers marital or family storms, difficult days, personal, social, or economic setbacks, or the hardships of separations, illness, mental or physical impairment, or death.

Married love is the most satisfying, joyful, comforting, and secure of all human experiences. It allows those in love to share in the most complete way their most important human dimension: the ability to give and receive love.

Christian Married Love

When Christians marry, says St. Paul, they marry "in the Lord." That is, Catholics believe that marriage is a sacred, sacramental act blessed by God through the baptism of the married partners. Christian married love, therefore, is the love of a Christian married couple enriched by their Christian faith. Not only does this love have the characteristics of mature married love described above, but it also has the added ingredient of religious faith.

Christian married love goes beyond the purely human. It goes beyond the sacredly sexual and beyond the love of friendship or kinship. It is love for the married partner because that person has been created by God, is loved by God, and is destined for a share in the Divine Life forever. It is love that is rooted in the reality of Christ in the life of the married couple.

Christian married love goes beyond the purely human. It goes beyond the sacredly sexual and beyond the love of friendship or kinship. It is love for the married partner because that person has been created by God, is loved by God, and is destined for a share in the Divine Life forever. It is love that is rooted in the reality of Christ in the life of the married couple.

Christian married couples love each other precisely because they are Christian. They understand, accept, and are aware of the religious dimension of their lives and their love. They practice their faith, live a spiritual life to the best of their ability, raise their children in a religious way, depend upon God, and relate their lives to the Lord. In their marriage, they make a conscious effort to live and love in a Christian way. Their Christian faith is a strengthening potion in their marriage. It makes their married love particularly special for them.

---

1. Describe the following kinds of love as used by ancient Greeks:
   storge   *eros*
   philia   *agape*
2. Describe married love.
3. Compare married love with Christian married love.

Summary

God inscribed in the humanity of man and woman the vocation and thus the capacity and responsibility of love and communion. Love is therefore the fundamental and innate vocation of every human being.

Pope John Paul II
Familiaris Consortio no. 11

- Marriage is a personal covenant that an individual makes with another person. The key to success in modern marriage is love—the love that two people have for each other which causes them to want to live together, to share all they have and are, and to become one.
- Marital love is communication: the communication of self to self. It involves an intimate self-revelation which embodies the entire self: body, mind, and spirit. It is upon each person's capacity to communicate—to give and receive the other—that marriage relationships depend.
- Marriage as a social institution provides the best conditions for the family to develop as a constructive unit of society. By setting up a family unit, a man and a woman set up a stable environment for their children and provide them with the best conditions in which to grow as human beings.
- For Catholics marriage is a sacrament because it is a way of life in which God is present in a special way in the lives of the two baptized persons joined with Christ in a union of love. It is a sacred action in which God is present with His special grace, offering His special assistance to help the married couple live their lives in a Christian way.
- Married love binds people together in all successful marriages, keeps the couple faithful to each other, and makes such marriages work. Christian married love is the love of a Christian married couple enriched by their Christian faith.

Review, Discussion, Research, and Reflection

1. How would you describe marriage?
2. What do you understand by "communication" in marriage? Why is it important? How important is "body language" in marriage?
3. Do you believe it is necessary for society to "legalize" marriages? Why? Why not?
4. Why is a stable family situation important for children?
5. In response to a question about marriage vows, a priest said: "The commitment of marriage gets us over the petty problems created by our human limitations. They prevent us from just walking out on our marriage partner." Do you consider that a good answer? Do you think it is true? Do you think people need marriage promises? Why? Why not?
6. Write a short essay giving your views on how to achieve happiness in marriage. Interview married couples if you like. Include in your article examples of how persons your age can prepare for this happiness at this period of their growth.
7. Discuss the difference between a marriage covenant and the agreement a young couple may have to live together. Do you think it is wise for a young man and a young woman who are not married to live together. Why? Why not? Who risks the most?
8. Name the various ways we communicate in nonverbal ways.

Projects

1. Conduct a survey among your peers about marriage. Ask them for their thoughts, their hopes, and their intentions. Report your findings to the class.
2. Try to interview four different married couples. Ask them to describe what marriage means to them—and if their ideas about marriage have changed since they were single. Ask them to describe what has kept their marriage together and how they cope with problems. Report your findings to the class.

Words You Should Know

Be sure that you can define the following words and can use them in a meaningful sentence:

sacrament
covenant relationship
erotic
vocation
married love
Christian married love
romantic love

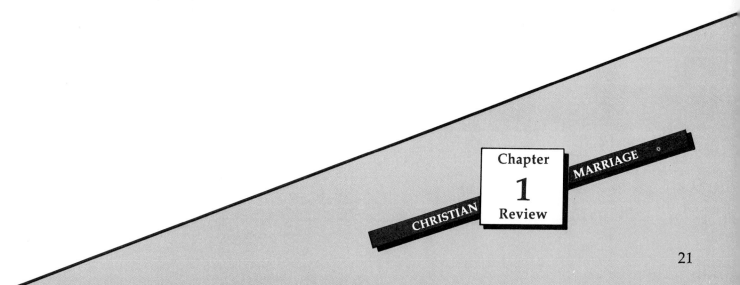

Chapter 1 Review

CHRISTIAN MARRIAGE

21

Chapter
2

CHRISTIAN MARRIAGE

Living in Marriage

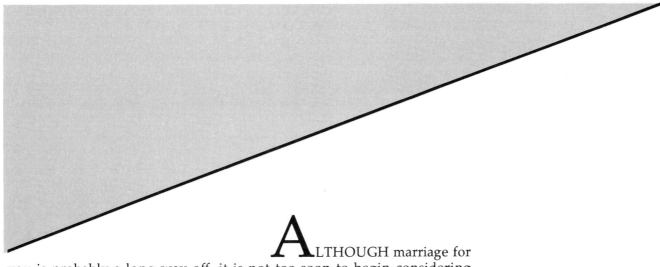

$\mathbf{A}$LTHOUGH marriage for you is probably a long way off, it is not too soon to begin considering the various aspects of marriage which will directly affect your life as a married person. Assuming for the moment that you are the marrying kind, some of the important questions about married life that you need to ask yourself are the following:

1. What kind of person do I want for my spouse?
2. What kind of person will my spouse be marrying?
3. What things will I expect of my spouse?
4. What things will my spouse expect of me?
5. What lifestyle do I want as a married person?
6. How will I handle the inevitable sexual challenges that I, as a married person, will undoubtedly face?
7. Am I ready to accept children? When would I prefer our first child? How many? How shall I accomplish my goal of family size?
8. What kind of parent will I be? What kind of parent will my spouse be?
9. How will I handle the problems that invariably crop up in marriage?
10. What shall I do if my spouse is seriously incapacitated or dies?
11. How shall I deal with my in-laws?
12. What priorities do I have for living in marriage?

All of these questions are worthy of thought and discussion because all of them will have a direct bearing on your marriage and how you will live as a married person. Think about them, answer them, discuss them with the teacher and the class, and then file your answers away for future reference.

On a separate sheet of paper, list three questions or areas not listed above that you think might cause problems in living in marriage.

Society of the Future

In looking forward to living in marriage sometime in the future, you will need to think about the changing structure of the society you live in because it will determine, in part, your role as a man or a woman within that marriage. Your role in marriage will also be determined, in part, by your abilities, your ambitions, the opportunities that are afforded you, your religious commitment, and how well you prepare yourself.

In primitive societies, food gathering needs established the pattern for family life and for society. Nomads, for example, moved around from place to place to meet this need. A style of family life evolved suited to transient existence.

As societal structures became more complicated and achievement became more sophisticated, society changed from being primarily concerned about food gathering to food production, and an agricultural society emerged. Political and cultural changes followed, and the role expressions of men and women in society changed also.

With the arrival of the Industrial Revolution in 1760, society in the Western World changed from an agricultural society to an industrial society. The roles of men and women in both the economic and family life areas of living changed again. Men moved from the farm to the factory and became subjected to a hierarchy of bosses. Although women were still the child-bearers and the homemakers, many extended their roles by employment in factories. Even children became employed in the factories. The Industrial Revolution drastically changed family structures and the role expressions of men, women, and children. Family life was never the same again.

When the age of technology blossomed after World War II (1945), industrialized society changed with it—and much more rapidly than ever before. Machines lightened the workload, labor unions shortened the workweek, and increased productivity brought about economic prosperity. Education broadened people's horizons and opportunities, and leisure time activity played a larger role in society's structure and expression. The roles and opportunities of both men and women changed radically to meet the demands of this new society.

Today, with the rapid growth of computers and their ever-increasing role in everyone's life, society is changing again. More labor-saving devices are changing the work patterns of people. New kinds of

job opportunities are offering people wider choices in their work fields and the future will offer even more jobs in the service fields than in the industrial or agricultural fields. Better and more instant communication techniques will raise the level of people's expectations, and more leisure time will be available for personal and family pursuits.

In addition, expanding educational opportunities, better health care, longer life expectancy, environmental concerns, and attention to conserving nonrenewable natural resources are changing lifestyles and priorities and affecting the quality of life that today's young people will experience in their most productive years. All these will affect the political and cultural expressions of society, the role expressions of men and women, and the patterns and experiences of family life.

Women's Expanding Roles in Society

The most dramatic change now taking place which will make the society of the future—your society—into a society radically different from the societies of the past is the concept and the expression of women's roles. Women will still bear children, of course, and in most cases will be the primary nurturers of their children. But they will no longer be only childbearers and homemakers. They will be an ever-increasing force in the wider world of economics, politics, and culture.

In earlier societies, women were primarily childbearers—having their children at an early age, and, on the average, dying earlier. (Life expectancy was only thirty-two years of age for women at the time of the American Revolution.) Their efforts were centered chiefly in and around the house.

Today, women live longer. They have a life expectancy of more than eighty years. They also marry later. On the average, they are more than twenty-four years old when they marry. Generally, they enter the work force before they marry and reenter it after their children are in school. Because only one-fifth of a modern woman's life is spent in childbearing and nurturing, she is able to devote much more time to other activities and interests. She has time to pursue personal, cultural, political, and economic interests of her own. These facts alone make the role of women in society much more dramatic than ever before and are changing the nature of role expressions in society for both men and women.

It used to be that men had the greater options in choosing jobs or careers and in selecting the direction of their lives. Since the mid 1960s, however, when social changes occurred and when women began questioning conventional sex roles, the social scripting has changed. It appears the options are greater not only for women but for men as well.

In addition, many women took jobs outside of the home because of financial necessity; perhaps their husbands were unemployed or unable to work because of illness.

Today, a woman can choose any or all of several different roles in society. She can choose to be single or married, a career person or a homemaker. She can combine one or more of these roles at the same time by being a married woman, a parent, a homemaker, and a career person. She can also elect to alternate her role by being a homemaker through the years her children are growing up, then becoming a career person.

Although future changes in the family could actually bring more rather than fewer problems, the resilience of the family amidst the changes, demonstrates the ability of the family to adapt to the changing world.

—Population Reference Bureau
Washington, D.C. 1984

Life expectancy for women was only thirty-two years of age at the time of the American Revolution.

By taking the initiative in examining the traditional assumptions of sex roles, women have created changes that affect men as well as women. While men have the same option of being single or married, they now also have the option of becoming more involved in the homemaking and childrearing aspects of family life. Career opportunities for men have been expanded, too, as a result of the changing role of women. Where society once placed restrictions on males to be involved only in so-called male-oriented jobs (doctor, pilot, construction worker), men are now able to become airline stewards, nurses, and clerical workers without social discrimination.

The Changing Structure of Marriage

Either directly or indirectly, the changes in society and in women's roles in society have resulted in a change in the structure of marriage. They have had an effect on the relationship between men and women, how each lives in society, and how each and both will live in marriage and in family life. The areas which appear to be more affected than others are family size, family responsibilities, and the incidences of divorce and remarriage.

Family Size

Larger family size was important when infant mortality rates were high and when more family numbers made work and economic burdens easier.

The number of children in the average American family today is about two per family. This decrease in the number of children to be cared for enables a woman to pursue interests outside the home either directly or indirectly related to her homemaking role: part-time or full-time employment, volunteer work in the school, parent-teacher organizations, child care facilities, Church and school functions, and social and political concerns directly related to family and child life. With both parents involved outside the home, there often evolves an increase in shared responsibilities.

Family Responsibilities

Directly related to family size in modern society and in the society of the future is family responsibility. Even though women are increasing their presence outside the home (they now make up more than 42 percent of the work force), they are still chiefly responsible for the smooth functioning of the family unit. In well over 90 percent of the homes, women are chiefly responsible for the care of the children. They are also responsible for the care of the home: they oversee the family budget, save for emergencies, prepare the meals, buy the groceries, chauffeur the children, attend the meetings, arrange the family social life, care for the sick and the elderly, and so forth. In most homes, they are the force that makes the family unit possible.

Today, one out of every five children lives in single-parent families.

It ought to be noted at this point that the number of single-parent families is increasing. Today, one out of every five children lives in a single-parent family. Although there has been an increase in the number of fathers who are assuming full-time custody of their children (known as the "custodial parent"), more often than not, the single parent is a

woman. As a result, family responsibility falls on the single parent, and the burdens of raising a family in such a unit are doubled. The single parent must not only provide the living for the family, he or she must fulfill a double parental role: provide for the care of the children during work hours and after school, oversee their upbringing alone, and see to it that their social and family life grows and expands.

Incidences of Divorce and Remarriage

Changes in society and in people's attitudes about marriage, sex roles, and family responsibilities have increased the divorce rate in Western-culture societies. The consequent increase in remarriage is resulting in more stepfamily situations. At the present time, fifty million Americans are in step relationships, and one child in six now lives in a stepfamily or blended family. In all likelihood, the number will increase in the future.

One child in six now lives in a blended family or stepfamily.

The process of divorce, and the resulting remarriage and creation of stepfamilies or blended families also affects family life. The negative emotional responses of all members of the family—father, mother, children—can be devastating and disruptive to the family unit. In addition, the roles and responsibilities of each member are often affected.

Family Life Is Important for Most People

In the midst of all these changes, one thing remains constant—as it has remained constant through all the centuries of human development: men and women are biologically, emotionally, and psychologically drawn to each other to form a societal unit we call the family. Well over 90 percent of the people say that family life is a very important priority in their lives and over 70 percent say they are very satisfied with the quality of their family life. This will remain so in the future.

What does all this mean to you as you contemplate the direction of your life in the society of the future? First, it means that you and your peers will be responsible for the society of the future. You will be its producers and its leaders. Second, most of you will, at one time or another, be married and form a family unit. These two things are your awesome responsibilities and your challenge. You can cope with them and make your life a happy, productive life if you prepare yourself now for your role in the society of the future.

---

1. Describe how the industrial revolution changed the roles of men and women in our society.
2. List several ways in which technological advances have influenced the roles and opportunities of both men and women in our society.
3. Give examples of how men's and women's life choices have been affected as a result of the expanding roles of women.
4. What areas within the structure of marriage have been affected by the changing role of women in our society?

Living in Marriage

In looking ahead toward marriage, you need to look at how your role as a man or a woman will affect your family life. You also need to look at the realities of living in marriage. In our society, it is easy to get married. It is not always so easy to live in marriage. Sometimes, in the enthusiasm of love, a young man and a young woman forget that they are marrying a person—warts and all, as they say.

What does it mean to marry a person? It means that you join your entire physical, intellectual, emotional, psychological, and spiritual person with another's physical, intellectual, emotional, psychological, and spiritual person. This is why it is so important, if you want to live a happy married life, to find out what kind of person you are and to ask yourself what kind of married life you want. Then you should ask yourself what kind of person you want to live with and what kind of life you look forward to.

Adam®   **by Brian Basset**

The kind of person you are now, and the kind of person you hope to become, involves learning how to make choices and right decisions as a young adult. For example, decisions you make now about your life-work—the money-making aspect of living—will affect decisions you make about your education. A person who wants to become a computer analyst should be taking courses now in computers and statistics. One who hopes someday to be in politics, should probably be taking courses in political science and history. The decisions you make about your education will determine what jobs you will be prepared for. The kind of job you are prepared for, will, to a large extent, also determine the life-style you will finally select—or have thrust upon you.

By the same token, the decisions you make now about the kind of person you want to become and the effort you make to be that kind of person will determine what kind of marriage partner you will be. If you are honest, considerate, trustworthy, and kind now, you will bring the same attributes into your marriage. Marriage does not change persons radically. The kind of person you are before marriage is the kind of person you will most likely be in marriage. The decision you make now about the kind of person you eventually want to live with will largely determine the kind of marriage partner you will someday have.

What does the future hold for you in marriage? There is no way to really know, but you do have some control over the direction your married life will take. Living *in* marriage will involve the major portion of your adult life. Because the stakes are so high and you have such high hopes for yourself as a married person, it is well to look ahead to what you want in and from marriage long before you become seriously involved with another person.

What Living in Marriage Really Means

Before becoming seriously involved with another person and certainly before **committing** yourself to another person in marriage, you need to ask yourself if you could live with that person every day on a down-to-earth level. You need to determine whether that person could be your friend—someone you like to be with, someone with whom you are compatible, sharing the same ideals, desires, ambitions, and loves in

the challenge of everyday living. How many persons do you know that you would like to be with day and night, year in and year out, in every circumstance of your life? That's what living in marriage means.

That is why social dating, dating a variety of persons, and reasonable engagement periods are important. They enable us to learn about people and to find out if we like them as persons. We can talk about our lives and what we hope for from our lives. We can explore ideas about life choices, finances, race, religion, sex, children, in-laws, and the thousand and one other things that involve relationships on a daily, nonromantic basis. We can find out if we can get along with another person because we genuinely like that person and want to share our life with him or her. We can learn if we are truly compatible.

Being compatible, being friends in marriage, does not mean that two people living in marriage cannot be themselves, cannot have independent ideas, or cannot differ, of course. It means that they respect each other and love each other as persons and that their differences are complementary rather than differences that cause them to clash or dislike each other.

Compatibility: The ability to exist together in harmony.

Compatibility means that two people get along well with each other no matter what happens. It means that they understand that there are differences between them, and they learn how to resolve them. It means that they are easily reconcilable, are happy together, are proud of each other. It means that they are happy and comfortable with each other whether they are alone or with others. It means that they are not demanding, not expecting too much, not requiring service, and not centered on self. It means that they communicate with each other on a deeper level than words and body language—they communicate on the level of feelings and spirit.

30

Living in marriage as friends means trust, patience, care, sacrifice, fidelity, and humility. Living in marriage means true married love. It means the kind of love St. Paul wrote about to the first Corinthian Christians:

> "Love is patient and kind; it is not jealous or conceited or proud; love is not ill-mannered or selfish or irritable; love does not keep a record of wrongs; love is not happy with evil, but is happy with the truth. Love never gives up; and its faith, hope, and patience never fail."
>
> —1 Corinthians 13:4–7

Living in marriage is a cooperative endeavor. While you are looking ahead to the kind of person you would like to have for your marriage partner, you must look at yourself to see what kind of marriage partner you will be. How do you get along with people? How patient, kind, forgiving, generous, restrained, courteous, and humble are you? Could you live with yourself every day and night of your life as you are in your unguarded moments? Are you your best self only when it suits your fancy or meets your needs?

Living in marriage means living with the ordinary frustrations of life, the common discourtesies, the thoughtlessness, the faults, the human weaknesses, and the limitations of ourselves and our marriage partner compounded by the unreal expectations of love and the intimacies of daily and unavoidable contact. It may mean coping with such things as sloppy eating habits, lack of personal cleanliness, carelessness with clothes, failing to cleanup, neglecting tasks, inattention, curt remarks, impatience, insensitivity, discourtesy, wastefulness with money, chauvinism, and the countless other things people do every day that irritate others.

Living in marriage also means, perhaps, facing and having to live with serious faults and problems that can plague a marriage. Not every marriage faces all the serious problems that can destroy a marriage or make it a less than pleasant experience, but many marriages suffer from one or more of them. Among the most serious are excessive drinking, the use of nonprescribed drugs, hypochondria, serious money problems, and prolonged and avoidable absence from home. Sexual incompatibility, extramarital affairs, abusive arguments, fighting, name-calling, jealousy, interference from in-laws, lack of growth in the marriage partner, and serious neglect of familial duties are other serious problems. A Jekyll/Hyde personality, a selfish concern for oneself alone, and spouse or child abuse can also destroy a marriage or make living in one miserable.

Every year two million wives are abused and more than one million children are abused.

Living in marriage means doing housework, washing dishes, doing the laundry, and keeping the lawn, the flowers, and the shrubbery in shape. It means cleaning windows, making beds, vacuuming, dusting, painting, changing diapers, sitting up with a sick spouse or child, going to the hospital, soothing hurts, and waiting up for latecomers. It means cooking meals, sewing on buttons, keeping track of mittens, worrying, running a shuttle service, giving of your time, and working hard, sometimes at two jobs, just to keep up with the bills. It means pacing yourself and cutting down on your social life, losing sleep, postponing vacations, and buying, buying, buying.

Most of all, living in marriage means growing together in love. It means sharing, supporting, admiring, and laughing together in love. It means loving companionship, security, peace, and the intimacy that only a trusting, loving, faithful relationship can give.

Living in marriage means two people live one life. If they have the same general goals, the same philosophy, the same values, and the same outlook on marriage and family living, living in marriage will be an adventure that will last a lifetime. Isn't that what every human being living in marriage really wants?

---

1. What does it mean to marry a person?
2. What aspects of your life will help to determine the kind of marriage partner you will be?
3. How can social dating have an affect on one's later life in marriage?
4. What does living in marriage mean?

Relationships with In-laws

When individuals marry, they not only marry a loved one; more often than not, they also marry "into" an extended family that includes many other people. Although young couples and their in-laws are usually compatible and get along reasonably well, in some instances, relationships with in-laws can provoke tensions for a married couple.

Sometimes, relatives make demands upon a couple or have certain expectations of them, or try to pressure them into doing certain things. For example, it is not at all unusual in this day and age for a young couple to decide to hold off starting a family until they feel they are more financially ready. As a result, many times they are subjected to pressures from in-laws, aunts, uncles, and others to have a baby.

Individuals contemplating marriage must look honestly at the nature of their relationship with their future in-laws and try to determine what kind of relationship will evolve with them. Above all, they must remember that it is their marriage and their relationship that are important. They should never let in-laws interfere with their lives and/or their marriage.

Extended Family: Any relative outside of the nuclear family, mother, father, and children.

Fidelity

In our society today, one of the most serious concerns facing young couples who are looking ahead toward marriage is infidelity. Fidelity in marriage means faithfulness. It means being true to one's spouse, one's promises, and one's marital obligations. It is an essential part of any marriage.

Yet infidelity, or unfaithfulness, appears to be a rather common element of many marriages in our society today. Cheating on one's spouse is even considered by some to be a normal part of the modern marriage scene. There is a double standard here. No one in marriage wants to be a victim of infidelity. However, because it appears as a frequent cultural presentation in movies and on the television, many people accept it as a matter of course in other marriages.

Infidelity has become so serious a problem that it has given rise to what many experts call "the maybe syndrome." By that, they mean that many couples contemplating marriage enter into it with reservations about its success or about their own or their spouse's faithfulness. Their observations of other unsuccessful marriages around them and their

Fidelity in marriage means faithfulness. It means being true to one's spouse, one's promises, and one's marital obligations.

32

"From many hours of shared anguish I know that lack of real commitment is where many marriages begin to fall apart. If husband and wife lose sight of the fact that their *decision*, their choice of committing themselves to each other, contributes something unique to the attraction they feel, then the marriage rests on a very fragile foundation.

"For many of these couples, there will be times when the attraction itself wears thin; there will be times when a new person will seem much more fascinating. If the awareness of the mutual commitment does not sustain a marriage through these difficult times, the particular marriage doesn't stand much of a chance. Nor will a second . . . or a third."

Excerpted from "Of Love and Nonsense" by John Reedy, C.S.C. *A.D. Correspondence*, Vol. 12, No. 4 (February 14, 1976). Copyright 1976 by Ave Maria Press, Notre Dame, Indiana 46556.

Prayer of A Husband and Wife

Keep us, O Lord, from pettiness. Let us be thoughtful in word and deed. Help us to put away pretense, and face each other in deep trust without fear or self-pity. Help us to guard against fault-finding, and be quick to discover the best in each other and in every situation. Guard us from ill temper and hasty judgment; encourage us to take time for all things, to grow calm, serene and gentle. Help us to be generous with kind words and compliments. Teach us never to ignore, never to hurt, never to take each other for granted. Engrave charity and compassion on our hearts.

awareness of the high incidence of divorce causes concern for them. They begin to see their commitment to *this* marriage as short-term and less than wholehearted.

This problem has affected the subconscious thinking of many young couples contemplating marriage. They wonder if their partner "really" loves them. They also worry about whether or not they will be a good marriage partner and express fear that their marriage will not last, sometimes giving the impression that they have little or no control over their future. Is it any wonder that many young people enter marriage with a "give it a try" attitude? They think to themselves that if it does not work, they will get a divorce and start over.

Lacking the cement of "until death do us part," such marriages have a difficult time surviving the inevitable difficulties that are part of any relationship, especially the intimate relationship of marriage. If people do not enter marriage with a "no matter what" determination, their chances of living in marriage for very long are slim.

One form of infidelity that is a major cause for the breakup of marriages in our society today is adultery—having sexual relations with someone other than one's spouse. Adultery is a seriously immoral act. It shatters the ego of one's marriage partner ("What's the matter with me?" one asks), is psychologically and emotionally harmful to the offended spouse, and is a gross affront to the promised fidelity spoken or implied in the marriage vow. As in all other instances of seriously immoral acts, adultery destroys the trust in a relationship and very often shatters family relationships.

Fidelity in a marriage encourages trust within the relationship and gives strength to the couple to grow within the relationship. It also eases the pains, heartaches, difficulties, and problems that accompany any marriage. It is the most prized of all marriage virtues and is the essence that makes the companionship aspect of long-term marriages so real. It is what makes each spouse in a successful marriage feel truly loved.

Fidelity in friendship is expected. In marriage, it is a positive necessity.

---

1. What influence should members of the extended family have on a couple's relationship within marriage?
2. What does fidelity in a marriage mean?
3. Describe "the maybe syndrome" as it refers to couples contemplating marriage.

Summary

- The ever-changing structure of society affects the role expressions of men and women and their patterns and experiences of family life.
- Either directly or indirectly, the change in women's role in society has resulted in a change in the structure of marriage and has had an effect on the relationship between men and women, how each lives in society, and how each and both will live in marriage and in family life. Areas particularly affected by this change are family size, family responsibilities, and the incidence of divorce and remarriage.
- Living in marriage means joining your entire physical, intellectual, emotional, psychological, and spiritual person with another's. Since it will involve a major portion of your adult life, it is important to know what you want in and from a marriage long before you become seriously involved with another person.
- Friendship in marriage requires trust, patience, care, sacrifice, fidelity, and humility. Most of all, it requires that two people live one life and grow together in love.
- An essential part of any marriage relationship is fidelity. It encourages trust within a relationship and gives strength to the couple to grow within the relationship.

Review, Discussion, Research, and Reflection

1. In an open forum, discuss the changing role expressions of women in today's society. Do you believe anyone benefits from the changes? Women? Men? Society? If you do, give examples of some of the benefits.
2. What do you see as the roles of men and women in society ten years from now?
3. When you get a chance, ask your parent(s) about how the roles of men and women in society have changed in the last ten years. What is their general attitude and the attitude of other people you know concerning women's increasing roles in society?
4. Who do you think should bear primary responsibility for the following tasks? Be sure to have good reasons for your responses. Compare your answers with your classmates:
   - a. Clean the house
   - b. Buy the groceries
   - c. Prepare the meals
   - d. Do the dishes
   - e. Cut the grass
   - f. Shovel snow
   - g. Take care of the dog
   - h. Care for elderly parents
   - i. Provide income for family needs
   - j. Nurture the babies
   - k. Hold principal governmental offices
   - l. Be fire-fighters
   - m. Fight in wars
   - n. Captain airline flights
   - o. Be law officers
5. Describe the different types of family units that exist today and compare their similarities and their differences.
6. Write an essay on what living in marriage means to you.
7. What is fidelity? Why is it so important in marriage?
8. Why do you suppose many TV shows and movies fail to treat fidelity in marriage as an important quality?

Projects

1. Survey five adults you know on the changing roles of men and women in marriage in our society. Ask them to reflect on their youth and compare what it was like then to what it is like now. Compile your answers and summarize.
2. Compile a list of eight questions an individual should consider in preparing for marriage. Put them in survey form and pass them out to your friends to answer without placing their names on the survey. Compile the results and summarize.

Words You Should Know

Be sure that you can define the following words and can use them in a meaningful sentence:

extended family
fidelity
commitment
compatibility

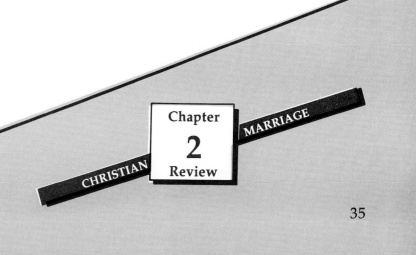

Chapter **2** Review

CHRISTIAN MARRIAGE

Chapter 3

CHRISTIAN MARRIAGE

Marriage: The Family Unit

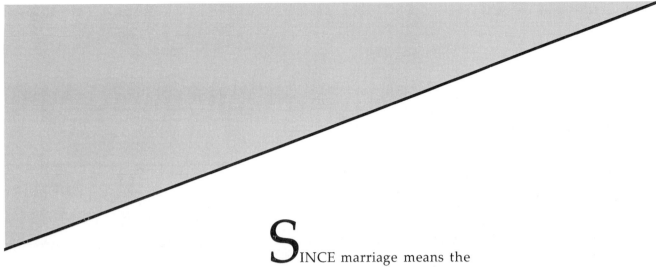

SINCE marriage means the joining of your physical, intellectual, emotional, psychological, and spiritual person with another and will likely involve a major portion of your adult life, it is important to know what you want in a marriage long before becoming seriously involved with another person.

Living successfully in marriage requires planning. If you choose to marry, decisions have to be made jointly by you and your spouse on a number of issues which will affect how your family lives and how family relationships will develop. The decisions made will depend on your basic values as a couple and on your ability to make the right decisions. They will also depend upon the kind of life you desire as a couple, the level of education you have, the availability of opportunities, and the kinds of sacrifices each of you is willing to make.

Courses you take in finance and economics in high school and college can help you prepare for marriage, not just for your occupation.

Take a moment to reflect on the kind of life you would like to have when you are thirty, and formulate plans for achieving that life. On a separate sheet of paper, write your thoughts and your plans, then file them away for review at the end of this period of study.

Among the more important areas in which decisions made will affect how your family lives its married life are your readiness for marriage, finances, parenting abilities, and family size (including the sensitive issue of conception control).

Readiness for Marriage

Persons thinking about marriage must ask themselves if they are ready for the total commitment that a good marriage requires. They must ask themselves if the conditions are right for them and for the person they may be marrying for establishing a family unit of their own.

In addition, they must ask themselves if they believe they are capable of assuming the responsibilities of a family, whether the conditions under which they will establish a family are right for the society in which they live, and whether they can provide the right environment in which to raise children. In other words, each person considering marriage must ask if he or she as an individual, and they as a couple, are

psychologically, financially, and socially ready for marriage. If they discover they are not, they should consider delaying the ceremony until they feel the time and circumstances are right. In this connection, it is important that if either partner is doubtful or hesitant about the relationship or the loved one, he or she should not allow others to pressure him or her into marriage.

For all persons, preparing for the commitment of marriage involves several processes. It involves a knowledge of themselves as human beings—likes and dislikes, needs and desires, goals and dreams. It involves an understanding of human nature and an awareness of which personality traits are attractive and desirable to them. It includes the process of maturing and the experiences that prepare them for a close, personal relationship with another.

It also includes learning how to make decisions that are based on their own likes and dislikes, needs and desires, goals and dreams. Most important of all, it involves the process of learning how to communicate those decisions openly and honestly with someone to whom they are emotionally committed. When it comes to learning good communication skills, it is important to know that there is a difference between being aggressive and being assertive. When individuals are aggressive, they can impose either physical or emotional harm upon another human being. They can be physically aggressive by punching or slapping another, or they can inflict emotional harm by emotionally manipulating a person, by calling someone a name, ridiculing him or her, or making a derogatory statement such as "You're stupid for doing that!" or using terms like "dummy" or "jerk." Statements of this kind can only cause another person pain.

However, when people are assertive, they express what they believe to be right in a positive and respectful manner. For example, it might be as easy as saying "No, thank you, I don't think I'll have any liver tonight!" or "I'd rather have a hamburger tonight instead of pizza"; or it could be something more difficult to say, such as "No, thank you, I don't do drugs" or "I care for you a great deal, but I'm not ready for any serious commitment right now."

All individuals need to know that they have a right to assert themselves in a polite and respectful manner.

Understanding their needs and desires and being prepared enough to take care of them is essential in considering their readiness for marriage.

Finances

Perhaps in no other area of family living is there more naiveté than in the financial aspect of living in marriage. In the bloom of young love, many people believe that "two can live as cheaply as one." Unfortunately, this just is not true, and tensions arise in *every* marriage about how money is to be spent.

Young couples contemplating marriage need to explore the financial costs of marriage, as well as the possibility of additional expenses that may arise when they become parents. They need to communicate about budgetary matters and decide *jointly* how money is to be spent. In addition, they need to realize that no matter who earns the money that comes in, it all belongs to both of them equally. Wise, careful planning about how money is to be used not only makes it possible for two people to live within their financial means, but it also gives them both a sense of responsibility for a venture that is a united effort in making a marriage what it should be.

Setting up a budget would help a young couple convert their dreams to realities. It would reflect their needs and wants, goals and desires. It should include items that are more or less fixed, such as rent, food, transportation, as well as items that are flexible or unexpected, such as entertainment, medicine, and clothing. Other items that should be included in a budget are insurance (whether it be automobile, health, or life), savings, and an emergency fund.

Since the majority of couples who marry today find themselves in the throes of parenthood within the first five years of their marriage, it is also important to explore the costs of raising a child in our society today. In economist Lawrence Olson's book *Cost of Children*, he calculates that on an average, a family in the United States should expect to spend $226,000 to rear a first-born to age twenty-two (in terms of 1982 U. S. dollars). He also estimates that it will cost approximately 2.2 percent more to raise a girl than a boy. Of course, parents have accomplished the raising of children since the beginning of the human race despite great obstacles; and they will continue to do so.

Planning for the future means planning *now*. Making a good future happen depends a great deal on self-discipline and self-direction. Self-direction involves setting goals for one's life; self-discipline involves living each day in a way that will get one to his or her goals. As a young adult, you can learn to work within your own personal budget. You can explore the advantages and disadvantages of installment loans and credit

Aggressive: Imposing either physical or emotional harm on another human being.

Assertive: Expressing what you believe to be right in a positive and respectful manner.

Perhaps in no other area of family living is there more naiveté than in the financial aspect of living in marriage.

cards and how different rates of interest can affect—and increase—the cost of an item. It can also be a time of learning about the perils of impulse buying, which implies a lack of planning and thinking about a purchase and may result in a situation of wasted money. Setting up your own personal budget and learning to live within your means now will help you to one day live successfully in marriage.

Parenting

Two people looking ahead toward marriage also need to explore their own feelings about being parents and their attitudes with regard to raising children, and they should discuss their feelings with their partner.

Raising children is not an easy task. It takes special skills, emotional control, foresight, and courage. Ideally, children should be raised in a family situation where there is mature, sexual love and a healthy physical and emotional atmosphere. In addition, there should be enough money to take care of basic family needs and an abundant supply of parental love and understanding. Like all of us, children respond best in a loving, accepting family situation.

For children to be raised in such an ideal situation, a married couple needs to be skilled in the art of parenting. However, although parenthood is a phase of life that most individuals encounter—whether a planned experience or not—very few receive any type of education in parenting. Being able to produce a child does not automatically provide the wisdom or the skill to be a good parent.

Good parenting includes all the skills both parents need to nurture, raise, educate, and prepare their children for life. It includes the love and respect the parents have for each other, the way they exhibit those qualities to their children, and the demonstrations of a wider love and respect for people outside the family. It also involves the demonstrating and sharing of values parents believe are important for their children to have. Above all, being a good parent requires self-discipline, patience, and sacrifice.

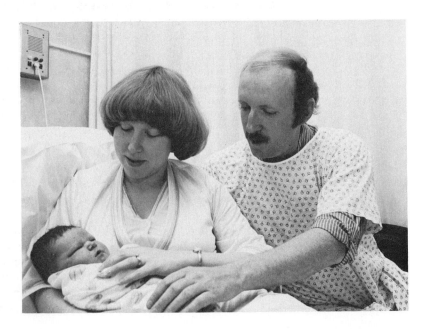

40

Couples looking ahead toward marriage ought to ask themselves if they as individuals and as a couple have the physical and emotional capabilities to raise children from infancy through adolescence into adulthood. Of course, most young people do not now possess many of the skills required to be good parents, but they can learn the skills and practice the virtues needed to become good parents.

Some of the skills inherent in becoming a good parent are the same skills that are present in every day interactions with others. Good communication skills, respect for others, being understanding and caring are all attributes that can be developed every day of one's life. In addition, courses, workshops, and books can help train a person for parenting.

Questions about Parenting Skills

To determine their readiness for raising children in a stable family environment, young couples should ask themselves certain personal questions such as:

- Do I like children?
- Do I want children?
- How many children do I think I can handle physically and emotionally?
- What do I want my children to be like?
- How will I help them achieve what I would like for them?
- How able am I to handle stress, disappointment, and failure?
- How able am I to handle success, money, ambition, flattery, and sexual and drug enticements?
- Do I have reasonable control over my emotions?
- Do I get angry often or lose patience?
- Do I have control over my tongue?
- Am I a complainer?
- Do I blame others?
- Am I outgoing or too self-centered?
- Do I volunteer my services easily?
- Am I willing to do whatever is necessary to make my family comfortable?
- Do I put other's welfare before my own?

In addition to asking themselves those personal questions to determine their readiness for raising a family, young couples should determine their skill readiness for marriage and parenting. To do so, they ought to seek information and learn from observation and reflection about the following:

- What the health needs of a pregnant woman are
- How to give birth to a baby
- How to clothe and diaper a baby
- How and what to feed a baby
- How to burp a baby
- How to wash, hold, and attend a baby
- How to cuddle, play with, and teach a baby
- How to cope with a handicapped baby
- How to handle a baby that cries incessantly
- What the health needs of a baby are
- What the symptoms of a mildly sick baby are

As a child grows, parents need to give attention to:

- The child's need for individual love and attention
- The child's health needs, and pre-school preparation
- The child's physical, emotional, and religious needs
- The child's need for discipline and encouragement
- The child's need for experiences outside the home and family
- The child's need to learn how to read, listen, pray, and share

Parenting during the Teen Years

As their children enter the preteen and adolescent years, parents should respect their growing need for independence while still letting them know what is expected of them. They should discuss sexuality and the role that sex should play in their lives. Parents should guide them in their choice of a vocation and help them develop the social graces, self-confidence, and ambition they need to succeed. They should make them aware of their role in society and their responsibilities to themselves, their family, their work and social groups, and to the world in general. Parents should prepare them for their political and cultural world and assist them to become self-reliant, honest, and true to their word. They should encourage their children to be themselves and to seek what they (the children) think is best for themselves.

At all times, parents should display love and affection for their children. They must show their children that they care for them above all else. They must be patient, understanding, and forgiving. Children learn about life and how it is lived from their parents.

---

1. Name some areas in which decisions will have to be made in planning for marriage.
2. How does one prepare for the commitment of marriage?
3. What does good parenting include?
4. State five questions young couples should ask themselves in determining their readiness for raising children. What kind of information should they seek?
5. What qualities do parents need to demonstrate when their children enter adolescence?
6. How does learning to prepare a budget as a young adult affect one's success in marriage?

Conception: The Miracle of Life

All of the physical changes that occur in the male and female reproductive systems eventually enabling a married couple to become parents lead to one of the most amazing phenomena in the created world: the creation of a new human being.

A new human life begins with the joining of a man and a woman in sexual intercourse. In sexual intercourse, the erect penis of the male enters the vagina of the female. The rubbing of the penis against the walls of the vagina brings the male to orgasm and semen is ejaculated into the upper end of the vagina. Some of the millions of sperm then

Education in love as self-giving is also the indispensable premise for parents called to give their children a clear and delicate sex education. Faced with a culture that largely reduces human sexuality to the level of something commonplace since it interprets and lives it in a reductive and impoverished way by linking it solely with the body and with selfish pleasure, the educational service of parents must aim firmly at a training in the area of sex that is truly and fully personal: For sexuality is an enrichment of the whole person—body, emotions, and soul. . . .

Pope John Paul II
Familiaris Consortio no. 37

A Father Reflects

OFTEN THERE flashes through my mind the comment carried on our book plate: "The paternal hearth, the gathering place of the affections." This quotation has impressed me deeply over many years, and particularly so in that it has been so richly realized in my own case. You cannot realize, nor can anyone, the measure of satisfaction to your mother and to me that all of the children are glad to come back to that modest place which we still call home. And to magnify that glow of satisfaction, the desire to come back has extended itself to all of the in-laws and to the grandchildren, I believe. I believe that we have a right to be proud that this is so, and I would not trade that possession for anything in the world that others might have.

There was a time in my life when we were considered well to do; that time has passed by. Years ago I had a much more responsible position than I do now, and I shall not be burdened with greater responsibility in the future, it is likely. . . . Happiness and contentment are to be found in the closely knit harmonious family unit . . . .

From a letter sent to John and Mary Steele, January 5, 1940, by Albert W. Wilkins.

enter the cervical canal and swim through the uterus and up into the fallopian tubes, looking for an egg on its way down from the ovary to the uterus. If an egg is present in the tube, only one sperm will finally penetrate it and move towards its nucleus. This is called conception or fertilization. Once this occurs, the fertilized egg resists the entrance of any other sperm cell trying to penetrate its surface.

As soon as the sperm enters the egg, the process of developing new human life begins. The process begins, not in the womb, but in the fallopian tube, when the cells begin to divide, roughly four to eight days before the fertilized egg takes root in the womb. (The fact that a new life begins and begins to develop even before the fertilized egg reaches the womb is important to the arguments of Right to Life proponents, who oppose abortion and its legalization. This new developing human life deserves the respect we give to other individual human life and may even deserve it more because it is so vulnerable. Moreover, human life is sacred, as is the reproductive process begun with the act of intercourse, and it is not to be violated or disrupted.)

But the miracle of conception does not end the miracle of the womb. In the womb itself, a thick, soft, spongy lining, rich in blood vessels has been made ready by the body chemistry of the woman. This becomes the "bed" for the fertilized egg. (If no fertilization takes place, the lining breaks down and the blood therein is expelled through the cervix. This is known as menstruation, or a woman's "period.") When conception takes place, the now fertilized egg multiplies in size and shape and travels down

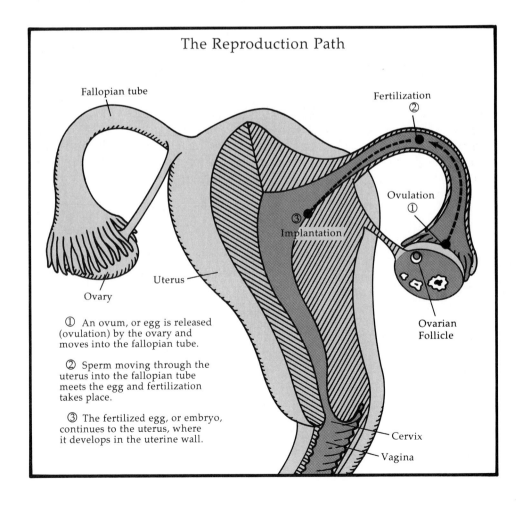

The Reproduction Path

Fallopian tube

Fertilization ②

Ovulation ①

Implantation ③

Ovarian Follicle

Uterus

Ovary

Cervix

Vagina

① An ovum, or egg is released (ovulation) by the ovary and moves into the fallopian tube.

② Sperm moving through the uterus into the fallopian tube meets the egg and fertilization takes place.

③ The fertilized egg, or embryo, continues to the uterus, where it develops in the uterine wall.

the tube to the womb where it attaches itself to the lining of the womb. This "attack" by a "foreign object" causes scar tissue to form on the womb which closes over the fertilized egg forming the protective home for the developing **embryo.** As the fertilized egg continues to develop—attached to the wall of the womb—its attachment to the womb becomes a kind of stalk, called the umbilical cord, and a bubblelike sac filled with fluid surrounds the embryo.

Meanwhile, the woman's body, responding to the miracle of pregnancy, creates the placenta, a thick disk-shaped collection of blood vessels and tissues growing on the inner wall of the uterus which provides for the nourishment of the fetus and for the elimination of waste products. Blood vessels, developing in the body stalk and soft lining signal the beginning of the baby's own circulatory system. Within one month, the **fetus** has simple kidneys, a digestive tract, a liver, a heart and blood flow.

During the period of growth in the womb, the fetus gets its nourishment (food and oxygen) from the placenta through blood vessels in the umbilical cord: two arteries leading from the baby to the placenta, and a vein from the placenta to the baby. These blood vessels branch out into the placenta with tiny leaflike fingers reaching out from each. The mother's blood, flowing in and through the womb walls, bathes these "fingers" so that they can dispose of waste matter and provide nourishment through the umbilical cord. The placenta thus serves as the baby's lungs, liver, kidneys, and intestines until the baby is born. It also serves the baby by providing hormones and producing ingredients that prevent infection.

During the nine months of pregnancy, the fetus lives in what is called the amniotic sac, a tough, transparent membrane filled with fluid. In a marvel of creation, this fluid is totally replaced every three hours, enabling the baby to live in a shock-proof, temperature-controlled environment. During the third month or so, the baby begins to practice breathing by inhaling and exhaling the fluid in the amniotic sac. It does not drown, however, because its oxygen comes from the placental activity previously described. Being in a state almost like weightlessness in this fluid, the developing baby begins exercising its muscle tissues, flailing its arms, kicking its feet, and turning somersaults—the actions which so surprise a woman pregnant for the first time, and fill her husband with awe as he feels the movement of the baby with his hand on his wife's abdomen.

During this time, of course, the woman's body is responding to the fetal activity. Her so-small womb expands as the baby grows within her (being able to accommodate a baby up to sixteen pounds—though the average is about seven pounds). When the time comes for birth, her body signals the muscles of her womb which begin a series of contractions (called labor), or waves of movement from the top of the womb to the cervix in clockwise and counterclockwise fashion. In the typical birth situation, the contractions are at first short and well-spaced, and as the body "practices" for the birth, they become more forceful and regular. When the body is ready [physiological and psychological factors determine this readiness], the baby is forced from the womb. Now the amniotic sac breaks, providing lubrication for the baby to pass through the neck of the cervix, and the vagina. The baby enters the "outside" world fully prepared to cope with the complexities of life outside the womb.

Embryo: The unborn in its earliest stages of development. In humans, the fertilized ovum during the first eight weeks of its growth.

Umbilical Cord: A flexible structure connecting the fetus and the placenta; navel cord.

Placenta: A thick disk-shaped collection of blood vessels and tissues growing on the inner wall of the uterus.

Labor: The contractions of the muscles of the uterus that first dilate the cervix and then, with the help of the abdominal muscles push the baby through the cervix and on through the birth canal.

With the birth of the baby, the umbilical cord and the placenta are also expelled from the womb. Shortly thereafter, the womb begins to contract to nearly its original size, and within a few weeks, it is ready to begin the process of getting ready for another impregnation.

Is it any wonder that people who understand the miracle of the womb have great respect for human reproductive powers and are dismayed when women are thought of, displayed, and used for a man's sexual pleasure alone? Christians understand the nature of sexual pleasure, but they see it as God's way of impelling people to participate in His creative process. They respect the reproductive organs of men and women as the means God has provided to enable people to "create" life—which, like God's own creative act, should be the result of true love. As Doctor Charles Bradford, a distinguished orthopedist, says:

> "The doctor observes the anatomical perfection of the hand, and the stabilizing microphones of the ear, and the television screens of the retina, and the multiple batteries of the electronic computers in the brain, and from all of these he gains a new reverence for the incomprehensible power that created man, so anxiously and so wonderfully wrought."

Conception Engineering

Modern medicine has made it possible that infertility in either a man or a woman is not necessarily a total bar to a couple's having children. In the past twenty years, the incidence of infertility has nearly tripled so that today, one in six couples in the United States is designated as infertile. (Science terms individuals infertile who have tried to conceive for a year or more without success.) For couples who seek to become parents, infertility can be frustrating and humiliating and can undermine the core of their relationship. It can also affect one's sexuality, self esteem, and self-image. It can even damage relationships with other family members and friends. At the same time, everyone knows that there are limits in the created world. Sometimes they cannot be overcome either physically or morally and must be accepted.

For women, the most common reason for infertility is an abnormality or blockage of the fallopian tubes where fertilization takes place. If the tubes are blocked or damaged by scar tissue, the egg will not be able to complete its journey toward fertilization. Also the postponement of childbirth until mid- or even late thirties, strenuous athletic activity, such as distance running, jogging, and some forms of dancing, and prolonged use of the contraceptive pill can sometimes cause temporary infertility.

It is now known that either the male or the female can be infertile, not just the female as was once usually thought. Research has found that in almost half the cases, men do not produce a sufficient amount of sperm to impregnate a woman. Ordinarily, about thirty million sperm must be produced to give one sperm a chance to penetrate and fertilize the egg. Other possible causes for infertility in both men and women are: working conditions, the effects of pollution, and medical treatment (X-rays, chemotherapy, some medications). Fortunately, with new advances in the scientific study of conception, the source of infertility in couples can be diagnosed in most cases. Half of all these cases can be treated.

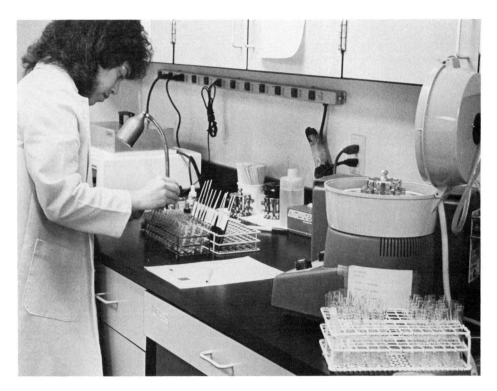

One of the most recent possibilities in the application of science to conception is in vitro fertilization (IVF). IVF involves the uniting of a sperm and an egg outside of the woman's body. Babies born as a result of this process are often referred to as "test-tube babies." IVF occurs in a variety of ways. A wife's egg may be fertilized by her husband's sperm; a wife's egg may be fertilized by a donor's sperm; or a donor's egg may be fertilized with the husband's sperm. It is also possible for a husband and wife to contribute their sperm and egg, but the embryo is carried by a third party who is donating the use of her womb.

In Vitro Fertilization: The uniting of a sperm and an egg outside of a woman's body.

At the present time, the success rates of this process vary from clinic to clinic, but even the best clinics offer little more than a 20 percent chance of pregnancy. Because of the high failure rate, in vitro clinics sometimes help nature along by administering drugs to the woman that can result in the development of more than one egg at a time. Then, when the egg is retrieved, a new process known as cryopreservation is used to freeze unused embryos in liquid nitrogen. The embryos can then be thawed and transferred to the woman's uterus if the first attempt at fertilization fails.

Unfortunately, becoming pregnant isn't the end to the infertility problem since one-third of the IVF pregnancies spontaneously miscarry in the first three months.

The Catholic Church has been very cautious in its evaluation of new fertility techniques, because the issues at stake are of such paramount importance. The fact that something is possible in the technical sense does not make it automatically right from a moral point of view. These are some of the questions the Church raises:

In vitro fertilization is experimentation with human lives. The technique is far from perfected, and many fertilized eggs die before they can be implanted safely in the uterus. If there are remaining fertilized eggs after implantation of one, sometimes they are "disposed of." Respect for the human procreative mystery is easily lost.

The donor situation creates still other problems of experimentation with human life. For example, in the case of the surrogate mother, the following questions remain unanswered and troubling: Who is the mother?—the donor of the egg or the woman who carries the child through pregnancy (if they are different)? What are the rights and responsibilities of each of the adults involved? What are the rights of the child? How is the child an expression of the love between the parents? Is this fertility solution one that justifies the expenditure of such large amounts of research money and energy compared to other pressing medical needs, especially of the poor?

The Church's traditional teaching stands: the reproduction of a human life should come about only from natural sexual contact, that is, intercourse between married couples. The sex act must be unitive as well as procreative. Science and technology can help it along, but it cannot replace it. Indeed there are some techniques and devices which do not violate the physical integrity of the act of marital intercourse to which the Church's official teaching has given its approval. Discussion of the moral problems related to fertility care will continue as the various techniques are developed.

Family Size

When a man and a woman are thinking about or planning marriage, they must discuss family size. They should know how the other feels about having children, adoption, foster parenting, and relationships with members of the extended family (in-laws, aunts, uncles, cousins, etc.). Family size does not involve only the number of children a couple might have. It might also include the probability of having to care for one or more of the couple's parents. Other members of the extended family such as grandparents, aunts, or cousins might show up unexpectedly and become a part of the family unit!

In society today, many couples make a decision regarding family size on existing world conditions and on the number of children they feel they can reasonably bring into the world, educate, and bring to maturity. With so much concern being raised over the economic, cultural, political, and environmental ramifications of living in a time of dwindling natural resources, some married couples are taking the time to consider the size of a family they can afford to raise to ensure that they can meet the purpose and function of a family in the modern world.

The decision regarding family size should also take into consideration the physical and psychological condition of each partner and their probable economic condition. Catholic hospitals, for instance, have approved programs to provide information and advice on genetic factors. Responsible parents will use these services if there are indications they are needed. They also need to know whether they are capable emotionally and financially of taking care of another human being. This decision can be made tentatively at the beginning of their marriage on the basis of probable expectations for their foreseeable future. As their situation changes, their needs can be reevaluated and perhaps decisions altered over the years as their circumstances change.

Children are a gift from God and, where possible, a vital part of the family unit. Children, however, must be looked at as persons to be loved, not as faceless things to be had. Therefore, parents must commit themselves to loving the children they have or plan to have.

Family Size and the Catholic Church

Over the centuries, the advances in medicine and the preponderance of improved health services have resulted in a decrease in infant mortality and an increase in birthrates and longevity. Therefore, parents need to plan their families carefully and try to arrange pregnancies in accordance with their physical, social, and psychological needs, and their

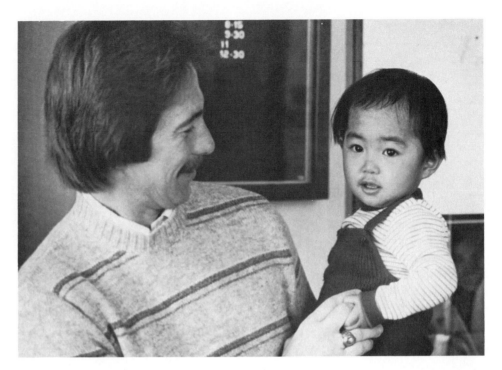

ability to raise their children and in accordance with their sense of God's call to parenthood for them. Recognizing this, Pope Paul VI instructed Christians to assume this responsibility:

> *Finally, it is for the parents to decide, with full knowledge of the matter, on the number of their children, taking into account their responsibilities toward God, themselves, the children they have already brought into the world, and the community to which they belong. In all this, they must follow the demands of their own conscience enlightened by God's law authentically interpreted, and sustained by confidence in Him.[1]*

This freedom to be *personally* responsible for the regulation of family size and growth has also been officially stated by the Church during Vatican Council II:

> *The parents themselves should ultimately make this judgment, in the sight of God. (50)*
>
> *For in view of the inalienable human right to marry and beget children, the question of how many children should be born belongs to the honest judgment of parents. (87)*
>
> *Only in freedom can man direct himself toward goodness. . . . For its part, authentic freedom is an exceptional sign of the divine image within man. . . .*
>
> *Hence man's dignity demands that he act according to a knowing and free choice. Such a choice is personally motivated and prompted from within.(17)[2]*

Responsible family planning between husband and wife is not the only means of determining the size of a family unit. As we have mentioned, it may also include *enlarging* the family by the addition of others

1. *On the Development of Peoples,* encyclical of Pope Paul VI, paragraph 37.
2. Walter M. Abbott, S. J. and Rev. Joseph Gallagher, "Pastoral Constitution on the Church in the Modern World," *Documents of Vatican II* (Chicago, Il: Follet Publishing Company, 1966).

from outside the family unit. Many couples feel that their family life is incomplete without a number of people to share the happiness of life with them. Others feel a social responsibility to enlarge their families, contributing their services to society at large and to individuals in particular. Both fulfill this need by adoption, by being foster parents, by accepting foreign exchange students, or by opening their homes to people in need of a place to stay. They welcome others into their homes, treat them as family members, and endeavor to help them lead useful lives.

With the medical advances increasing individual life spans, and costs of living increasing at an annual rate, a very real possibility that every young couple must face is the care of elderly parents. As so often happens, one or both parents of a couple may live to an age where they will need *family* care. Responsibility for this care rests on all members of a family, of course, but oftentimes it becomes the responsibility of just one person. Planning the size of one's family must take this eventuality into consideration.

The essence of planning a family is the creation of a meaningful family.

It must always be remembered in planning a family unit that *the essence of family planning is the creation of a meaningful family.* It includes much more than determining the spacing and number of new members in the family. It includes the whole lifestyle of the family in view of the unique individuality of man and wife, their social, economic, and political environment, and the potentiality of each person in the family unit.

---

1. Describe the process of developing a new human life.
2. State several reasons for the increase in infertility in the United States today.
3. Describe the in vitro fertilization process.
4. Christians respect the reproductive organs of men and women as the means to do what?
5. Why does your book call human conception a "miracle"? Could you call animal reproduction a "miracle", also? If you think so, state why. If not, why not?
6. Why are some couples taking the time to consider the size of a family they are called to produce and raise?
7. What responsibility does Pope Paul VI instruct Christians to assume when planning a family?

The Catholic Church and Family Planning

The Catholic Church believes that all human relationships ought to be life-giving and love-giving. A life-giving relationship at its fullest in marriage is one in which the individuals co-create new human life with God, and help each other and the child or children to grow as persons, to become more fully human, more fully alive, and thus, more holy and more whole. Such a relationship is, of its nature, unselfish, for it seeks the good of the other person.

A love-giving relationship between a husband and wife calls out for sharing, generosity, and fruitfulness. The couple's relationship will grow as they share their love with each other and with others. If having a child is possible for a couple, this is the most natural and sublime way for them to fully express the life-giving and love-giving qualities of their relationship.

In his encyclical, *Humanae Vitae*,[3] Pope Paul VI described the characteristics of married love this way:

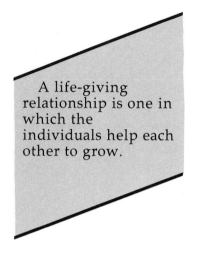

A life-giving relationship is one in which the individuals help each other to grow.

> *This love is first of all fully* human, *that is to say, of the senses and of the spirit at the same time. It is not, then, a simple transport of instinct and sentiment, but also, and principally, an act of the free will, intended to endure and to grow by means of the joys and sorrows of daily life, in such a way that husband and wife become one only heart and one only soul, and together attain their human perfection.*
>
> *Then, this love is* total, *that is to say, it is a very special form of personal friendship, in which husband and wife generously share everything, without undue reservations or selfish calculations. Whoever truly loves his marriage partner loves not only for what he receives, but for the partner's self, rejoicing that he can enrich his partner with the gift of himself.*
>
> *Again, this love is* faithful and exclusive *until death. Thus in fact do bride and groom conceive it to be on the day when they freely and in full awareness assume the duty of the marriage bond. A fidelity, this, which can sometimes be difficult, but is always possible, always noble and meritorious, as no one can deny. The example of so many married persons down through the centuries shows, not only that fidelity is according to the nature of marriage, but also that it is a source of profound and lasting happiness.*
>
> *And finally this love is* fecund *for it is not exhausted by the communion between husband and wife, but is destined to continue, raising up new lives. Marriage and conjugal love are by their nature ordained toward the begetting and educating of children. Children are really the supreme gift of marriage and contribute very substantially to the welfare of their parents.*

As Pope Paul describes it in his encyclical, sexual expression within marriage is meant to be unitive and procreative. Catholics believe that sexual intercourse is proper only to marriage because it is only within such a committed relationship that all of the qualities of love mentioned above are possible. Within the marriage relationship, they also believe that sexual intercourse ought to express and promote the unity of the couple and be open to life in whatever ways that are possible.

Although the Catholic Church believes that marriage and conjugal love are by their nature ordained toward the begetting and educating of children, it also recognizes that there are times when a couple can or must choose not to have children. This decision, the Church points out, ought to be made only for unselfish and serious reasons. Among such reasons are (1) the inability of the couple to support children—or another child—for financial or psychological reasons; (2) the health of the

3. An encyclical is a formal letter or document sent by the Pope to all the bishops of the Roman Catholic Church. Its material applies to all Catholics. *Humanae Vitae*, the first words of Pope Paul VI's letter, means "of human life." This encyclical deals with the moral aspects of marriage, birth control, and abortion as viewed by the Roman Catholic Church. (*Humanae Vitae*, no. 9)

mother and/or father; and (3) social responsibility. The Church Fathers at Vatican II put it this way:

> Parents should regard as their proper mission the task of transmitting human life and educating those to whom it has been transmitted. They should realize that they are thereby cooperators with the love of God the Creator, and are, so to speak, the interpreters of that love. Thus they will fulfill their task with human and Christian responsibility. With docile reverence toward God, they will come to the right decision by common counsel and effort.
>
> They will thoughtfully take into account both their own welfare and that of their children, those already born and those which may be foreseen. For this accounting they will reckon with both the material and the spiritual conditions of the times as well as of their state in life. Finally, they will consult the interests of the family group, of temporal society, and of the Church herself.[4]
>
> This council realizes that certain modern conditions often keep couples from arranging their married lives harmoniously, and that they find themselves in circumstances where at least temporarily the size of their families should not be increased.[5]

As a method to avoid pregnancy, or to space pregnancies for the good of the family or of society, the Catholic Church morally approves methods of natural family planning, which keep intact the unitive and procreative aspects of their sexual expression. With a properly informed conscience regarding the Church's teaching on conception control (also known as birth control), a married couple must choose a method of family

4. Walter M. Abbot, S. J. and Rev. Joseph Galagher, "Pastoral Constitution on the Church in the Modern World," *Documents of Vatican II* (Chicago, IL: Follett Publishing Company, 1966) number 50.

5. *Documents of Vatican II*, number 51.

planning that is both life-giving and love-giving to the greatest extent possible for them at a particular time.

> *For in view of the inalienable human right to marry and beget children, the question of how many children should be born belongs to the honest judgment of the parents. The question can in no way be committed to the decisions of government. Now since the judgment of the parents supposes a rightly formed conscience, it is highly important that everyone be given the opportunity to practice upright and truly human responsibility. This responsibility respects the divine law and takes account of circumstances and the times. It requires that educational and social conditions in various places be changed for the better, and especially that religious instruction or at least full moral training be provided.[6]*

Conception Control

An awareness of the beauty and complexity of the human reproductive system and knowledge of the patterns of fertility and of the methods for control of conception are essential for responsible parenthood.

Conception can be controlled by natural or artificial means. Two natural family planning methods are the Billings Ovulation Method, or the mucus method, and the basal body temperature method, or the temperature method.

Artificial means of conception control include the use of mechanical or chemical materials of various kinds. In either case, most pregnancies can be avoided or spaced according to the wishes of the married couple. The only certain method of controlling conception, of course, is abstaining from sexual intercourse during a woman's fertile period.

6. *Documents of Vatican II,* number 87.

Natural Family Planning

As we have said, the various natural methods of conception control in the natural family planning process (method) are based on an awareness of fertility and a thorough understanding of the reproductive system. These methods allow couples to live with their natural life-giving powers rather than interfere with them. To use either of these methods of fertility awareness to avoid a pregnancy, a couple abstains from sexual intercourse for several days during the time of the woman's monthly cycle when she would most likely be able to conceive. A couple planning on having a child can also use the methods to pinpoint more accurately the time when the woman ovulates; that is, when she is fertile.

The **Billings Ovulation Method** was developed by Doctors Evelyn and John Billings in the late 1960s. The method is generally taught to couples in small groups by competent instructors, often through local hospitals. Several earlier studies and their own study led the Billings to the conclusion that the mucus discharge from the vagina differs at various times during a woman's cycle.

Day one of a cycle is the first day of the menstrual period. After the period ceases, a woman can observe the color, texture and quantity of the natural mucus discharge. The yellowish, viscous mucus that is normally present before and after the fertile phase of the menstrual cycle becomes thinner, clearer, stringy, and more profuse as a woman approaches her fertile time (about half-way through a normal twenty-eight day period). The mucus becomes a slippery, stretchable, clear discharge, much like a raw egg white during ovulation as a result of a low saline content and a high estrogen level.

Most fertile women are able to notice these fairly regular changes in the vaginal mucus and can pinpoint the time of ovulation in each cycle. In addition to indicating the approach of ovulation, the presence of the mucus apparently assists in the preservation of the male's sperm cells and in their transport to the site of fertilization.

The change in mucus texture usually begins about six days before ovulation. If a pregnancy is not desired, intercourse must be avoided from the beginning of the fertile time. The most fertile time of the cycle is the last day of the fertile-type mucus. Three days after the return to the pre-fertile-type mucus or the disappearance of the mucus, it can be assumed that the time of ovulation has passed and that the woman is in the infertile final stage of her cycle.

Couples using the Billings Method often keep a monthly chart to record the significant changes. Note that, unlike the so-called "Rhythm Method," the focus is always on the current reproductive cycle. One is not predicting the time of ovulation for the current cycle based on past cycles, but measuring as well as possible the current cycle, using data about past cycles only insofar as it may be helpful.

A second natural method of conception control is the **basal body temperature method,** commonly called the BBT method. The basal body temperature is the lowest temperature reached by the body of a healthy person during waking hours. By noting this temperature daily at the same waking time and before rising out of bed, a woman may determine her time of ovulation after she has recorded her BBT on a chart for three to four successive months. Although there can be striking variations between the chart characteristics of different women, the majority of women will find their temperature chart to be fairly consistent from month to month. In any case, the focus is always on one couple determining one particular cycle, using data only insofar as it may be helpful.

Immediately preceding ovulation, the BBT of some women drops slightly; other women do not notice any drop. From twenty-four to seventy-two hours after ovulation, however, a noticeable rise in temperature takes place, usually four to six tenths of one degree Fahrenheit. Her temperature will then remain high until the next menstrual period begins.

Some women have one or more other regular signs of ovulation, such as a mood change or a brief spotting of blood. Some of these signs are helpful to the individual but are not general enough for common use. Once a woman determines when ovulation occurs in her menstrual cycle, she can abstain from sexual activity for eight to ten days surrounding that period of time or until the fourth day of the sustained temperature rise.

The sympto-thermo method combines the mucus signs and the temperature pattern and adds one more fertility indicator: the cervix sign. The safe period after ovulation is judged from three days of raised temperature after the mucus dries up or returns to the nonfertile state. The cervix (lower part of the uterus) provides an additional guide to the fertile time in a woman's cycle, as it changes in position and texture during ovulation. During a woman's infertile time, the cervix, which can be felt by inserting a finger into the vagina, is closed, low in the vagina, and firm to the touch. At the time of ovulation, the cervix feels open, higher, and soft to the touch. The changes at the time of ovulation are due to the increase in estrogen as that time approaches. At ovulation, progesterone increases and causes the cervix to return to its former condition.

Some couples add one more indicator to chart the last safe day for intercourse without risking pregnancy prior to ovulation. This is the twenty-one-day rule and is similar to the method used in bygone days—the rhythm or calendar method—before other fertility indicators were researched. To use the twenty-one-day rule, a woman must know the number of days in her shortest cycle of the last twelve cycles (or better yet, eighteen or twenty-four cycles). If, for example, her shortest cycle was twenty-seven days, she would subtract twenty-one from twenty-seven, which would be six. Her last safe day, counting from the beginning of her period, would be day six. Other indicators would be used to verify this and to determine the length of her suspected possibly fertile time in each given cycle. The twenty-one-day rule would be ignored if the mucus sign contradicted it, because the mucus sign is based on the present cycle while the twenty-one-day rule is based on past cycles. Some couples successfully use a combination of the temperature method and the twenty-one-day rule.

Although abstinence, per se, is not usually listed as a natural method of natural family planning, it is a very commonly used method of conception control. Many people choose abstinence for moral, religious, and ethical reasons. No matter what a person's age, it is important for him or her to know that it's not necessary to have intercourse and that decisions about having sex are important ones that should be made very thoughtfully and in the context of their moral and ethical values. At the same time, refraining from intercourse for long periods of time can cause severe strain on a marriage, which, after all, ordinarily includes physical sexual love.

The natural methods of birth control require a high degree of communication, moral discipline, and cooperation between a husband and wife. In addition, they require a couple to have a better than usual un-

Announcements
NOVEMBER 6

| 7 00 AM | PACE WORKSHOP | 6TH FL AUD |
| 9 30 | MERCY SERVICE CLUB | 6TH FL BD RM |

NATURAL FAMILY
PLANNING CLASS
ROOM 638

derstanding of their reproductive powers and to be truly in control of those powers. Love is both required and deepened by these methods. Moreover, they involve no health risk to the wife, in contrast to several artificial methods of birth control that carry with them significant health risks.

Note that these methods can also be used to increase the chance of conception in cases where there are fertility problems. They can even be used to plan the exact occasion of conception. An added bonus is the fact that by becoming knowledgeable about her body and its patterns, a woman can often promptly recognize abnormal situations that may require medical attention. Overall, because of these natural family planning methods, couples develop a respect and appreciation for the human body, for nonphysical forms of expressing love, and for the miracle of human fertility.

The Church forbids the use of artificial methods of birth control for her members because these methods interfere with the procreative aspect of sexual intercourse. The Church teaches that complete love-making between a husband and wife is love-giving and life-giving, unitive and procreative. On this point, Pope John Paul II wrote the following:

"The inseparable connection between the unitive and procreative aspects of marriage is founded on the intimate structure of the marriage act itself, which enables a husband and wife to generate life according to the laws inscribed in the very being of man and woman. By safeguarding both these essential aspects, the marriage act preserves in its fullness the sense of true mutual love. At the same time, it remains faithful to God's design for the purposes of marriage in directing husband and wife toward their high calling of parenthood."[7]

7. Quoted in *Florida Catholic*, August 31, 1984, page 14.

Almost 40 percent of today's twenty-year-old women have had at least one pregnancy in their teens.

Out-of-wedlock teen births tripled between 1960 and 1980.

It is for these reasons that the Catholic Church approves as a moral means the use of natural family planning rather than any of the following artificial methods. It is important to know about these artificial methods if only because there are other reasons to avoid these forms in addition to the Church's prohibition based on the nature of the marital act. Whether it is "children having children" (teen pregnancies) or adults having children, knowledge of patterns of fertility and its control are essential for responsible parenthood.

It is a tragic fact that teenagers in the United States are having babies, often out of wedlock, at an alarming rate. Almost 40 percent of today's twenty-year-old women have had at least one pregnancy in their teens.[8] Out-of-wedlock teen births tripled between 1960 and 1980, creating a social problem that cannot be ignored.

The reasons for the high incidence of teenage pregnancies are multiple and vary from individual to individual. Certainly the problem will never be solved by conception control or abortion. Societal changes must occur before the teenage pregnancy problem is solved. No matter what the ages, however, adults and teenagers alike need information on their reproductive systems and on family planning to assist them in making responsible decisions about parenthood. It should also be noted that figures which compare death rates for a method of artificial contraception

8. *Fact Book on Teenage Pregnancy. Tables and References for Teenage Pregnancy: The Problem That Hasn't Gone Away* (New York: Alan Guttenbacher Institute, 1981).

with the death rate of mothers who give birth are scientifically questionable. This is because mothers who die sometimes do not get good medical care; it is not clear how many would have died with good medical care and so it is doubtful whether the statistical comparisons are valid.

Artificial Methods of Conception Control

Artificial methods of conception control act in a variety of ways to prevent a pregnancy. Some suppress ovulation. Some prevent implantation of the fertilized egg in the uterus. (These do not involve conception control since conception would already have occurred. They are abortifacient, causing abortion.) Some include chemicals that destroy sperm, and still others create a barrier within the woman's body to prevent the sperm from reaching the ovum. None of these methods is 100% effective. In general, a key factor in the effectiveness of any method of conception control is the individuals using it: whether the method is used both the way it is prescribed and also every single time sexual intercourse occurs.

The contraceptive pill utilizes the synthetic hormones estrogen and progestins to manipulate the woman's menstrual cycle in controlling fertility. Estrogen is responsible for inhibiting ovulation; progestins cause changes in the mucus in the cervix that hamper the movement of sperm and decrease the ability of sperm to penetrate the cervical mucus. The pill is considered to be the most effective artificial method of birth control because it suppresses ovulation. If ovulation does not occur, there is no egg for the sperm to fertilize; hence, conception does not take place. Side effects from use of the pill may be minor (weight gain, bloated feeling, mild depression) or major (high blood pressure, headaches, increased risk of thrombophlebitis and infertility).

Research is constantly being conducted on oral contraceptives for men. But because of complications (the slowness with which male antifertility agents begin to take effect, the slow return to fertility after discontinuing use, and difficulties in the ways of administering these agents) most researchers agree that no male oral contraceptive pill will be marketed within the next few years in the United States.

A second artificial method of conception control used by women is the intrauterine device, or IUD. IUDs are made of plastic or metal. They vary in shape and size and may or may not contain other ingredients such as copper or progesterone. Inserted in a woman's uterus by way of the vagina, the IUD is suspected of increasing the movement of the egg in the fallopian tube, making it more difficult to fertilize. It is also believed that the body's inflammatory response to this foreign object prevents the implantation of the fertilized egg in the uterus. Because its effectiveness is not always from preventing the sperm and egg to meet, however, it is not a barrier method, that is, a method which acts only by preventing the sperm and egg from meeting and uniting.

Since the IUD does not always prevent fertilization, it is considered to be an abortifacient, that is, it causes very early abortions. An uninformed woman will mistake these for an ordinary menstrual period. Some of the more serious side-effects of the IUD are infection, severe pain, the piercing of the uterine wall, heavy bleeding, complications when pregnancies occur, miscarriages, permanent sterility as a result of some infections, and death.

There are also several foams, creams, jellies, and vaginal suppositories that contain chemicals (spermicidal agents) that destroy sperm and thus prevent conception. These spermicidal agents are inserted into the woman's vagina before intercourse and can be used either alone or in connection with other devices. Because they are chemicals, they can sometimes cause an irritation or an infection. And they can possibly cause birth defects.

The diaphragm and the cervical cap are barrier contraceptive devices for women. A diaphragm is a rubber dome-shaped, cup-like device with a flexible rim that is placed inside the vagina and covers the cervix. The cervical cap is thimble-shaped and fits over the cervix. It is held in place by suction between its firm, flexible rim and the surface of the cervix. Both must be fitted by a doctor or health technician for correct fit and effectiveness, and both barrier methods are used with contraceptive jellies that contain spermicidal agents to destroy any sperm that come in contact with it. Inconvenience, discomfort, possibility of improper fit, and difficulty in using them are negative factors.

A fairly new barrier-type contraceptive is the sponge, which is placed inside the woman's vagina and rests against the cervix as a barrier. It contains a spermicide as well. Unlike the diaphragm and the cervical cap, the sponge is used only once and then disposed of. The woman who uses the sponge as a method of contraception risks getting toxic shock syndrome, especially if the sponge is not removed within twenty-four hours after intercourse. It is too new to be sure what its statistical effectiveness in conception control is.

Another barrier-type artificial method of conception control—the only one available to men—is the prophylactic or condom. It is a thin, rubber sheath that is worn over the erect penis to prevent the transmission of semen into the vagina. Its relatively low rate of effectiveness, including from breakage, is a negative factor, besides having negative aesthetic factors.

Permanent forms of birth control, known as sterilizations, are the most common methods of conception control for both men and women in our society today. Known as a vasectomy for men and a tubal ligation for women, they are performed to stop conception from occurring.

Sterilization: Permanent forms of birth control.

The vasectomy is a surgical procedure for men by which a small incision in the scrotum is made so that the vas deferens can be lifted out and about an inch of it can be cut away. The ends are then tied, thus blocking the passage of sperm from the testicles to the ejaculatory ducts. It can usually be performed in about twenty to thirty minutes on an outpatient basis under general or local anesthesia. The procedure is generally irreversible, so it is a very serious decision for a couple. A man who has had a vasectomy can still have sex, of course, but his sperm is not ejaculated. It is absorbed by the body and/or eliminated through the bladder.

Tubal ligations may be done either by an incision in the woman's abdomen or through the vagina. In either procedure, the fallopian tubes are cut or blocked. Because of this, ova cannot make their way down the tubes and ordinarily cannot be fertilized by the male sperm. A tubal ligation requires a hospital or clinic stay of several hours or overnight. Again, there is no sure method of reversal. Neither form of sterilization (vasectomy or tubal ligation) is effective in all cases. And no surgery is risk-free.

Another procedure which leaves a woman sterile but is most often performed to correct certain abnormalities or malignancies is a hysterectomy. A hysterectomy is the surgical removal of the uterus and may or may not include the removal of the fallopian tubes and ovaries. Following a hysterectomy, a woman ceases to have her menstrual cycle and she is no longer capable of reproducing. A longer hospital stay and period of recovery is required.

There are other surgeries and medical treatments for men and for women which may cause sterility as a side effect or as an unintended effect.

The Abortion Issue

Abortion is such a serious social issue with physical, emotional, moral, and religious ramifications that it should be discussed by couples contemplating marriage. Clearly, if you reject abortion and your partner does not, the difference is too severe for a marriage to take place. In the United States in 1982, more than 1,600,000 abortions were performed on women of childbearing age. Almost eighty percent of these were by unmarried women. In 1983, more than one million teenage girls became pregnant, and more than 400,000 of them elected to have an abortion. These figures do not include unreported pregnancies, miscarriages, or

Abortion: The termination of a pregnancy before the fetus ordinarily is capable of living on its own. It usually causes or is followed by the death of the fetus.

self-induced abortions. Abortion has become a common form of birth control and is the standard policy of some governments throughout the world.[9]

Abortions became legal in the United States in 1973 when the Supreme Court ruled that a woman had a right to privacy which implies her right in consultation with her physician, to terminate a pregnancy. Until that time, abortions were illegal except (in some states) in cases where the life or health of a woman was in jeopardy. It was a crime punishable by law. It was not a question of "the fetus," "the embryo," "the ovum," or "the product of conception;" it was the question of an unborn child. To destroy the child in the womb was to destroy human life.[10]

In order to change the law and justify its position, the Supreme Court had to get around the legal tradition against abortion, the meaning of the word *abortion* in common usage, and the declared rights of the unborn. It shifted attention from "mother-and-unborn child" to "woman" and referred to the child in the womb in neuter terms, like "it".

The 1973 decision meant that it was legal anywhere in the United States for a woman to terminate a pregnancy at any time during a pregnancy. Later rulings provided that a dependant girl does not need the consent of her parents.

Since the Supreme Court decision, there have been major efforts by groups (known as "Pro-Life" or "Right to Life") to have the United States Constitution amended to prohibit abortion entirely and to affirm the unborn's right to life and protection under the law from the moment of conception.

Almost 80 percent of the 1,600,000 abortions performed in 1982 were procured by unmarried women.

9. In India, at least 15 million abortions are procured every year. In China, abortion forced by the government has been practiced to attain their goal of one child per couple. Accordingly, some Chinese couples also practice infanticide, the killing of children already born, usually females.

10. See *A Private Choice: Abortion in America in the Seventies*, (New York: Macmillan, 1979) by John T. Noonan, a legal scholar at the University of California in Berkeley.

I wish to affirm that the basis of our opposition to abortion is established by themes which should be compelling for the Catholic conscience because they are so centrally located in Catholic moral and social teaching.

The basic moral principle that the direct killing of the innocent is always wrong is so fundamental in Catholic theology that the need to defend it in the multiple cases of abortion, warfare, and care of the handicapped and the terminally ill is self-evident. This is why one cannot, with consistency, claim to be truly pro-life if one applies the principle of the sanctity of life to other issues but rejects it in the cases of abortion.

Cardinal Joseph Bernardin
Bishops' Committee for
Pro-Life Activities

Pro-Lifers maintain that from the moment of conception the fertilized egg is an individual human life. It has its own unique genetic inheritance. Its mother merely provides it with nourishment and a place to grow from the moment of fertilization until birth. In addition, they maintain that because this human life is harmless and innocent, it has a right to life as much as if not more than any other innocent human being and deserves the protection of the law. Society has no right to kill it, Pro-lifers say; to do so is murder. They believe that the Supreme Court decision has provided justification and legalization for an unspeakable crime.

John T. Noonan says:

> "How far the masking goes on, depends on whether there is a social imperative to conceal. In the case of abortion, the social pressure has been enormous and the need for a socially acceptable sponsorship has been proportionately high. "The famous editorial on the new ethics in California Medicine describes the masks and their sponsors in these terms: 'The very considerable semantic gymnastics which are required to rationalize abortion as anything but taking human life would be ludicrous if they were not put forward under socially impeccable auspices.' "[11]

In other words, some scientists saw they would have to twist human language (and they admitted it in the editorial). Because they were scientists, they were able to have some success in covering over what abortion is, even though the facts are obviously different than the false ideas and terms they put forth. It's a kind of brain-washing or propaganda.

It is important to remember in all the rhetoric surrounding the "Pro-choice"/"Pro-life" debates that abortion is (1) not a right; it is an option, or something people do and (2) abortion destroys human life, no matter what the child in the womb is called. This is the heart of the issue.

The Catholic Church and Abortion

The population of the world is growing at a rapid rate. It is estimated that if nothing more is done about this growth, there will be more than eight billion people who will have to be fed, clothed, and housed by the year 2025.

One of the principal means used for controlling population in some countries even by governments is abortion, because standard birth control measures have not worked and because appeals to people to refrain from having children have fallen on deaf ears. In the United States, some people use abortion as a "solution" to terminate an unplanned, untimely, unwanted pregnancy.

The Catholic Church recognizes the problem of overpopulation, appreciates the anguish and concern of individual women, and understands the need for governments to make policies and decisions concerning their people and the growth in population. Through its teaching authority, however, it says that abortion is an unacceptable solution to

---

11. *A Private Choice: Abortion in America.*

overpopulation and unwanted pregnancies. Natural Family Planning, abstinence from nonmarital sex, a fairer distribution of the world's goods, and increased economic growth are among the solutions the Church favors.

Abortion is an unacceptable solution to overpopulation and unwanted pregnancies.

The abortion question is not simply a Catholic issue.[12] It is a human issue. In the view of the Catholic Church, abortion is morally wrong because it is the killing of a human being. "Respect for human life," wrote Pope Paul VI, "is called for from the time the process of generation begins. From the time the ovum is fertilized, a life is begun which is neither that of the father nor of the mother. It is rather the life of a new human being with its own growth. It would never be made human if it were not human already."

The Catholic Church in the United States bases its moral position on abortion on four foundation footings:

1. The inherent dignity of every human being regardless of its chronological age or stage of development.
2. The divine potential of every human being created to share God's life forever.
3. The constant tradition of human experience which holds human life sacred.
4. The Constitution of the United States which, properly interpreted, guarantees the right to life of every human being regardless of age, sex, creed, race, or social status.

12. The Catholic Church's moral position is supported by most religious bodies and by various nonreligious organizations supporting children's rights.

64

In responding to the Supreme Court decision and the immediate widespread procurement of abortions, the bishops of the United States stated:

> It is therefore as ironic as it is tragic that, in a nation committed to human rights and dignity, the practice of legalized abortion is now widespread. Every human life is inviolable from its very beginning. While the unborn child may not be aware of itself and its rights, it is a human entity, a human being with potential, not a potential human being. Like the newborn, the unborn depend on others for life and the opportunity to share in human goods. Their dependence and vulnerability remind us of the social character of all human life: to live and thrive as a human being, each of us needs the help and support of others.
>
> To destroy these innocent unborn children is an unspeakable crime, a crime which subordinates weaker members of the human community to the interests of the stronger. God who calls us to Himself loves the helpless and weak; like Him we should affirm the unborn in their being, not close our eyes to their humanity so that we may more easily destroy them. Their right to life must be recognized and fully protected by the law.[13]

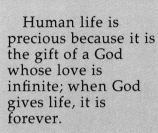

Human life is precious because it is the gift of a God whose love is infinite; when God gives life, it is forever.

Pope John Paul II

1. When do individuals who adhere to the "Pro-Life" movement believe that human life begins? Express the philosophy of the "Pro-Life" movement with regard to the abortion issue.
2. What is the Catholic Church's view on abortion?
3. Describe your own personal philosophy on abortion. Are there ever any exceptions to your own personal moral position? Do you hold one set of standards for your own behavior, but another set of standards for others?
4. Discuss how morality must enter into political discussion and decision-making.

Together with other religious and nonreligious groups and people, the Catholic Church hopes to see the legal status of abortions changed in the United States. Already payment for abortions with federal and some state funds has been stopped. Meanwhile, the Church does all it can through Catholic Charities, other agencies, and volunteer groups to provide aid and counselling to pregnant women so that they will not choose abortion. And it helps mothers after birth in countless ways.

In addition, the Catholic Church favors, promotes, and carries out responsible sex education programs for people of all ages so that (1) unplanned pregnancies can be avoided as much as possible and (2) pregnancies will be brought to term in order that precious human beings in God's image will be given the chance at life that their parents have had.

The only exception Catholic theologians make to the moral prohibition of abortion is in cases such as an ectopic pregnancy (the egg is fertilized but becomes implanted in the Fallopian tube rather than in the womb). In such a case, not only will the fetus die, it also poses a clear

13. Excerpted from "To Live in Christ Jesus." A Pastoral Reflection on the Moral Life: National Conference of Catholic Bishops: November 11, 1976.

threat to the life of the pregnant woman. In such a case, it is considered moral to remove the fetus from the mother's body in order to save the mother's life. Even though the fetus will thus ordinarily die, the intent was not to directly attack that life but to save the mother's life in the only way possible. In addition, the age at which the child can be kept alive outside the womb by technology gets lower and lower.

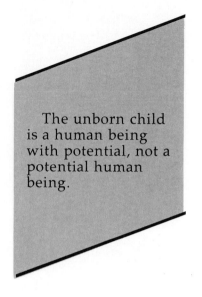

The unborn child is a human being with potential, not a potential human being.

Summary

- Living successfully in marriage requires planning. A couple's readiness for marriage, finances, family size, and parenting abilities are some of the more important areas where decisions made will affect how a couple lives its married life.
- All persons contemplating marriage must ask themselves if they are ready, as individuals and as a couple, for the total commitment of marriage. They must also determine if the physical and psychological condition of each partner and their probable economic condition are right for establishing a family unit of their own.
- One of the most amazing phenomena in the created world is the creation of a new human being. Conception engineering, or in-vitro fertilization, appear to be just the beginning of advances in the science of conception that provides new physical ways of conception for childless couples. The question is always whether the physical means is a moral means.
- The ability to determine whether and when to have a child is an important right of every human being, and there are various methods of natural and artificial conception control devices available to assist families in controlling their fertility. But as Pope Paul II stated, "The natural regulation of fertility is morally correct and contraception (that is, artificial means) is not morally correct." Since human life begins at conception, the Catholic Church also strongly teaches that abortion is morally wrong. To destroy these innocent unborn children, says the Roman Catholic Church, is an unspeakable crime.

Review, Discussion, Reflection, and Research

1. In an open forum, discuss requirements for being a good parent.
2. What do you understand by discipline in the home? What kind of discipline do you think is necessary and useful at various stages of child development?
3. Discuss the moral arguments concerning conception engineering.
4. Describe the various methods of natural and artificial contraception. Discuss the moral and other dimensions of each method.
5. Talk to your parents about the Supreme Court decision legalizing abortions in the United States. Does it seem to you to be the morally right decision?

Projects

1. Research the various alternatives that are available to an unmarried couple who find themselves with an unplanned pregnancy. Give your personal views on the moral dimensions of each option.
2. Research the pro-life vs. pro-choice viewpoints on abortion. Write a two-page objective report on their views.
3. Prepare a sample budget of a young couple getting married today. Estimate personal income and determine fixed and average family expenses. Include at least ten items in the budget. Use the sample below as a guide.

Name _____ Monthly Income _____

Fixed Items	Cost
Nonfixed Items	Cost
Possible Luxury Expenses	Cost

Words You Should Know

Be sure that you can define the following words and can use them in a meaningful sentence:

aggressive
assertive
conception
fertilization
embryo
fetus
umbilical cord
placenta
labor
contraception
in vitro fertilization
sterilization
abortion
abstinence

CHRISTIAN MARRIAGE

Chapter 3 Review

Chapter 4

CHRISTIAN MARRIAGE

The Question of Divorce

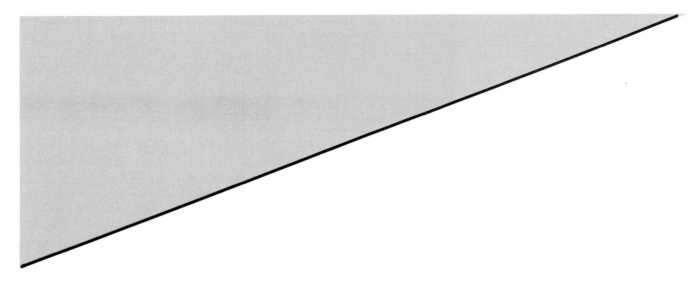

1. In the United States, a large percentage of marriages end up in divorce. In an open forum, discuss what you think are the principal causes for divorce and for the increase in divorce in the past twenty-five years.
2. Discuss what you think the effects of divorce are on the couple, their children, their relatives, and on society in general.

Divorce: An Admission of Failure

Marriage is romanticized in literature, films, on television, and in people's minds. And well it should be. It is a bonding relationship of love—the most powerful and most commonly sought-after need of the human spirit. Most marriages, of course, do not measure up to the unrealistic expectations and the romanticized pictures presented.

Most married couples find a good deal of happiness in their marriages. Many find some happiness and contentment. Many, however, find marriage to their particular partner not very good. In marriage, as in most human endeavors, human limitations take their toll.

Some marriages, unfortunately, just do not work out as had been hoped. Many teen marriages, for example, seem doomed from the start, and end up in divorce within three years. But marriages can begin to unravel almost anytime—divorce among couples married for more than twenty years has quadrupled in the last ten years!

Whenever a divorce occurs, it is an admission of failure. One or both parties come to realize that what most likely began with love and hope has now ended up being totally different than they had planned.

Divorce: A judicial declaration dissolving a marriage.

Causes for Divorce

Divorce is a process that begins with rather continuous distress in a marriage and involves a chain of events that includes legal, social, emotional, psychological, economic, and sexual changes and problems for the couple and for each one as an individual.

As one reviews in divorced couples the period of courtship before marriage, the evolution of the family, including the birth of children, and the course of the marital failure, no single answer can be given for the dramatic increase in the number of failures of so many marriages. Members of divorcing families no longer include only those suffering from loneliness and isolation, with each family member going his or her own way. They also include members who share a rich history, common recreational interests, and religious beliefs.

Some husbands and wives live together as strangers for many years. Communication between them is poor or almost nonexistent. For many couples seeking divorce, there is a pervasive sense of being uncared for, of having important and pressing needs which are unacknowledged and unmet by their partner. As a result, divorcing couples tend to blame one another for the failure of the marriage. Most researchers believe that the single most common cause for divorce stems from dissatisfaction with a particular spouse and not from marriage itself. The fact that most divorced people remarry within three years reinforces this statistic.

Among the causes for this dissatisfaction and the consequent failure of a marriage are the following:

- Lack of commitment to the marriage by either party.
- Keeping score on real or imagined hurtful actions.
- Blaming the partner for whatever caused the problem.
- Unrealized expectations, especially in teenage marriages.
- The failure of one party to grow and develop along with the other.
- The awakening of latent abilities and desires.
- Intolerable family situations.
- Personality traits that were unrecognized before marriage.
- Job requirements keeping the husband or wife away from his or her spouse for long periods of time.
- Infidelity—mostly, but not always, sexual.
- Excessive drinking and/or the use of drugs in a way that interferes with job efficiency or causes abuse and vulgarity.
- Financial problems—caused by excessive spending or squandering money on foolish or low priority items.
- Sexual temptations arising from changing customs and mores—causing both men and women to seek sexual gratification with a person other than their spouse (adultery).
- Shifting of marital priorities.
- Abuse of the spouse or of the children.
- Lack of personal cleanliness.
- Differences in religion.
- Lack of preparation for marriage—just sliding into marriage.
- Immaturity—sexual, emotional, or psychological.
- Selfishness of one or both of the parties.
- One partner's refusal to have children.
- Easy availability of marriage.
- Easy availability of divorce.
- Lack of effort to make the marriage work.
- Unsuitability—personality traits that clash.

Infidelity: Unfaithfulness to one's spouse.

Adultery: Seeking sexual gratification with someone other than one's spouse.

There are other causes ("As many as there are people seeking divorce," says one lawyer handling hundreds of cases per year), but these seem to be the most common.

Of course, not every couple experiencing one or more of these problems opts for divorce, but those who do, generally, find their relationship eroding bit by bit until there is little, if any, love relationship remaining.

If there is no love relationship—on any level—should the couple stay together? Only the couple can say whether they should or should not stay together, but only after due consideration and counsel, lest their emotions plunge them into a situation they may later regret.

The Effects of Divorce

Without a doubt, there are some people who would be better off not married, and there are some marriages that just do not work out as hoped. In both cases, divorce may be necessary. Divorce is not easy, however, even though it may be necessary.

Divorce ranks second—behind death—as the most severe trauma that an individual can experience. It signals the end of what began with so much hope. In divorce, everyone suffers. More often than not, the psychological and social obstacles that confront divorcing couples and their children are formidable, and the road back to personal, emotional, social, and economic tranquility can be a long one.

Divorce ranks second—behind death—among the most severe traumas that an individual can experience.

Divorce affects everyone involved in a particular marriage relationship. First, of course, it involves the married couple. Then it affects the social, economic, and psychological well-being of any children of the marriage. Finally, it involves the in-laws, relatives, friends, the Church, and society.

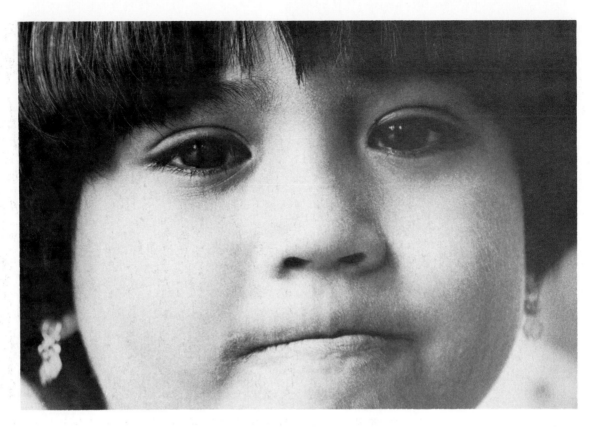

As far as the married couple is concerned, in all but a few cases, divorce is an admission of failure. Divorcing couples admit first to themselves that their marriage has failed. Then they admit to others, either openly or by their actions, that they are part of a failed or failing marriage.

The erosion of the love and trust with which a marriage began is usually slow and gradual. While it is true that some divorces are the result of some major problem or difficulty in one or both of the married persons, most often divorce begins with little things that gnaw at the trust and affection that were present at the beginning of the marriage. Soon, resentment at the cause, or causes, for the erosion of trust sets in. This is often followed by resentment toward the person who seems to be the cause of the erosion of trust and then the resentment is followed by anger.

If the cause, or causes, for the anger and resentment is not addressed and settled or compensated for, a strong desire to be rid of the cause sets in. This is followed by fear of the consequences.

These negative feelings soon affect the personalities of individuals and spill over into their conduct, communication, body language and voice. Guilt feelings, self-blame, and feelings of inferiority compound the trauma. Soon the situation occupies the time, energy, and productivity of the one, or ones, suffering.

Children of Divorcing Parents

If there are children involved in the failing marriage, the relationship between the parents and children does not always mirror the unhappy marital ties, and the stresses of the marriage do not necessarily spill over into the parents' relationships with the children. Sometimes, parents maintain a relatively conflict-free atmosphere with the children—though this is not always the case. Parents sometimes use their good relationship with their children as a means of offsetting their marital unhappiness.

This does not mean, however, that children do not suffer as a result of their parents' divorce. Most children suffer severe trauma and tend to blame themselves, at least partially, for the breakup of their parents' marriage. They can feel severely rejected by the divorcing parent and fear that they will be abandoned or deserted by both of their parents. It is also very likely that their lifestyle will be altered because their parents' financial status will change—an income that once supported one household is now responsible for supporting two.

Children of divorcing parents can experience a range of emotional reactions. On the one hand, they can feel resentment and anger toward their parents, while at the same time fantasizing about their parents' remarriage. They can also suffer from the taunts of their peers and from the stigma of their parents' "failure."

It is estimated that 50 percent of the children born in our society from now on will be raised in single-parent families and that at least half will not see their fathers for more than a year. "What's happening to kids is a howling shame," says University of Chicago law professor Franklin Zimring. "Parents used to think more of the kids when contemplating divorce or separation. Now they think mostly of themselves."

Divorce Changes Lifestyles

By the time the divorce has been legally completed, it becomes evident that there are definite changes in the lifestyles of all members of the family. Besides affecting the couple and their children, divorce also affects relatives, friends, in-laws, and the lifestyle of the couple and the children. First of all, the family has only a single parent for its anchor and role model. Secondly, increased stress is placed on both the single parent and the children.

Despite joint custody situations that make the news, in most cases, women have the legal custody of the children, and most children continue to live with their mothers. Men will most likely have visitation rights and, for a time, become "weekend fathers." They are frequently responsible for child support payments.

Women are often better able to live alone after a divorce because they have already mastered the skills needed for living alone. They have had considerable experience in shopping, cooking, cleaning, managing a house, and more often than not, parenting. Men, on the other hand, generally suffer more from loneliness, since they are without a spouse or any children.

In a good percentage of the cases, both men and women experience a substantial decline in their financial status. The harsh realities of socioeconomic change following the separation continue after the divorce. As a result, most women become employed fulltime. At the same time, it can be noted that one-third of all persons living in poverty have a female householder without a husband present. The sad results of divorce in America, together with unmarried parenthood, are easy to see in these terms.

Most children suffer severe trauma and tend to blame themselves, at least partially, for the breakup of their parents marriage.

It is estimated that 50 percent of the children born in our society from now on will be raised in single-parent families.

Divorce's Common By-product: Stepfamilies

After a divorce, it is very likely that one or both partners will remarry. As a result, a good percentage of the children will find themselves living with a new stepparent and possibly with stepbrothers and stepsisters. This new family is sometimes called a blended family.

The formation of such a new family unit involves major adjustments for all concerned. Sometimes remarriage improves the lives of all in some ways. The members may feel a sense of relief at being a two-parent family again, and the children get a new sense of security—especially if they like the stepparent. The economic situation usually improves, and the members of the new family have more opportunities.

More often than not, however, the formation of such a new family unit creates a situation in which members must learn to deal with a whole new set of circumstances. On the one hand, for example, it is not unusual for the new parent to experience fear of rejection. To deal with it, he or she might put up a protective shield by showing some kind of coolness or a tentative approach to the whole situation.

Likewise, the new parent may not take on the role and responsibilities of a parent and may shirk the duties of parenting. Then again, the new parent may work too hard at the role, and a child may feel instant affection from the new parent that he or she is not yet ready to accept. In addition, a child may resent a new parent acting as a substitute for someone who is very real, though not present: a stepparent does not automatically become one's "parent."

Two other critical areas of adjustment for the new family unit are authority and "sibling" rivalry. The stepchild has to learn how to deal with a new authority figure and the way in which authority is exercised. It is not unusual for children to resent the "other" person and the authority he or she is trying to exercise over them. "Sibling" rivalry can occur when there are children on both sides of the family who compete not only for their parent's affection but with each other.

There is no question that remarriage and the formation of a new family unit involves an adjustment period for all family members. Open, honest communication and respect for others are keys to resolving any conflict early in the relationship.

Society Suffers, Too

In addition to the personal and family suffering that accompanies a divorce, society suffers, too. One of its units has broken down. Complicated legal, economic, and social forces must be brought in to repair the damage, often at staggering cost. Friends and relatives have to shift gears. Mailing lists, bank accounts, credit cards, party arrangements, and the thousand and one things that go to make a couple one in society must be rearranged.

There are no winners in a divorce situation, but sometimes divorce is better than enduring an intolerable marriage. It becomes a matter of choosing the lesser of two evils. The question is, is it better for persons to change or for them to change persons (i.e., change partners)? The former is preferable to the latter, no matter how you look at it, but not always possible.

---

1. Why is divorce considered to be an admission of failure? In the United States, what percentage of marriages end up in divorce?
2. List some of the causes for divorce. Can you add any to the list that are not there?
3. What are some of the effects of divorce on the married couple? Their children? Relatives?

Most people who get divorced think the decree ends their marital problem. More often than not, it's just the first phase in their court fight.

Before the divorce, a man and a woman can fight each other for nothing. After the divorce they have to pay lawyers to do it for them.

This year, about 30,000 couples will file for divorce in Cook County. But 36,000 divorced couples will be back in court fighting over their children or alimony payments or some other matter disguising a rage for vengeance.

"We get 72,000 blaming screamers [36,000 couples] in here this year even though they've already had the big remedy," exclaimed I. A. Burch, director of the county's Divorce Conciliation Service. "It's a plague. And there's an equal number of kids involved. That's 150,000 people!"

Judge Charles J. Fleck Jr., presiding judge in Divorce Court, said the rate of returning to court after divorce is "ballooning." He's assigning additional judges and hearing cases himself.

Burch and his staff of six counselors try to reconcile divorce-bound couples. Now the postdecree counseling takes 30 to 40 percent of their time.

We talk with Burch every year or so because he's on the firing line in marital troubles, and he doesn't talk in "sociologese."

"You only get a good divorce when both admit they are at fault," Burch stated. "Blaming the other person is a fake solution. And you don't get a good divorce if some legal schmegal says it's just a matter of finance.

"They're back in court because the legal remedy didn't solve anything. As for this Mickey Mouse thing called no-fault divorce, where the complaints are just buried, if there's no fault, why split?

"People think it's okay to mess around and jump from sack to sack with no commitment. The postdecree court is where it all hits the fan."

Burch is convinced after talking with 55,000 married people and witnessing countless divorces that unless both parties admit they were at fault in the breakup, and share the blame for the failure of the marriage, they're inevitably headed back to court at great emotional and financial cost.

"People are told to blame the other person when they get a divorce," he said. "That it's just a matter of who gets the car, as if it were a financial transaction. I say a divorce won't do any good unless you see your former mate as your victim and not your enemy.

"Divorce is one contract you can't cancel, because the children just won't go away. Many of the postdecree fights are over child custody and support. A woman gets a new boyfriend who turns out to be a child abuser, or a man finds out his wife is living with a man, so he's back in court because he wants the kids back.

"A lot of people go back to court to get even. They have the illusion they're perfect and their ex-spouse is vicious. But they're tied together permanently because of the kids.

"Divorce is a superficial remedy. A fraudulent remedy. It lets us blame others for our unhappiness. During a counseling session, if I ask somebody what their faults are, they'll say they're too generous, too patient, too loyal.

"Each person has to understand their private definition of love, a relationship, and the unfair demands we put on the other person. Most people's definition of love is sick. Until I find out what is meant by love, don't give me any more of it."

Judge Fleck said the issues in postdecree court "generally are flatout money or custody. Revenge is the motive in some cases."

The emergence of the father's demanding custody of the children is a growing factor. In the past, women automatically would get the children. Now men are fighting for them.

This is complicated by increasing mobility of our society. A lot of women now petition the court to move out of state with the children, particularly to the Sun Belt. "We don't see any requests to go to Pittsburgh or Detroit," the judge commented.

These are the toughest decisions because they essentially end the relationship between the children and the parent who stays behind. "Those are the heart-breakers," said Judge Fleck.

Another consideration in the increase in cases may be lawyers. The more they go to court, the more money they make. When a divorced client calls in distress, the lawyer may counsel to cool down and talk things over. Or he may file a motion.

—Jack Mabley

The Catholic Church and Divorce

There are about eight million divorced Catholics in the United States. That is about 25 percent of the Catholic adult population. This is the same percentage of divorced persons found in the general population of the United States. The causes for divorce among Catholics are the same as for those who are not Catholic.

There are eight million divorced Catholics in the United States.

Many Catholics, especially younger Catholics thinking about marriage and married Catholics whose marriages are in turmoil, have some misconceptions about the Catholic Church and divorce. They think, for example, that Catholics who divorce or are thinking of divorce, or whose marriages are in trouble, are automatically "bad" or "less worthy" Catholics. This simply is not true. Some think that if they are divorced they are automatically excommunicated (that is, put out of the Church). Some also think that if they are divorced and remarry without approval, they are put out of the Church. These misconceptions also are false.

Divorced Catholics who do not receive an annulment from the Church, but who remarry outside the Church, are living in a civil marriage that is not recognized by Church law. They are free, however, to attend Mass, and may be allowed to serve in various capacities in the Church requiring the services of Catholics. They may not, however, receive the sacraments.

Annulment: A declaration by Church authorities that a marriage was not a valid marriage and that a person is free to marry "in the Church" with the approval and blessing of the Church.

Because of misconceptions about the Church and divorce, some Catholics choose to ignore the role of the Church concerning divorce and Catholics. "I don't see why the Church is against divorce," said Debbie, a senior in one of San Diego's larger high schools. "Sometimes it's better for them to separate."

"I agree," said Billie. "If I get stuck with some guy who treats me like his slave or hurts me, I'm gonna leave him. And marry someone else, too, I hope."

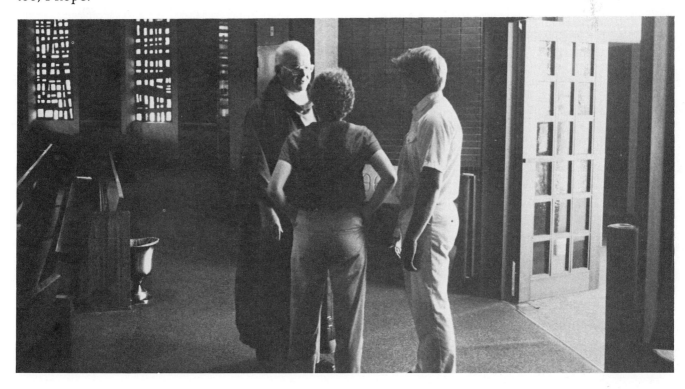

"Well, I agree," said Juan. "You shouldn't have to live with somebody who's no good. But I wonder if making it easier will help marriage. Maybe the Church is telling us something. But I think you should be allowed to remarry if your marriage breaks up. How can a guy not marry again, especially if he made a teenage mistake."

"Yeah," said Les. "Is it better to forgive and forget than to have some guy sleeping with every dame he meets simply because he can't get married again? If the Church can forgive murder, why can't it forgive divorce?"

"I'd like to know why the Church is so much against divorce," said Teresa. "Maybe if we knew, we'd understand what this whole thing is about. I think that sooner or later the Church will have to give in."

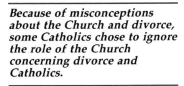

Because of misconceptions about the Church and divorce, some Catholics chose to ignore the role of the Church concerning divorce and Catholics.

Debbie, Billie, Juan, Les, and Teresa reflect the thinking of many people. It is not that they are "for" divorce or that the Church is "against" divorce. It is just that they do not understand the reasons for what they think is the Church's attitude about divorce, and they hope that someday it will change.

What they do not understand, or do not think about in a discussion regarding divorce and the Catholic Church, is that very few people, in or out of the Catholic Church, are "for" divorce. Even those who advocate divorce are not "for" divorce. They are "for" marriage. That is, they want marriage to be what it is supposed to be. When it is not, and hasn't been from the start, they are saying, "This is not marriage, so why pretend that it is? Let's untangle the legal problems involved in this relationship and start over."

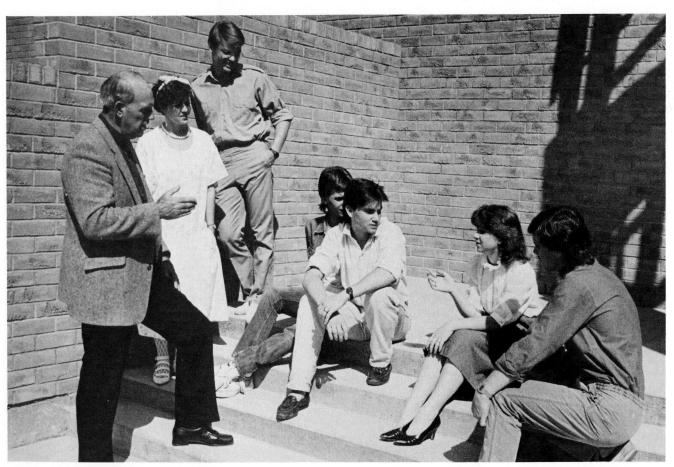

So, it is not that "everybody" is for divorce, and the Church is against it. It is just that the Church (that is, the teaching office of the Church) continues to speak out against divorce just as it speaks out against adultery, fornication, and other sexual deviations which directly attack the sacredness of sex, human dignity, and the seriousness of marital commitment.

The Catholic Church believes as Jesus did that "easy" divorce trivializes marriage. It believes that marriage is a serious commitment of major importance in the lives of those who marry, in the lives of whatever children they may have, in the life of the community in which they live, and in the life of the entire human race. It believes that easy divorce attacks the very institution of marriage and undermines both the commitment and the confidence couples should have when they marry.

Furthermore, the Catholic Church teaches that marriage is a sacrament. It is a way of life in which God lives and acts in the relationship of those who are married. For Catholics, marriage is a sacred, creative union. What the Church is telling Catholics by its teaching on marriage and its laws concerning divorce is that while divorce may be necessary in some cases, for Catholics, it is not a good in itself. For the Catholic Church, divorce is only a final step in a desperate situation.

Biblical Basis for the Church's Position on Divorce

The reasons for the Church's strong stand against divorce are Biblical, historical, and sociological.

The Church as the Body of Christ attempts to be Christ to the world. It attempts to reflect the *mind* of Jesus in whatever situation it finds itself, and attempts to reflect the *actions* of Jesus in dealing with people as individuals. In other words, the Church, like Jesus, presents an ideal and norms to apply to the real.

The question of divorce is not a modern question. It is as old as recorded history. When the problem of divorce was presented to Jesus, he said:

> "What law did Moses give you?"
> Their answer was, "Moses gave permission for a man to write a divorce notice and send his wife away."
> Jesus said to them, "Moses wrote this law for you because you are so hard to teach. But in the beginning, at the time of creation, 'God made them male and female,' as the Scripture says. 'And for this reason a man will leave his father and mother and unite with his wife, and the two will become one'. So they are no longer two, but one. Man must not separate, then, what God has joined together."
>
> —Mark 10:3–9

This was such a revolutionary thought for most of the Jewish people of Jesus' day that he was questioned further. He not only restated his original premise, he also included something unheard of in Jewish society. Jesus said:

> "A man who divorces his wife, and marries another woman commits adultery against his wife. In the same way, a woman who divorces her husband and marries another man commits adultery."
>
> —Mark 10:11–12

There were two opposing schools of thought about divorce among the Jewish people of Jesus' time, one allowing divorce and remarriage for the husband even for light reasons and the other allowing divorce and remarriage only for serious reasons.

79

What Jesus is reflecting in these two passages is his attitude about *marriage*—as much as divorce! He recalls, for his questioners, what marriage is and why the Jewish people were "allowed" divorce by Moses. Jesus was restating God's original intent. He was presenting the norm and ideal, restating the ideal—for those who would accept what he had to say.

Jesus was quite firm in restating the principle. He recalled it because he was aware of the abuses to which the decree of divorce, so easily obtained, gave rise. He saw the effects of divorce on women and on families, and witnessed the sexual sins that went on. He knew that women were usually blamed for marriage difficulties when, in reality, they were rarely at fault in that culture. It is evident that he despised the male chauvinism prevalent in the culture of his time. That is why he reminded the men present that they, too, commit adultery if they divorce their wives and remarry.

The Catholic Church, through the centuries, has tried to reflect this mind of Christ concerning marriage. Its most recent and authoritative documents continue to reflect this:

> *Sealed by mutual faithfulness and made holy above all by Christ's sacrament, married love remains steadfastly true in body and in mind, in bright days or dark. It will never be profaned by adultery or divorce. Firmly established by the Lord, the unity of marriage will radiate from the equal personal dignity of wife and husband, a dignity acknowledged by mutual and total love.[1]*

Are There Any Exceptions?

With this ideal as its norm, the Church, like Jesus, faces the *reality* of human living. The Church has always recognized that, the human condition being what it is, there are exceptions to the ideal when the ideal is impossible to attain. It has taken its cue in this regard from the practice presented in Matthew's recollections and adaptations of Jesus' comments as presented in 19:9 and St. Paul's advice given in his first letter to the Corinthian Christians. In both, we find exceptions to the ideal. For instance, Matthew writes:

> *Because of your stubbornness, Moses let you divorce your wives . . . but at the beginning it was not that way. I now say to you, whoever divorces his wife (lewd conduct is a separate case), and marries another woman commits adultery, and the man who marries a divorced woman commits adultery.[2]*
>
> —*Matthew 19:8–9*

---

1. Excerpted from *The Documents of Vatican II*, Constitution on the Church in the Modern World, paragraph 49. eds. Walter M. Abbot and Msgr. Joseph Gallagher. Follett Publishing Company, Chicago.

2. In the original version, the word now used, "lewd," meant immorality, fornication, even incest. Though the specific action is now unclear, it was clearly an exception to the general rule against divorce in some sense. Some argue that the situation involved is one where there was no marriage in the first place. But through the ages there have been opinions that stated that this is a more straight forward exception. Clearly, it does not say the same thing as Mark's Gospel and the addition by Matthew may reflect some practice in his community at the time he wrote his Gospel (after A.D. 70).

In the same vein, St. Paul also grants exceptions to the rule:

To the others I say (I, myself, not the Lord): If a Christian man has a wife who is an unbeliever and she agrees to go on living with him, he must not divorce her. And if a Christian woman is married to a man who is an unbeliever and he agrees to go on living with her, she must not divorce him. For the unbelieving husband is made acceptable to God by being united to his wife, and the unbelieving wife is made acceptable to God by being united to her Christian husband. If this were not so, their children would be like pagan children; but as it is, they are acceptable to God. However, if the one who is not a believer wishes to leave the Christian partner, let it be so. In such cases, the Christian partner, whether husband or wife, is free to act. God has called you to live in peace. How can you be sure, Christian wife, that you will not save your husband? Or how can you be sure, Christian husband, that you will not save your wife?

Each one should go on living according to the Lord's gift to him, and as he was when God called him. This is the rule I teach in all the Churches.
—1 Corinthians 7:12–17

Understanding that there are marriages that encounter serious difficulties, and that, regrettably, some will end in divorce, the Catholic bishops of the United States wrote:

Since the following of Christ calls for so much dedication and sacrifice in the face of strong, contrary social pressures, Christ's Church has a serious obligation to help his followers live up to the challenge. In worship, pastoral

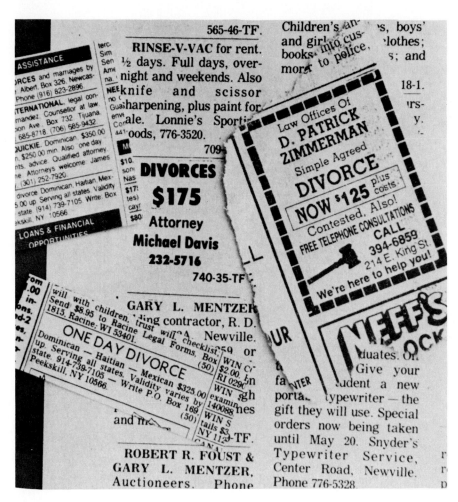

care, education, and counseling, we must assist husbands and wives who are striving to realize the ideal of Christ's love in their lives together and with their children. Young people and engaged couples must be taught the meaning of Christian marriage. Married couples must have the support and encouragement of the Christian community in their efforts to honor their commitments.

It remains a tragic fact that some marriages fail. We must approach those who suffer this agonizing experience with the compassion of Jesus Himself. In some cases, romanticism or immaturity may have prevented them from entering into real Christian marriages.

But often enough 'broken marriages' are sacramental, indissoluble unions. In this sensitive area, the pastoral response of the Church is especially needed and especially difficult to formulate. We must seek ways by which the Church can mediate Christ's compassion to those who have suffered marital tragedy, but at the same time, we may do nothing to undermine his teaching concerning the beauty and meaning of marriage and in particular his prophetic demands concerning the indissolubility of the unions of those who marry in the Lord. The Church must ever be faithful to the command to serve the truth in love.[3]

3. Excerpted from "To Live in Christ Jesus," National Council of Catholic Bishops, United States Catholic Conference, 1976, page 16.

Annulments

Throughout its history, the Catholic Church has granted annulments when the circumstances were proper to warrant them. The Church has always maintained the ideal of marriage and made it difficult for people to obtain a divorce, believing that they should attempt to work through their problems, not throw in the sponge because difficulties arise. On the other hand, if the situation was impossible, the Church accepted the lesser of two evils and permitted people to separate. Special retreats and support groups are recent examples of the Church's effort to minister the compassion of Jesus to divorced people in these situations.

Today the Church, listening to the sociological and psychological realities of modern living, maintains the ideal of marriage for all people and discourages "easy" divorce. But it advises its ministers to adopt a pastoral attitude and to consider each problem individually, applying the biblical norms to each case.

The Church and Nonsacramental Marriages

The Church realizes that some marriages between Catholics may not have been truly sacramental for a variety of reasons. If such a marriage is shown to not be sacramental, the Church will declare the marriage null and void (meaning that a sacramental marriage did not really exist) and proceed to provide the married couple with a solution to their nonsacramental "marriage." In these cases, the Church grants those in such a marriage an annulment, which gives them either the freedom to marry someone else in the Church, or the possibility of making their "marriage" a sacramental union.

Some causes for marriages being declared nonsacramental are:

- Mental illness of one of the partners
- A hidden intention to not fulfill one of the promises made at the time of marriage (to remain faithful, to consider marriage permanent, or to be open to having children)
- A previous legal or sacramental marriage which still binds one of the couple
- A physical illness that would make sexual intercourse perpetually impossible
- A formal vow of celibacy (a vow not to marry) from which the person marrying has not been dispensed by the Church

Other causes for some marriages being declared nonsacramental and therefore null and void are:

- Psychological inability to give a full, mature consent
- Failure to have intercourse during the marriage
- Inability to make a lifelong commitment to another person
- Lack of discretion (one or both did not understand the seriousness of the commitment—sometimes the case with teen marriage)
- Alcoholism
- Homosexuality
- Failure to obtain the necessary dispensation to marry someone who is closely related by blood, marriage, or adoption

- Failure to obtain the necessary dispensation to marry an unbaptized person
- Undue pressure to marry (pregnancy at the time of marriage is sometimes judged to have involved a lack of freedom in particular cases.)
- Marriage for money or social status or other unworthy reasons.

The annulment process involves a serious investigation by the Church of the facts surrounding a marriage in question. Catholics who have any reason to think their marriage was not valid by Church sacramental criteria are encouraged to contact their parish priest to see about applying to their local bishop through the marriage tribunal for judgment in their particular case.

The Church believes that marriage is for normal, mature people able and willing to give and receive love, union, and fulfillment in their marriage and in whatever family they may eventually have. Each person comes to a marriage as a person created by God for happiness both in this life and in the next. Marriage is not a cure for unhappy people nor is it an escape from an otherwise intolerable condition of life. Marriage must not be used *for* something. It must be entered into *as* something: a deep, lasting, and very personal relationship between two persons who truly love each other.

At the same time, the Church judges that a sacramental marriage exists, it greatly admires the nobility of people who remain faithful to their partners in imitation of Christ's fidelity to us by not taking a new partner—even though society might say the first marriage no longer exists.

---

1. Describe some of the misconceptions many Catholics have about the Catholic Church's views on divorce.
2. How does the Catholic Church view Catholics who are divorced without an annulment? Can they receive the sacraments?
3. What are the reasons for the Catholic Church's strong stand against divorce?
4. Are there any exceptions to the Catholic Church's views on the indissolvability of marriage? If so, describe them.

Summary

- For any one of a variety of reasons, some marriages just do not work out as hoped and divorce occurs. Unfortunately, divorce affects the social, economic, and psychological well-being of the family unit and members of the extended family as well.
- The reasons for the Catholic Church's strong stand against divorce are biblical, historical, and sociological. It teaches that marriage is a sacrament, a way of life in which God lives and acts in the lives of those who are married. Because marriage is a sacred, creative union, the Church tells Catholics that while divorce may be necessary in some cases, it is not good in itself. For the Catholic Church, divorce is only a final step in a desperate situation.
- An annulment recognizes that, at the time of marriage, one or more of the criteria for a sacramental marriage was lacking.

Review, Discussion, Research, and Reflection

1. Look at the causes for divorce listed on page 70. Which three would you find it most difficult to cope with in your own marriage?
2. Find out from whatever source you can what the incidence of divorce is in your area. Try to find out the causes, then compare them with the causes given in this book.
3. What do you think are good reasons for a person's seeking a divorce?
4. What is the Catholic Church's teaching on divorce? What does the Church mean by "married in the Lord"?
5. Discuss the reasonableness of the Church's stand on divorce and annulment. In preparation for this discussion, ask your parents or some adults you trust what their views are.
6. One marriage counselor said: "Not everyone can or should get married." What did he mean by that? Do you agree? Why? Why not?

Projects

1. During the course of a week, watch several TV shows dealing with family situations. Take notes on the following: What was the main theme of the shows? Were they realistic? Were the characters "real"? Was marriage depicted in a positive or negative way? Elaborate on your answers and give examples.
2. Ask six adults individually who they think are most affected by a divorce—the husband, the wife, or the children. Ask them why they think as they do. Prepare a report on their answers and be prepared to make a report to your classmates.
3. If you know any teens whose parents have been involved in a divorce, ask them how they felt before, during, and after the divorce. Ask them how they coped with the situation as it unfolded. Be sure to keep their responses confidential unless they give you permission to reveal them.
4. Talk to someone who has been through the annulment process and is willing to share the experience. What was involved? How much time did it take? Did the process serve any other purpose for the individual (such as healing)?

Words You Should Know

Be sure that you can define the following words and can use them in meaningful sentences:

divorce
annulment
adultery
fidelity in marriage

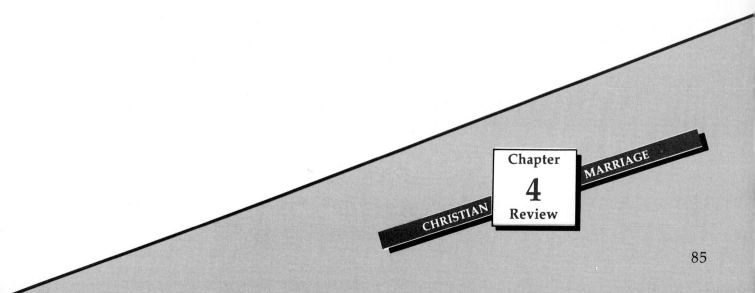

CHRISTIAN

Chapter

4

Review

MARRIAGE

Part 2

Preparing Oneself for Marriage

It remains each person's duty to retain an understanding of the whole human person in which the values of intellect, will, conscience, and fraternity are preeminent. These values are all rooted in God, the Creator, and have been wonderfully restored and elevated in Christ.

— Constitution on the Church in the Modern World no. 61

Developing Your Own Personality

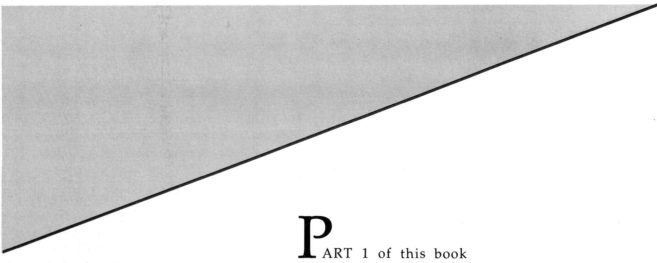

PART 1 of this book stressed the fact that marriage is too important a commitment in life to be entered into lightly. A person should know what it is, think about it in all its complexities, and prepare to face its challenges. Part 2 will discuss some of the personal aspects involved in preparing for marriage.

On another sheet of paper, write what you think are the three most important things a person needs to do to prepare himself or herself personally for living in marriage. Be prepared to discuss your selections with your classmates.

You know what the word personality means, but can you say what it really is? What kind of person do you like best? Are you, in effect, describing that person's personality? What kind of person do you like least? Is that, too, a description of personality? What, then, is personality? In an open forum, discuss personality with your classmates.

What Is Personality?

You have probably become aware as a young adult that you are experiencing greater independence, and with that independence comes more responsibility about the choices you make. Each choice you make, and every action you perform, contributes to *your* total person—each going to make up what people commonly call personality.

Personality, then, seems to be the sum of the personal characteristics you show to people. It is included in the kind of person you are. It is shown by your general emotional and behavioral patterns. It is the you that you show to others.

Personality: The total sum of the physical, mental, emotional, and social characteristics of an individual.

Although there are exceptions, a person's general pattern of behavior is consistent with his or her philosophy of life, value system, and the attempt to achieve a personal ideal of what it means to be a man or a woman. That is, you act on what you believe. Because this is so, it is important to sort out your philosophy of life, select the values that will motivate your constant choices, and determine what kind of person you want to be as a mature man or woman.

Your philosophy of life will be determined, ultimately, by what your concept of life is. Your values will be determined by your philosophy of life, and the kind of person you want to be will be determined by your value system. All three will influence the kind of personality you will develop.

Your Philosophy of Life

Philosophy: A system or set of principles used as guides in living.

As you grow into adulthood, you will be offered many philosophical options—or ways to look at life and what it means. Some are admittedly far-fetched, but most are enticing and make at least some kind of sense. For example, the philosophy of materialism does, on the surface, make sense. So do hedonism, existentialism, and secular humanism.

If a person is a materialist, financial gain dictates the course of action in all areas—political, financial, social, or sexual. If a person is a hedonist, pleasure alone dictates the options and mode of action. If a person is an existentialist, he or she will define options and actions in terms of personal freedom. For a secular humanist, purely human, pragmatic values will determine the course of action. Other philosophies such as Marxism, socialism, fascism, and capitalism, as well as Christianity, Buddhism, and Hinduism, make sense to their adherents. No matter what the philosophy, each one gives a person a certain view of life and each affects how he or she relates to others.

For Christians, life is ultimately sacred because, for them, it comes from God and is completed in God. This is the message of Jesus who, recognizing the difficulties of life, the allurement of secular philosophies, and the reality of human weakness, kept the ideal of what it means to be human uppermost in his message:

> *"Look at the birds: they do not plant seeds, gather a harvest and put it in barns; yet your Father in heaven takes care of them! Aren't you worth much more than birds? Can any of you live a bit longer by worrying about it?"*

Hedonism: The philosophy that pleasure or happiness is the highest good.

Materialism: A philosophical theory where there is emphasis on material objects and needs and a disinterest in spiritual values.

Secular Humanism: Any system of thought in which worldly human interests and values are taken to be of primary importance.

Existentialism: The belief that people have absolute freedom of choice.

"And why worry about clothes? Look how the wild flowers grow: they do not work or make clothes for themselves. But I tell you that not even King Solomon with all his wealth had clothes as beautiful as one of these flowers. It is God who clothes the wild grass—grass that is here today and gone tomorrow, burned up in the oven. Won't He be all the more sure to clothe you? What little faith you have!

"So do not start worrying: 'Where will my food come from? or my drink? or my clothes?' (These are the things the pagans are always concerned about.) Your Father in heaven knows that you need all these things. Instead, be concerned above everything else with the Kingdom of God and with what He requires of you, and He will provide you with all these other things."

—*Matthew 6:26–33*

Jesus was not counselling laziness. He was calling on his followers to realize that they are uppermost in God's design. He was telling them that they are called to look beyond the affairs of earth, to transcend their earthly humanity, to strive to be better than they found themselves because God wills them to be better than they are.

Jesus reminded them that God made them capable of growing and developing into the kinds of persons they were created to be. He was teaching them that life is worth living because God made it so. He was saying that they should have a religious view of life rather than a secular view. He was urging them to keep God in view in all their affairs. He was inviting them beyond nondivine existence.

Those who adopted his philosophy of life became happy persons. They did not escape sorrow and suffering, as you well know; they simply did not become bogged down by it. Their happiness came from an inner peace, a strong sense of self-worth, and a confidence that stemmed from their knowledge that they were God's and God was theirs.

It is important to sort out your philosophy of life, select the values that will motivate your constant choices, and determine what kind of person you want to be as a mature man or woman.

1. Be sure that you are clear about the essential differences among the various philosophies mentioned in your book: *materialism, hedonism, existentialism, humanism.*
2. What is the essential difference between a religious and a nonreligious philosophy?
3. What is Jesus' main point in the Sermon on the Mount as cited in the text? Why do you think he said what he did?

Your Values and Your Personality

For Christians, **values and ideals**—the things that are really important or worth having, the things that are motivating principles in their choices of action—are religious values because Christians live by faith. They accept Jesus as God's Son, the Second Person of the Trinity, who assumed a human nature to demonstrate what it means to be truly human and show how to attain the ideal of humanity. They accept his value system, motivating their lives by the principles he expressed and living by the power of his Holy Spirit.

They know that the principles by which he lived worked for him. They know that his magnetism came not from *who* he was (people did not know that he was the Son of God) but from *what* he was: a human

Go placidly amid the noise and haste, and remember what peace there may be in silence. As far as possible without surrender be on good terms with all persons. Speak your truth quietly and clearly; and listen to others, even the dull and ignorant; they too have their story. Avoid loud and aggressive persons, they are vexations to the spirit. If you compare yourself with others, you may become vain and bitter; for always there will be greater and lesser persons than yourself. Enjoy your achievements as well as your plans. Keep interested in your own career, however humble; it is a real possession in the changing fortunes of time. Exercise caution in your business affairs; for the world is full of trickery. But let this not blind you to what virtue there is; many persons strive for high ideals; and everywhere life is full of heroism. Be yourself. Especially do not feign affection. Neither be cynical about love; for in the face of all aridity and disenchantment it is perennial as the grass. Take kindly the counsel of the years, gracefully surrendering the things of youth. Nurture strength of spirit to shield you in sudden misfortune. But do not distress yourself with imaginings. Many fears are born of fatigue and loneliness. Beyond a wholesome discipline, be gentle with yourself. You are a child of the universe, no less than the trees and the stars; you have a right to be here. And whether or not it is clear to you, no doubt the universe is unfolding as it should. Therefore be at peace with God, whatever you conceive Him to be, and whatever your labors and aspirations, in the noisy confusion of life keep peace with your soul. With all its sham, drudgery and broken dreams, it is still a beautiful world. Be careful. Strive to be happy.

being who centered his life on the principles of his Jewish faith: love of God and deep respect for people. They know that if they live as he did, they will be admired and imitated—they will make friends, establish their relationships on trust, and become the kinds of persons they really want to be. They have the secret of what it means to be truly human: They care about others as much as they care about themselves.

Your Self-image and Your Personality

The third ingredient necessary for developing your own personality is a good self-image. You need to think well of yourself for others to think well of you.

For Christians, self-worth is based upon the divine value of being human. In the Christian concept, each human person is sacred not only because God created that person, but also because humanity is the vehicle through which the Son of God entered creation and, in so doing, brought it to its ultimate dignity: incorporation into the Divine.

Because God created human nature to be worthy of expressing the Divine in creation, every person, regardless of his or her situation, condition, or circumstances, shares in the dignity of what it means to be human. All are created in God's image.

For Christians, the marvels of God's creation—the universe, the glories of the earth, the miracle of life, the complexity of the human body, the intricacies of the human psyche—pale in comparison with what it means to be capable of sharing the Divine Life. Each of us has a unique body, a mental capability, a potential to develop self and the world into the kind of world every person longs for. This in itself gives every person a worth that cannot be measured. But over and above all that, Christians see the reality of being incorporated into Christ, a fact of life which makes each human being God's singular treasure and a reality that can be more fully realized in all human beings. As St. Paul said:

> It is through faith that all of you are God's sons in union with Christ Jesus. You were baptized into union with Christ, and now you are clothed, so to speak, with the life of Christ himself. So there is no difference between Jews and Gentiles, between slaves and free men, between men and women; you are all one in union with Christ Jesus. If you belong to Christ, . . . then . . . you will receive what God has promised . . . so that we might become God's sons.
>
> To show that you are His sons, God sent the Spirit of His Son into our hearts, the Spirit who cries out, "Father, my Father." So then, you are no longer a slave but a son. And since you are his son, God will give you all that He has for His sons.
>
> —Galatians 3:26–29; 4:5–7

The Key to a Good Self-image

Many young adults (sixteen to eighteen years of age) are plagued by self-doubts. They are uncertain of themselves, uncertain of how to act in new situations, uncertain of what the future holds for them. This is natural because they are entering a new phase of their life cycle. What they need to remember is that no matter who they are, how they look,

Christian values and truly human values are not opposed or contradictory—they are complementary. Christian values are religious; that is, they are based upon God's revelation in Christ of what it means to be human. Humanistic values are based upon the human concerns of a secularist society. Both, carried to their ideal, have a common goal: the development of truly human persons who are concerned about the welfare of human society. Christianity recognizes the source of the human and religious values and depends upon God and worship of God for the power to realize them. Secular humanism becomes more complete when it becomes Christian humanism.

what their accomplishments are, or what others say about them, as human beings they are the zenith of God's creation. As Jesus reminded the "average" person of his day: "Look at the birds: they do not plant seeds, gather a harvest, and put it in barns; yet your Father in heaven takes care of them! Aren't you worth much more than birds?" (*Matthew* 6:26).

It is because Christians sense their own natural and supernatural worth that they feel they are called to a life of joy—a life of inner happiness and contentment that pervades their thinking and their behavioral patterns. They do not delude themselves into thinking that because they are Christians there will be no more conflict, no more pain, no more suffering or sorrow or alienation. They accept these as part of the human condition, as part of what it means to live in a world that is limited, limiting, and sinful. Their joy stems from their faith in the fulfillment of God's eternal plan, their hope for a world made better by those who cooperate in God's design for having people create a better world, and their basic love for all people.

It is in this context that your human sexuality—your being the particular man or woman that you are—becomes most fulfilling. For Christians, life is not to be endured with stoic passivity, or filled with a frantic search for pleasure, self-fulfillment, or ego-fulfilling roles. It is not to be shrivelled by fear of death, fear of God, or fear of the unknown. It is to be lived to the full—enjoying pleasure, understanding pain and disappointment, sharing with others, giving of self, and relating to God. Christians know that life is bigger than self, more important than self-seeking, more durable than momentary pleasure, and they know that it reaches beyond the grave.

Being a truly human man or a truly human woman fulfills God's plan for you and your innermost desire for yourself. This is the highest human aspiration and God's hope for you.

Christians know that their being the man or woman God created them to be is God's design. They know that to strive to be anything less is falling short of their potential to be the human person they long to be. They know that they fulfill all their human (including their particular sexual) needs, their needs as male or female, by responding to the call of their nature to be the man or woman that is theirs to become.

They know that their sexual needs are not simply biological or principally biological; they encompass their entire person. This is what Christians understand by their sexual nature: the combination of physical, intellectual, emotional, psychological, and spiritual components that are uniquely theirs as men or women, and given to them alone by God, who calls them to be the best man or best woman each can be in the circumstances of time and place that are theirs alone.

An important aspect to consider in developing a good self-image is the matter of integrating your sexual nature into your total life experiences at this point in your growth to maturity. Peer pressure, much of the media, various social agencies, your natural curiosity, and strong sexual drives may bring pressure upon you to become "sexually active." On the other hand, personal considerations, religious convictions, conscience, parental concerns, the advice of informed adults, and the inevitable guilt feelings experienced by most young adults when involved in intimate sexual activity may cause you to hesitate to become sexually active.

What you need to think about is the effect a sexually active life will have on your view of yourself and the view others will have of you if you do engage in genital sexual activity. You need to ask yourself what effect this will have on you as a person.

An important aspect to consider in developing a good self-image is the matter of integrating your sex life into your total life experiences at this point in your growth to maturity.

Your Actions and Your Personality

The fourth ingredient in developing your own personality is deliberately choosing to do those things which enable you to get along well with others. This does not mean that you have to "go along with the crowd" and go against your own values just to please others. It means being a caring individual who is easy to get along with and who respects the rights and responsibilities of others as well as himself or herself.

Doing those things which enable us to get along with others and others to get along with us involves two things: (1) acquiring personal qualities which everyone recognizes as appropriate to what it means to be human, and (2) treating others with the respect and dignity they deserve as human beings (whether we feel that they deserve it or not). Some of the qualities which people expect to find in persons who are truly human are honesty, integrity, confidence, charity, restraint, cheerfulness, kindness, courage, perseverance, humility, purity, warmth, sympathy, and manliness or womanliness.

Treating others with the respect and dignity they deserve means making them feel accepted by you. It means taking a sincere, personal interest in them as they are and expressing praise and appreciation for things done. It means learning how to give criticism without sarcasm, hostility, or contempt. It means being sensitive to another's needs in both great and small situations. It means never embarrassing or putting another person down, or making the person feel inadequate. It also means observing the common amenities, and never using someone for personal gain.

It is not always easy to treat people with respect and dignity, especially if they treat us in ways we do not like or if they have characteristics which irritate us. Because most of us have an innate sense of self-protection, a fear of being held in contempt, and a desire to justify ourselves in the eyes of others, our initial reaction is to strike back. When we do feel like seeking revenge (and revenge is not always expressed in physical violence), we need to muster all the self-discipline we can to avoid seeking self-justification. Our actions reveal and realize our personalities—they are what people see and experience.

---

1. A person's personality, or general pattern of behavior, is determined by what three ingredients?
2. How did Jesus' message to Christians describe what it means to be human?
3. Why are values for Christians religious values?
4. Why did Jesus assume a human nature?
5. Describe why self-worth for Christians is based upon the divine value of being human.
6. Describe the components of a Christian's sexual nature.

Your Christian Vocation

There is one more area you ought to think about seriously in your quest for understanding yourself. Your spiritual self.

Your spiritual self is your nonmaterial self. It is your incorporeal (not body) self—that part of you that religious people call your soul or your nonorganic life principle. It is what psychologists call your psyche, and theologians call your innermost being. Whatever it is called, it is that part of you which is spirit. It is your "within." It is that mysterious part of your total nature which is not physical. In other words, you are not simply a material being. You are a spiritual being, also. Your bodily nature and your spiritual nature make up your human nature.

It is your human nature, of course that is in touch with God, but it is your spiritual self that makes you aware of His divine presence in your life and enables you to relate to God directly. The reality of God-in-your-life may or may not be part of your conscious life to any great degree. It is a reality, however. God is present in the world and in your life. God has created you through the act of love of your parents and has called you to be a Catholic Christian through your baptism.

Your baptism is a sign of your membership in the Catholic Church and a sign of your receiving the Divine Life in a special way. More than that, however, your baptism is a sign to you of your Christian vocation.

You have been baptized not simply for yourself. You have been baptized for others also. Just as the first followers of Jesus were not made disciples for themselves alone but to spread the good news of his coming, so you, too, were baptized as a Catholic to be his witnesses in your world.

Spiritual self: The part of ourself that is creative and idealistic, which makes us aware of God's divine presence in our life and enables us to relate to Him directly.

96

Faced with problems and disappointments, many people will try to escape from their responsibility: escape in selfishness, escape in sexual pleasure, escape in drugs, escape in violence, escape in indifference and cynical attitudes. But today, I propose to you the option of love, which is the opposite of escape. . . . Whatever you make of your life, let it be something that reflects the love of Christ. . . . Whatever you do, remember that Christ is calling you, in one way or another, to the service of love: the love of God and of your neighbor. . . . Love demands effort and a personal commitment to the will of God. It means discipline and sacrifice, but it also means joy and human fulfillment. Dear young people: Do not be afraid of honest effort and honest work: do not be afraid of the truth.

—Excerpt from "New World Sayings of John Paul" (*Time*, October 15, 1979)

You are called to make Jesus and his message known by your life, your words, and your actions. In other words, you are called to be holy, as Jesus said, even as God, your heavenly Father is holy (Matthew 5:48).

As a Catholic, by your baptism, you have been made a member of God's special people, as St. Peter, Jesus' principal apostle, reminded those he had baptized in Jesus' name:

> *Praised be the God and Father of our Lord Jesus Christ, He who in His great mercy gave us new birth. . . . You however are a "chosen race, a royal priesthood, a holy nation, a people He claims for His own to proclaim the glorious works" of the One who called you from darkness into His marvelous light. Once you were no people, but now you are God's people.*
>
> —1 Peter 1:3; 2:9,10

To be God's witness of Jesus' saving acts means being your best self—the self you were created to be. It means living your Catholic life in concert with the best the Church has to offer you. It means being a Catholic in thought, word, and action. It means understanding the Catholic faith, participating in the Catholic liturgical life, and following the moral guidance of the Catholic Church. In this way, you show your "Christian" personality: You display your Christian values.

By living the life you are called to live in the Catholic Church, you are being a witness to the Kingdom of God in your world and you are fulfilling your Christian vocation.

Personality and Interpersonal Relationships

The more comfortable you are with yourself as a human being, the better your interpersonal relationships will be.

If you are a good person, you will attract good persons. You might be taken advantage of occasionally, it is true, but if your constant pattern of acting stems from your wanting to be a good person (and a good person is not a wall flower, a stick-in-the-mud, or a faceless nothing; a good person is one who is truly human, seeking the ideal of what it means to be truly human), and you work at it, you will be a good person. Others will like you for what you are and will accept you as one who reflects in his or her actions what it means to be truly human.

There is, of course, a difference between wanting to be a good person and wanting to be popular. There is nothing wrong with being popular, but giving up one's principles, surrendering one's goodness, or doing what is contrary to the general thrust of human nature to gain popularity is self-defeating. It may gain us the acceptance of those who are equally unprincipled, but because it is based upon the shaky, uncertain grounds of having to conform—to buy popularity, as it were—and is not based on our own values, it cannot have substance, and is certainly not based upon respect.

James C. Coleman, a respected authority on human behavior, put it this way:

> The desire for popularity can be a booby trap if it leads the individual to conform rigidly to popular tastes, expectations, demands, and pressures—if he [or she] feels that he [or she] must act and even think like the others in his [or her] peer group. The person who keeps up a busy social life while failing to build more meaningful relationships with his [or her] family and a few close friends cannot be called socially competent. The striving for popularity as an end in itself usually indicates a selfish orientation and a lack of sureness about one's own adequacy and worth. The person who knows himself [or herself] and is at ease with himself [or herself] is relatively independent of the need for this kind of approval. At the same time, he [or she] enjoys a greater capacity for both giving and receiving the satisfactions that only interpersonal relationships can afford. Ultimately the ability to get along with others rests upon the ability to get along with oneself.[1]

And, of course, Christians would add that self is essentially related to God, so getting along with oneself likewise depends on getting along with God.

Acceptance based upon the respect people have for a truly human man or woman is what makes people genuinely popular. And this is the heart of the matter. You relate to others as a man or as a woman and as the kind of man or woman you are.

Your relationships with people will vary from time to time and from place to place, but you will project your manhod or womanhood no matter what the circumstances of time and place may be. You may have family relationships, social and recreational relationships, political, financial,

---

The more comfortable you are with yourself as a human being, the better your interpersonal relationships will be.

religious, or medical relationships, short-term or long-range relationships, casual friendships, or deeply emotional relationships, but all of them will be colored by the kind of man or woman you are.

A Special Kind of Relationship

Among the interpersonal relationships you need to consider, make judgments about, and establish modes of conduct for are with others which have a purely physical sexual inspiration.

Most of the time your relationships with others will not be inspired simply by the physically sexual. With some people, you will have only casual relationships; with others, such as family members and special friends, you will have relationships which are much deeper, much more personal. There are some relationships, however, that can only be described as "glandular"—relationships based upon a physical, sexual attraction. In such relationships, body chemistry and psychological needs ignite a reaction ranging from an almost insignificant sparkler to a full display of fireworks. In this kind of relationship, behavioral decisions are most demanding. In other kinds of relationships, you are primarily concerned with your person—the kind of man or woman you are. In a strongly sexual relationship, you are also concerned with what you should do, especially sexually. Eros changes things.

As young adults, you are learning to handle this kind of relationship. You may feel drawn to express a sexual relationship to a degree in keeping with your physical feelings, but you will attempt to relate these strong drives to your emotional feelings and your conscience. You will constantly be faced with challenging questions that require difficult, and often immediate, answers.

You might ask yourself, "How shall I handle this situation?" "How far shall I go in this relationship?" "Why shouldn't I do this or that?" You might ask, "What is wrong with doing what I feel like doing?" "What is right about doing what I want to do?" You may wonder, "How shall I tell him (or her) that I do not think I should do what we both feel like doing without hurting him (or her) at this point in our relationship?" "Is it right for me?" "What does my religion tell me about this choice? Why?" These and other questions will arise almost every time you enter a physically charged sexual relationship.[2] You need to explore your own thoughts, feelings, and values and find the right answers for you.

As a male or female, you are provided by nature with the capability of performing certain bodily functions and you are created with certain drives to move you to act in certain ways. You have eyes which respond to light to bring images to your brain. You have a brain that responds to signals enabling you to make choices. You have ears which respond to sound. You have fingers and toes, arms and legs, a heart, lungs, intestines, and a whole host of internal bodily organs which respond, each to its own kind of stimulus.

---

2. These questions will arise throughout your life. Even though a person is married, and has, to some extent at least, answered these questions relative to a marriage partner, he or she will be faced with these questions, and a thousand variations of them, with regard to other persons who affect them physically and psychologically.

You also have genital organs which respond to sexual stimuli. At this stage of your growth, you may have found that the copulative function of your genitals is most urgent, not because it is more important than the others, but because it is most intense—and most physically pleasureful. You have become used to your eyes and ears, arms and legs, and fingers and toes, and your internal organs work without your having to do much about them. But you have not become used to your reproductive drive. When it knocks on the front door of your consciousness, your instinct is to answer.

But it is not your reproductive capability that is most important; it is how you use it. Just as you can use or misuse your other bodily capabilities (Is constant, intense light good for your eyes? Can excessive radiation exposure from the sun damage your skin? Does exposure to deafening sounds have an effect on your hearing? Does excessive use of alcohol have an effect on a person's kidneys?), so you can use or misuse your reproductive capability.

Having bodily capabilities does not make you a human person, but using them to express who you are as a person does. You are a person with bodily functions through which you express your being as a human person. This is the challenge of your sexual nature.

---

1. Describe what you understand as your spiritual self.
2. What is Baptism a sign of for Catholics?
3. What does it mean to be God's witness of Jesus' saving acts?
4. What does it mean to treat others with the respect and dignity they deserve?

Summary

• Each choice you make and every action you perform contributes to your total person—each going to make up what people commonly call personality. An individual's general pattern of behavior is consistent with his or her philosophy of life, value system, and the attempt to achieve a personal ideal of what it means to be a man or a woman. The more comfortable you are with yourself as a human being, the better your interpersonal relationships in all areas of your life will be.

• In your quest for understanding who you are and developing your own personality, it is important to realize that you are also a spiritual being. It is your bodily nature and your spiritual nature that make up your human nature. By acknowledging your spiritual self and living the life you are called to live in the Catholic Church, you are being a witness to the Kingdom of God in your world and you are carrying out your Christian vocation.

Review, Discussion, Research, and Reflection

1. Discuss in an open forum what personality characteristics make one person more appealing than another. List the five characteristics that are most appealing. Discuss what makes them so.
2. Describe the various influences you believe have contributed to your present philosophy of life.
3. How do you believe values influence a person's behavior? Do you believe it is easy to adhere to one's values when making a decision?
4. What do you believe individuals can do to improve their feelings of self-worth? Be specific with your suggestions.
5. How does your book describe the difference between wanting to be a good person and wanting to be popular? Do you agree or disagree? Support your point of view.
6. Review some of the questions your book suggests young adults ask themselves when they feel drawn to expressing a sexual relationship. List other questions you believe an individual should ask him or herself when placed in this particular situation.
7. Discuss in an open forum your book's statement: "Acceptance based upon the respect people have for a truly human man or woman is what makes people genuinely popular." Do you agree or disagree? Support your point of view.

Projects

1. Make a list of ten items which you believe your peers value today. Survey ten students and ask them to rate these items on a scale of one to ten (one = best; ten = least). Compile your answers and draw a conclusion.
2. Research five different cultures to determine what makes an individual popular in that culture. How do they all compare with each other? with the society you live in?
3. In the next week, watch five regular television shows you like. What kind of person plays the hero or heroine? What kind of person is portrayed as the villain? Why are those particular images given to the person portrayed?

Words You Should Know

Be sure that you can define the following words and can use them in meaningful sentences:

personality
philosophy
spiritual self
materialism
hedonism
values
existentialism
humanism

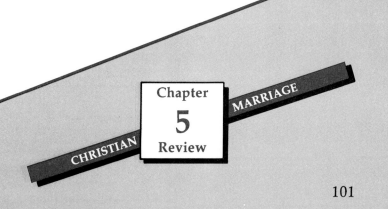

Chapter
5
Review

CHRISTIAN MARRIAGE

CHRISTIAN MARRIAGE

Chapter 6

Sexuality: An Expression of You

Copyright, 1983, Universal Press Syndicate. Reprinted with permission. All rights reserved.

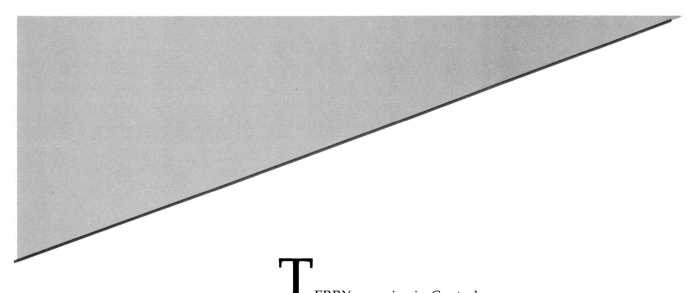

T ERRY, a senior in Central High School, walked resolutely to the front of his speech class and placed his folder on the teacher's desk. He faced his audience for a brief moment and then turned to the chalkboard. In large, bold letters he printed SEX. Once again, he turned to face his audience, and, after a slight pause, said, "I'm not going to talk about sex. I just wanted to get your attention!"

The students caught their breath. Then they looked cautiously at their teacher seated in the back of the room. When they saw him laughing quietly behind his hand, they burst into laughter.

1. In an open forum, discuss why sex, a mention of the word "sex," or a reference to sex are such attention-getters among all people, not simply teenagers.
2. When you hear or see the word *sex*, what comes to your mind? Are there other uses for the word *sex*? What are they?

Interest in Sex Is Natural

There is no question that Terry had the right idea. In today's society, the word *sex* **is** an attention-getter. Perhaps it is because the word and the thought of sex, sexual activity, and sexual matters stir up various levels of response in most human beings and because it receives so much emphasis.

For some people, it creates thoughts of pleasure, excitement, fun, and games. For others, it is a means for exploitation, money, power, or domination. For many, it means a special relationship, while for others, it means an expression of love and a tender, total commitment to another person expressed in nature's most intimate union.

It is not unusual for a person to blush or giggle or feel embarrassed by sex—nor is it unusual for a person to be angry at the sometimes outrageous or indignant manner in which the topic of sex is presented.

It is unusual, however, for an individual to feel comfortable with the topic of sex and be able to cope with the various ways sex is approached. It is rare because with very little open, honest communication about sex, the majority of people narrowly view it as "an intimate act" rather than as a part of one's sexuality—or total self.

Sex and *sexuality* are two different words that have two different connotations. Knowledge about both is vital if men and women are to develop positive self-images as sexually competent human beings, and if they are to function fully in life and be in control of themselves. It is also necessary if a person is to establish moral values and make responsible decisions about his or her sexuality.

Once you know what sex and sexuality are, you will need to explore what role sex will play in your life. This is the key question for you at this stage of your growth as you prepare yourself for marriage in the future.

Understanding Your "Selves"

To appreciate the role of sex in your life you need to be aware of and understand the several "selves" that make up your total person.

There is your physical self, your intellectual self, your emotional self, your social self, your sexual self, your moral self, your spiritual self and your religious self. In addition, there is your imaginary self—the one you think you are—and your wished-for self—the one you would like to be. Each of them and all of them together make you the unique person that you are.

Your physical self, of course, is your body. You present to the world around you a particular kind of body build, a particular kind of bodily health, a particular image of concern for and care of your body. Your genetic makeup has determined in large part your particular body build, but your environment, your personal habits, and your physical exercise have determined much of the condition your body is in at this stage of your growth. What you do with your body and how you present it (clean, neat, and so forth) tells the world around you what you think of yourself and the regard you have for others.

Your intellectual self is the self which knows, understands, and makes judgments. It is your mental capacity self. Intellectual capacity, or mental ability, varies from person to person and from time to time, and its powers or abilities can be cultivated or neglected. Some people are smarter than others, some know more than others, and some learn faster than others. A person's intellectual ability is only one of the many things that make him or her a human being.

Your emotional self is the self that reacts to a stimulus—a thing that excites you or moves you to action. Your emotional self is your feeling self—the self that shows joy or sorrow, love or hate, anger or concern, hope or despair, anxiety or resignation, and all the other feelings that show your reaction to things that come into your life. To show your best emotional self to others, you need to direct your emotional reactions toward social good. Because your emotions are what move you to action, you ought to train yourself to act in moderation and learn to control what are called your negative emotions—the ones that might move you to antisocial behavior. It is on your emotional self, generally, that people make judgments about your personality.

Your social self is the self you show to others. Whether you realize it or not, you have several social selves. There is, for example, the one you show to people in general as you walk down the street, enter a store, or go to church. There is the social self you show to your parents and the one you show to your teachers. There is the one you show to people you like and the one you show to people you do not like. There is the one you show a person you want a favor from, the one you show when you are caught doing something wrong, and the one you show when you are lost in an angry crowd. You know how you show yourself to others in a variety of situations. Which one is your real social self? What should it be? What would you like it to be?

Your sexual self is the self you show to others as a man or woman. It is how you express yourself as male or female. It is all your other selves being expressed as the man or woman you are. It is your personality being expressed through your maleness or your femaleness.

Your moral self is the you acting in the face of a moral challenge. It is easy to be moral if you are not tempted to do something wrong or antisocial. It is often difficult to be moral when temptations arise, pressures mount, and opportunity beckons. The habitual choices you make when under pressure to do something immoral determine your "morality quotient." If you generally choose to do the right thing, you are a moral person. If you do not, you may be tending to become immoral.

Your spiritual self is the you that is creative and idealistic. This element of humanity urges you to want to be better and gives you the means to be better, to reach your ideal if you so wish. It is your spiritual nature that allows you to go beyond the material to establish a relationship with God.

Physical self is your body.

Intellectual self: The self which knows, understands, and makes judgments.

Emotional self: Your feeling self—the self that reacts to a stimulus and shows joy or sorrow, love or hate, anger or concern, hope or despair, anxiety or resignation and all the other feelings that show one's reactions.

Social self: The self one shows to others.

Moral self: The self acting in the face of a moral challenge.

Spiritual self: The self that is creative and idealistic.

Your religious self puts you and your relationship with God into a form expressed by some religious group, though not everyone who is religious belongs to a religious group. When you belong to a religious group (such as the Catholic Church), you respond to the religious values of the group insofar as it is possible for you. You value the collective wisdom of your Church and make use of that wisdom in making your decisions. Thus your religious self has a direct effect on your moral self.

Sex and Sexuality

There is a difference between sex and sexuality. The word *sex* may signify an impersonal designation of being male or female as, for example, on your driver's license or on an application form. It may also mean a composite of qualities which ordinarily are a part of someone's personality, as when it is said that a person has "sex appeal." It may signify the act of making something more attractive or interesting, as, for example a person might try to make an outfit "more sexy." Most of the time, however, sex is used as an umbrella term signifying a wide variety of physical activities of a specific nature. The most common is an intimate physical action involving two people called "sexual intercourse."

Sexuality, on the other hand, is a word that describes how you express yourself in your role as male or female. That includes how you walk, talk, act, think, and dress. It encompasses your whole person and also includes not simply your basic anatomy, but all that you have learned, and all your thoughts, ideas, values, and experiences.

Like every aspect of human behavior, the way you speak, your attitudes, and your habits and practices are strongly influenced by those among whom you live and associate.

The process of sexualization is an ongoing process that begins the day you are born. You are constantly learning through observation, by experience, and by being taught. Your parents are the first to influence the formation of your sexuality in the way they treat you and hold you, and in the way they express themselves when it comes to their expectations of you as a male or female. It is not unusual for parents to expect their sons to take out the garbage and mow the lawn while assigning their daughters such chores as dusting and dishes. By dressing you in a certain way and purchasing toys and games of a particular kind, your parents gave a clear message that you are to behave in a certain way. Moreover, your parents are the strongest models to you of what it means to be a male or female human being, of what it means to be masculine and feminine.

As you enter adolescence, your peer group begins to exert more and more influence on your emerging sexuality. They have certain expectations of you, not only in the way you behave but in your appearance. Not long after entering adolescence, it becomes apparent to you that physical attributes such as good looks, muscles, and height for guys and being shapely and voluptuous for girls increase one's chances of becoming popular. Labels such as "sissy," which imply a "boy is acting like a girl," or "tomboy," which identifies a "girl who is acting like a boy," are often used by peers to taunt another's behavior—behavior which they believe to be inappropriate for one's sex!

Religious self: The self that puts one into a religious group and responds to the values and wisdom of that group.

Sex: One of two divisions, either male or female, into which human beings and animals are divided; also, a term for sexual intercourse.

Sexuality: How one expresses oneself as male or female.

Adolescence: The period of life between puberty and adulthood in human development, extending, mainly, over the teen years.

The process of sexualization is an ongoing process that begins the day you are born.

Society also influences your behavior. Messages from the media often put a big value on sexual attractiveness and performance, and popularity and success are often associated with being "macho" for males and "sexy" for females.

Adult relatives, teachers, coaches, or a dance or music instructor may also influence the formation of your sexuality. Sometimes teachers have certain expectations of students merely because of their sex. For example, teachers often expect boys to do better in math and science and to be mechanical, while they expect girls to do well in music and dance, to be neat, and to do well in reading and spelling. At a young, impressionable age, a person will respond to these expectations and model their behavior accordingly.

When you reach late adolescence, the emergence of your sexuality is a unique blend of your physical, mental, emotional, and biological characteristics. The differences between men and women are not in their human natures but in their sexual natures. Both have the same kind of body cells, the same mental processes, the same emotional reactions, and the same ambitions, desires, and ideals. They are basically different only in their anatomy and their biochemistry because of the role each sex plays in reproduction.

Sexuality is so much more than genital activity. It is an aspect of personality which lets us enter other persons' lives as friends and encourages them to enter our lives. The dimension of sexuality must be developed by all men and women not only because it is, as we have just seen, a gift making us more like God, but is also so very necessary if we are to follow Jesus' command to become "lovers" (Matthew 22:36–40). It is a relational power which includes the qualities of sensitivity, understanding, warmth, openness to persons, compassion, and mutual support. Who could imagine a loving person without those qualities? . . .

There may be no convincing way to say this to someone who does not want to listen. We know, however, that the experience of countless human beings and sound psychology support the wisdom of the Church teaching regarding both the goodness of sexuality and the unfortunate ambiguity related to its genital expression. Although each of us is called to live our *sexuality* in the sense of the human qualities and relationships seen above, its *genital expression* (physical sexual contact, arousal, orgasm) needs a special context before it can serve human love and live generously and without deception.

Human Sexuality, Bishop Francis J. Mugavero; Bishop of Brooklyn, New York; February 11, 1976.

107

Sexual Attitudes

Our feelings and attitudes about sex and sexuality have a great influence on our decision-making capabilities—and ultimately, our behavior. In truth, sexual attitudes set the stage for sexual behavior. The expectations and demands of any culture produce a wide variety of attitudes toward sexual matters. All cultures place specific restrictions on the expression of sexuality, and changes in what a culture considers acceptable behavior are often very slow to occur.

Human society, for the most part, has been and is male dominated. Even though, in some parts of the world, various women's groups have made inroads into male-oriented societal structures, for the most part, males determine society's attitudes and practices in regard to most things, not the least of which are sex and sexual matters and practices of both men and women.

Often in our society, men are expected to be much freer sexually than women. (Of course, women may pay a higher "price" than men for sexual miscues, such as an unplanned pregnancy; hence, there is a sense

in which they need to be more cautious!) We can generalize by saying that men expect and are expected to dominate women sexually. They are expected to know more. They are expected to brag more (though some women talk more about sex and sexual matters than men do). They are expected to show sexual prowess and to demand more sex. Men are expected to show a macho image in everything, including sex. For these reasons, young men are expected to know more, do more, and be more excited by sex than they might actually be at any given time.

But the message society conveys and what, in reality, exists are often two different things. One of the reasons for this is that men have been, for the most part, extremely secretive about their real sexual behavior. They may talk a lot about women and their conquests, joke about sex, and make allusions regarding their sexual conquests, but they usually do not discuss their personal concerns or ask questions. In addition, most men have the tendency to think that all other men are having a better time sexually than they are, and that other men do not have the questions or worries they have.

Another reason for the bravado some men display when discussing sexual issues may have to do with the way they were raised. In some cultures and in some families, young men are denied the open expression of some very important feelings such as, love, sadness, fear, and affection. As a result, they keep silent or they learn to fake it. They fake their feelings, pretend to be confident when they are not, pretend to know something when they do not, and pretend to enjoy when they do not feel enjoyment.

But men do have concerns about sex. Almost all have questions about their sexuality and about how they feel and function, especially with the onset of puberty and the physical changes that accompany it.

On the other hand, girls, when growing up, often hear such statements as "aren't you pretty" or "don't you look pretty today" and they learn that they are appreciated and recognized for their sexual attractiveness and their bodies. We can generalize by saying that since there are not supposed to be any explicit discussions about sex, whether it be about the basic reproductive system or something as important as sexual behavior, women have little opportunity to practice moral reasoning about it.

But the development of one's reproductive system and secondary sexual characteristics is real for **both** males and females. Information in this area is vital if both are to develop positive self-images as sexually competent human beings, if they are to function fully in life, and if they are to be in control of themselves.

1. Why is knowledge about sex and sexuality vital to a man and a woman?
2. Name and describe the several "selves" that make up one's total person.
3. Describe the different ways sex can be defined.
4. Describe the various influences on your emerging sexuality.
5. What are the differences between what society expects of men in the way of sexual behavior and what actually exists?
6. Why do women have little opportunity to practice moral reasoning about sexual behavior?

Sexual Identity and Decisions

If "sex" is used to designate a person as male or female, then it becomes apparent that *sex is not primarily something that you do; it is what you are.* Each and every one of you identifies with a sex, whether it is male or female, and your sexual identity evolves as a result of how you see yourself in that role. Your sexual identity is also greatly influenced by other family members, your friends, teachers, coaches, and society.

People begin to see themselves more clearly in their role as male or female with the beginning of adolescence and the onset of puberty. At this time, there occurs the development of secondary sexual characteristics that outwardly make a woman more shapely and a man more muscular and that internally enable both to reproduce.

What also appears to evolve at this time is a close relationship between one's sexual identity and one's self-worth. If a man's growth spurt in adolescence begins early, and he becomes tall and muscular either before or at about the same time as his friends, and a woman begins to menstruate and becomes more shapely like her friends, then they are more likely to have favorable feelings of self-worth.

However, the variations in growth patterns for adolescents is so great that sometimes a young man does not begin his growth spurt until he is sixteen or seventeen, and some females do not begin to menstruate when their friends do and are not as shapely as they would like to be. Often these aspects of growing up, along with others such as being over or underweight, or suffering from acne, can detract or take away from one's feelings of self-worth.

Puberty: The stage of development at which a young man's or a young woman's reproductive organs become functionally operative and the secondary sex characteristics develop.

Secondary Sexual Characteristics: The physical characteristics—other than the external sex organs—that distinguish a male from a female.

Self-image and Decisions

How comfortable you become with yourself can influence the way you make decisions and it can influence your behavior. If you feel good about yourself, you may not find it necessary to "borrow" other's decisions and "go along with the crowd." You like who you are and feel confident. If, on the other hand, you do not like what you are, you may seek acceptance by acting to please others—even if you know it is not right. If this is how you receive acceptance, you might conclude: "If others like me, then I must be OK!"

But seeking acceptance through others may backfire if the decision you make contradicts your own personal values or conflicts with the values of some of the important people in your life. Imagine a classmate coming to you and saying, "Let's skip school today!" You may want to say yes for the sake of friendship or being liked, but you also know it's against school policy, your parents would be upset, and you really do not want to skip school. Of course, the first elation of skipping school will sooner or later change to fear of being caught and worry about your parent's reaction, and possibly a guilty conscience. And what if it really does not turn out so well? What if the "friendship" you sought does not materialize? How would you feel about yourself?

Being able to make a decision that is right for you is not influenced only by your self-image. It can also be influenced by your emotional maturity, your personal experiences in making decisions, the amount of information you have, and, ultimately, the situation you find yourself in when you have to make a decision. Each of these elements plays a key role in your decision making.

1. Emotional and Moral Maturity

Being emotionally and morally mature means having the ability to personally handle, within reason, the responsibilities and consequences of any situation.

Two aspects of maturity that influence decisions are your level of independence and the values you have established. As a young adult, you find yourself becoming more independent in all aspects of your life with each passing day. Your activities outside the home place you in decision-making situations. When out with your friends, it is up to you to act appropriately; your parents will not be around to guide you. It is the same as if you were swimming somewhere without adult supervision; it is up to you to determine when you are out too deep. There is no question about it: **with independence comes a greater responsibility to decide what is right for you to do.**

As an individual, you also have an obligation to root yourself in true values. It is up to you to determine what you like and what you do not like, value and do not value. Whether it is something as simple as chocolate or vanilla ice cream, one style of shoes over another, or something more complex, such as how to respond in a sexually stimulating situation, the decision is yours. There is an old cliche that says: *"Stand for something . . . if you don't, you'll fall for anything!"* Once you've clarified your values, respect them, and stick to them.

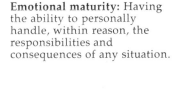

Emotional maturity: Having the ability to personally handle, within reason, the responsibilities and consequences of any situation.

2. Personal Experiences

Another influence in your ability to make a decision is the experience you have had in making them, the results of those decisions, and the knowledge you have gained from making past decisions.

Some families seldom give young people the opportunity to make decisions; the parents make all the choices and direct behavior. Other families not only give opportunities to make decisions, but also give opportunities to express them. Sometimes, expressing a value that is morally right for you is not an easy thing to do, especially when it does not conform to what others believe or want. For example, you may not like to speak negatively about another person, so you do not gossip or say malicious things about another to your friends. Or you may not feel right about cheating on a test that your friends plan to cheat on. In both cases, they may chide you for not doing what they are doing. You may feel left out, despite the fact that you have chosen to live by your beliefs.

If you have ever been asked to do something—perform a simple task, such as babysit a child, run an errand, or the like—and you really wanted to say "no" to, but said "yes" to it instead, then you have found yourself in a common human condition. Upon consideration, you have probably also arrived at the conclusion that it is not always easy to say "no." In fact, sometimes it takes a great deal of courage and inner strength. Learning how to express your thoughts, feelings, and values and doing what is right for you to do is a very important part of learning how to make right decisions.

3. Information

The information you have is as important as emotional and moral maturity and experience in the decision-making process. This includes not only the information you have on the subject, but also your awareness of the consequences should you make a decision as well as your responsibilities to yourself and others affected by your decision.

Many young adults today rely upon their peers to be their primary source of information on any topic, and especially on sex. Unfortunately, your peers are not necessarily any more knowledgeable than you are. You have to find reliable information that will help you weigh the pros and cons of a decision. Only then can you explore your own values in order to make a right decision.

4. The Situation

Becoming an adult means assuming added responsibilities. With an increased independence that comes with being an adult, you will find yourself in decision-making situations that will determine your behavior.

In this regard, there are two important factors to keep in mind. First, when you face the actual situation of a decision-making challenge, you will not be able to ask permission of anyone. For example, when faced with a decision regarding sexual activity, you most likely will not be able to go home and ask your parents for permission. You will make the decision yourself, and you will thereafter be responsible for that decision.

A second important factor in decision making is to realize that there is no guarantee that a decision you make will not hurt—even if it is a decision that is right for you and corresponds with your value system. For example, you may care deeply for a member of the other sex who wants a sexual relationship. If you choose not to become sexually involved because of your value system, you may experience the painful loss of the relationship. However, in time, the personal strength and growth gained from the experience will far outweigh the initial pain.

As a young adult, you will be greatly concerned about your own sexual values and habits. There is a need to evaluate the conflicting signals you receive from various sources of information about sex and sexual matters before you select and integrate into your life those values and practices which will best serve your true needs and lifestyle. At this stage of life, determining which values and practices are really best for you in the long run is difficult, as you may not have enough prior experience to make an individual judgment or decision. In any case, decisions regarding such an important part of your life should not be based on fear, ignorance, or the desire to please.

You were created to be unique—one of a kind. No one looks exactly like you, nor does anyone have the same fingerprints as you. Do not work at becoming a carbon copy of someone else. Develop your conscience and your Christian philosophy of life, become rooted in Christian and human values, and do what is right for you to do.

1. Why do individuals begin to see themselves more clearly in their role as male or female with the beginning of adolescence and the onset of puberty?
2. How does one's sexual identity affect one's feelings of self-worth?
3. Your decision-making abilities are influenced by a number of factors. What are they?
4. What two aspects of your emotional and moral maturity may influence the decisions you make?
5. What are two important factors young adults should remember when making a decision that will determine their behavior?

Catholic Interpretation of Human Sexuality

Catholics derive their philosophy of the human reality of sex from the answers to two basic questions:

1. Where does human sexuality come from?
2. What is the purpose of the male and female expressions of humanity?

For their answers, they can turn to Scripture, both the Old and the New Testaments of the Bible, to see what God has revealed about His divine plan for men and women. In it, they find two significant passages.[1] The first is from Genesis 1 and 2. The second is from Matthew 19.

> In the beginning, when God created the universe, the earth was formless and desolate. . . . God commanded, "Let there be light"—and light appeared.
> Then God commanded, "Let there be a dome to divide the water and to keep it in two separate places"—and it was done. . . .
> Then God commanded, "Let the water below the sky come together in one place, so that the land will appear"—and it was done. He named the land "Earth," and the water which had come together he named "Sea.". . . Then he commanded, "Let the earth produce all kinds of plants, those that bear grain and those that bear fruit"—and it was done. . . .
> Then God commanded, "Let lights appear in the sky to separate day from night. . . .
> Then God commanded, "Let the water be filled with many kinds of living beings, and let the air be filled with birds."
> Then God commanded, "Let the earth produce all kinds of animal life: domestic and wild, large and small"—and it was done. . . .
> Then God said, "And now we will make human beings; they will be like us and resemble us. . . ." He created them male and female, blessed them, and said, "Have many children, so that your descendants will live all over the earth and bring it under their control. . . ." God looked at everything he had made, and he was very pleased.
> —Genesis 1:1–3, 6, 9–11, 14, 20, 24, 26–28, 31

1. There are other passages, of course, dealing with male-female relationships. These two are given because they establish the general biblical attitude about the origin and meaning of human sexuality.

When the Lord God made the universe, there were no plants on the earth and no seeds had sprouted, because he had not sent any rain, and there was no one to cultivate the land. . . .

Then the Lord God took some soil from the ground and formed a man out of it; he breathed life-giving breath into his nostrils and the man began to live.

Then the Lord God planted a garden in Eden, in the East, and there he put the man he had formed. . . .

Then the Lord God said, "It is not good for the man to live alone. I will make a suitable companion to help him." So he took some soil from the ground and formed all the animals and all the birds. Then he brought them to the man to see what he would name them; and that is how they all got their names. So the man named all the birds and all the animals; but not one of them was a suitable companion to help him.

Then the Lord God made the man fall into a deep sleep, and while he was sleeping, he took out one of the man's ribs and closed up the flesh. He formed a woman out of the rib and brought her to him.

Then the man said,

"At last, here is one of my own kind—Bone taken from my bone, and flesh from my flesh. 'Woman' is her name because she was taken out of man."

That is why a man leaves his father and mother and is united with his wife, and they become one.

—Genesis 2:4–5, 7–8, 18–24

When Jesus finished . . . he left Galilee and went to the territory of Judea on the other side of the Jordan River. Large crowds followed him, and he healed them there.

Some Pharisees came to him and tried to trap him by asking, "Does our law allow a man to divorce his wife for whatever reason he wishes?"

Jesus answered, "Haven't you read the Scripture that says that in the beginning the Creator made people male and female? And God said, 'For this reason a man will leave his father and mother and unite with his wife, and the two will become one.' So they are no longer two, but one. Man must not separate, then, what God has joined together."

The Pharisees asked him, "Why, then, did Moses give the law for a man to hand his wife a divorce notice and send her away?"

Jesus answered, "Moses gave you permission to divorce your wives because you are so hard to teach. But it was not like that at the time of creation. I tell you, then, that any man who divorces his wife, even though she has not been unfaithful, commits adultery if he marries some other woman."

His disciples said to him, "If this is how it is between a man and his wife it is better not to marry."

Jesus answered. "This teaching does not apply to everyone, but only to those to whom God has given it. For there are different reasons why men cannot marry: some, because they were born that way; others, because men made them that way; and others do not marry for the sake of the Kingdom of heaven. Let him who can accept this teaching do so."

—*Matthew 19:1–12*

> The Bible is a spiritual and religious interpretation of human reality. Catholics believe it is God's revelation of the meaning of creation.

Catholics believe that Genesis and Matthew reveal God's plan in creating human beings male and female.

First of all, sexuality, sex, and marriage are sacred and come from God (Genesis 2:22; 1:27; Matthew 19:4). These passages reveal the mutual affection the two partners have for each other and take note of the fact that they have the same basic human nature and dignity (Genesis 1:27; 2:21–23; Matthew 19:5,6).

The strong physical awakening and desire that draw a man and a woman together in love is God-designed. Sexual intercourse is willed by God as a means to enable a man and a woman to express love and affection for each other and to reproduce children in a loving marital situation. This will enable whatever offspring there may be to be raised in a loving home (*Genesis* 2:23–24; 1:28; *Matthew* 19:6,9).

Finally, according to the Bible, the ideal marriage is a husband and a wife who love and respect each other, constantly awakened to enthusiastic and loving response in the joyful discovery that they love each other and are loved. They express their love fully and completely in absolute trust for as long as they live (*Genesis* 2:24–25; *Matthew* 19:11).

Catholics believe that the biblical attitude toward sexuality, sex, and marriage is the norm for sexual conduct. It reveals God's purpose. It expresses the innermost desire of every man and every woman and places sexuality, sex, and marriage at the very heart of what it means to be truly human.

Catholics believe that people are created by God to seek love and express love as men or women in keeping with the nature and purpose of loving relationships. The biblical attitude keeps sexuality, sex, and marriage in perspective by reminding people that their instinctual sexual feelings are God-given. Catholics believe that, in the final analysis, God is the cause of it all.

1. Where do Catholics turn to find spiritual and religious answers to the questions "Where does human sexuality come from?" and "What is the purpose of the male and female expression of humanity?" Why do they go to this source?
2. What do Genesis and Matthew say to Catholics about sex and sexual feelings? On a separate piece of paper, quote the passages illustrating what Genesis and Matthew say about sex and sexual feelings.

Summary

- Knowledge about sex and sexuality is vital if men and women are to develop positive self-images as sexually competent human beings, if they are to function fully in life and be in control of themselves, and if they are to be rooted in moral values and make responsible decisions about their sexuality.
- Catholics turn to Scripture, both the Old and New Testaments of the Bible, to see what God has revealed in His divine plan for men and women. Catholics believe the biblical attitude toward sex, sexuality, and marriage is the norm for sexual conduct. They believe it reveals God's purpose.

	Parents	Church	Teachers	Peer Group	Some media
Premarital sex					
Fooling around					
Teen marriage					
Contraception					
Homosexuality					
Teen pregnancy					
"Sex" magazines					
"Sex" movies					
Rock music					
Sex education					

Review, Discussion, Research, and Reflection

1. Discuss in an open forum what the book means when it says the differences between men and women are not in their human nature but in their sexual nature.
2. Discuss in an open forum the following statements: "Sex is not something you do; it is what you are," and "stand for something . . . 'cause if you don't, you'll fall for anything."
3. The book says it sometimes takes a great deal of courage and inner-strength to say "no." Do you agree or disagree? Give examples. Are some decisions easier to make than others? Give examples.
4. In the chart on the previous page, tell what you think is the attitude of your parents, your Church, your teachers, your age group, and many television shows, magazines, movies, and music regarding the items listed in the column on the left. In the appropriate box after each, put "approve," "disapprove," "encourage," "discourage," or "don't know" where these words apply.
5. Most likely, an examination of your responses and your classmates' responses would reveal rather sharp differences in some categories in the list above. In an open forum, discuss, first, why the differences occur. Then discuss whether you agree or disagree with the attitude you think each group on the chart has in each category.
6. Consider all of the various influences that have contributed to your emerging sexuality. Then list them in the order of which contributed the most, which the least.
7. Why are some movies rated "G," "PG," "PG–13," "R," or "X." Do you agree with the rating system as it exists and the restrictions it places on who can view certain movies? If so, why? If not, why not?

Projects

1. Young adults today are faced with many important decisions, some of which could seriously alter their lives. State what you consider to be three of the most important decisions they might have to make and describe a decision-making process that would enable them to make the right choice for each decision.
2. Look for a minimum of five articles in newspapers and magazines that deal with the subjects of sex and sexuality. Note the name of the publication and the date of the article. Describe what you believe is the message that is being conveyed. Are all the articles trying to convey the same message? Summarize your findings.

Words You Should Know

Be sure that you can define the following words and can use them in meaningful sentences:

sexuality
sexual identity
adolescence
puberty
secondary sexual characteristics

CHRISTIAN MARRIAGE

Chapter
6
Review

Chapter
7

Looking Ahead toward Marriage: Dating

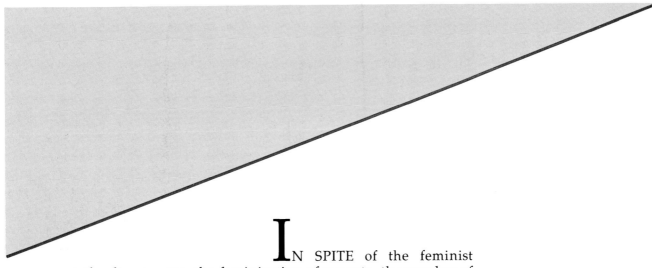

IN SPITE of the feminist movement, the divorce rate, the feminization of poverty, the number of teen pregnancies, the number of women in the work force, the number of single parent families, and the realities of economic life in America, most teenage girls in the United States still expect "Prince Charming" to come along some day. They expect to have a beautiful home in suburban America, have two trouble-free children, and lead a life of carefree leisure. Most refuse to believe that they will be a part of the harsh realities of adult living.[1]

In an open forum, discuss the following questions:

1. Do you think that what Ms. Bingham says is true of the young women you know? How do you know? Do you think it is just a fantasy for young women or do they really believe in it? Where do you think such fantasies come from?
2. What are some of the realities men and women preparing for marriage should be aware of? Are some applicable to only one sex? Which ones?
3. What three things would you not tolerate in a prospective mate?
4. How can you find out if someone who wants to date you has personal, financial, philosophical, psychological, or religious problems that might cause difficulties if you decided to marry that person?

The Purpose of Dating

The fact that young men and young women date is an observable fact. What they do when they date is culturally conditioned. Why they date is at once a psychological and biological phenomenon.

Everyone has a deep psychological need for acceptance. This need is fulfilled, nurtured, strengthened, and satisfied by a mother's loving care, a family's acceptance, casual and close friendships, and the inclusion of a person in a particular society's economic, political, and cultural

1. Excerpted from a talk given to the California State Division of the American Association of University Women by Melinda Bingham, executive director of the Girl's Club of Santa Barbara and author of *Choices: A Teen Woman's Journal for Self-Awareness and Personal Planning*. (Reported in the Sarasota, Florida, *Herald Tribune*, August 2, 1983.)

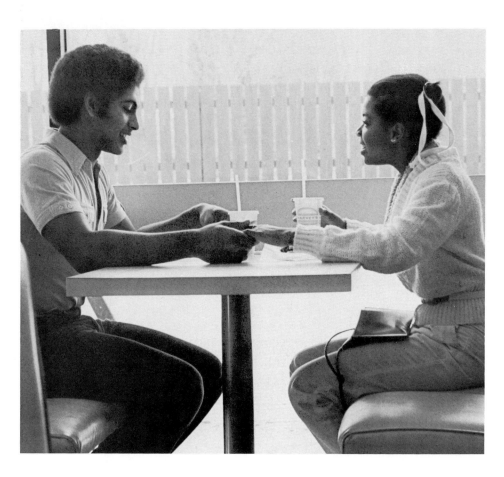

life. Acceptance reaches its highest point and most satisfying fulfillment through an exclusive and loving relationship with one particular person.

Dating is a step in the acceptance process leading to the type of relationship that desires intimate union. Whether or not such a union is consummated is a different question, but the fact that the urge toward such a union is part of the psychological and biological makeup of every human person is hardly disputable.

In both old and young, dating is for companionship, leading to sharing. It is also a time for social and sexual growth. In young persons, it is a time for general social experience and general sexual growth. As people grow older, it is for learning about the other person in greater depth and for sexual adjustment within the restrictions of that relationship.

Dating is the usual process for finally selecting the one person we want to live with in the exclusive lifestyle we call marriage. However, not every date—or even serious dating—leads to marriage. For example, one person might date simply for companionship. Another might date for convenience, or for protection, for money, as a token of esteem, to fulfill a social obligation, for sex, or for any of a dozen reasons. Regardless of the reason, the chances are high that dating will eventually lead to exclusiveness, and exclusiveness will lead to marriage.

Since marriage is such a totally demanding relationship, with love balancing among many tensions, it is important to enter marriage carefully. Two major factors to be considered when marriage is contemplated are maturity and compatibility, both of which are learned in the dating process.

Dating: A step in the acceptance process leading to the type of relationship that desires intimate union.

Companionship: A fellowship; individuals who are frequently in the company of one another.

Compatibility: The ability to live together in harmony.

The formative years for older adolescents and young adults can be the most important period of their lives as far as marriage is concerned. It is during these years that they develop a maturity for marriage and learn what compatibility means in a relationship. This does not mean that a marriage early in life is doomed to failure. It simply means that developing these two most important ingredients prior to marriage can make the adjustment to married life much easier.

Preparation for marriage is very important because of its human ramifications and, for Catholics, its Christian dimension. Dating is an essential part of that preparation. It gives us the opportunity to explore our own feelings with regard to the type of person to whom we want to make a commitment, and it gives important clues about our prospective partner. More importantly, when we are older it helps us decide if we can actually live with that person in the totality of the relationship of marriage.

The formative years for older adolescents and young adults can be the most important period of their lives as far as marriage is concerned.

---

1. What is the purpose of dating, according to your book?
2. Discuss what your book means by "culturally conditioned" dating practices. Do you know of any such customs in the United States? in other countries?
3. What are two major factors to be considered by a couple when they are contemplating marriage?
4. What does your book mean by "dating is at once a biological and psychological phenomenon"?
5. The following is part of a discussion held by one of the authors and a group of juniors and seniors in a San Diego, California, high school. The general subject was relationships between young men and young women in their senior high school years. The material quoted below deals with dating. Discuss whether or not it reflects your own experiences.

Matt: I think that's the problem. It's like a contest. Dating ought to be fun. You ought to go out with somebody because you like them not because of what you can get.

Juan: I think most guys do. But it's kind of expected that you at least try. You think, what's she going to think if I don't at least try? She'll think you're scared, or something.

Ed: You're darn right. If I don't try, the girl'll think she's a dud. That's why I say it's up to the girls to say yes or no.

Maria: Is that what the guys think?

Ed: Most of them do.

Matt: That's why it's a problem. Sure I think it's up to the girls in that respect. I mean, what's a girl going to think—about you and most of all about herself—if I don't at least try to kiss her? She'll think she's got bad breath or something.

Jennifer: But if you say no, what do they think?

Matt: That's why it's a contest. Why does everybody think you've got to *do* something? Shouldn't whatever you do be natural and just come from being together? Why is everybody just hung up on sexual intercourse? I just like to go out with girls. What's the big deal? Do I have to prove something?

Maria: I wish it were that way, too. But you're expected to. . . .

Jennifer: That's why I said it's cultural. They tell you what you're supposed to feel like and do.

Anna: If two people like each other, it shouldn't be a contest. But I agree with Ted. It seems like it's a contest.

David: I don't even think about it. I just like to go out with girls, but I don't have to go out with them to have a good time, and I don't expect anything from them just because they go out with me. Why should I? And why should they feel they have to pay me? If we went out together because we like to go out, there's no debt there either way.

Sarah: That's the way most girls want to feel, too, I think.

David: Why can't they?

Jennifer: Because they think the boys think the girls think you have to.

Sarah: That's right. I think everybody'd be better off if they knew what dating is.

Anna: That's what Ted meant by a contest. Dating ought to be going together. Why have to worry about should I or shouldn't I?

Maria: I wish it was that way. But sometimes you feel like having sexual intercourse and you'd like to do it but in the back of your mind there's always the idea that you shouldn't. I wish I knew.

Matt: I didn't say it wasn't natural, but I think it shouldn't be a contest, that's all.

Juan: That's what's hard. How can you tell?

The Importance of Dating

Dating on more than a casual basis helps two people decide whether or not they are mature enough to marry (maturity does not necessarily develop with chronological age) and if they are compatible with each other.

Maturity does not necessarily develop with chronological age.

Compatibility means that two people are able to relate well together. It means that they like each other as persons, have similar interests, enjoy each other's company, communicate well with each other, are tolerant of each other's weaknesses, and like to do things together.

How can two people who seem to be in love and are drawn to each other on the physical level tell if they are compatible? One sure way is if they can get along without sex—not once, but for a long time. If sex is the glue that holds a relationship together, how can a couple tell if it is a biological urge or a response to genuine affection? They cannot. *This is the role that dating without sex plays: it tells two people if they can get along*

124

with each other, have fun together, be good companions, and grow together as persons. They will know they are not merely using each other for sexual release.

There is little doubt that people in the first bloom of attraction and dating can get along well together and like to be in each other's company. Most people try to be polite and courteous and accommodating of another's feelings when the encounter is in a new relationship. It is also not unusual for two people, in the excitement of early love, to overlook what appear to be small differences and indiscretions in their partner. But what happens when excitement gives way to the routines of daily living?

Nobody's perfect, of course, and people in love must expect differences. There are, however, certain areas in which differences can be discussed and issues resolved by a couple before reaching the engagement level of a relationship. These are:

- Personal habits
- Family tensions
- Religious differences
- Racial background or nationality
- Lifestyle aspirations
- Maturity level

None is an automatic barrier to happiness in marriage, of course. Each in its own way, however, produces subtleties within the relationship which neither person can completely offset unless one is an exceptionally strong, compassionate, and well-integrated person. The only way a person can tell if one or more of these areas can cause a problem in a marriage relationship is through extended dating. This may very well be the most important part of the dating process.

Personal Habits

As your relationship evolves into a more serious commitment, it is important to tune into your partner's personal habits. Almost anyone can get along well with a person who is considerate, polite, kind, patient, honest, and respectful of others. But what do you do with a relationship when your partner begins to exhibit qualities that are unattractive to you? In the first blush of a romance people often put their best foot forward. However, it is usually only a matter of time before "the real person" shows up. What would you do if you began to notice that your partner was becoming selfish, rude, inconsiderate of your feelings, violently impatient, or unclean?

First and foremost, it is important to take the time to discover what qualities you admire and which ones you do not admire—not only in yourself, but in others. Remember that sometimes a relationship is like a mirror: it reflects you back to you. Whatever you require or demand, your partner will respond to. If you are polite and considerate, your partner may reflect the same qualities. If you are critical and rude, however, you may elicit the same negative response!

Each of us has some aspects of human weakness that will annoy others. If, however, a person you are dating consistently exhibits negative personality and character traits which would make you avoid that person in ordinary circumstances, there is little reason to think you could live with such a person in marriage. It is a grave mistake to enter a serious relationship with the idea that you can change an individual's personal habits. Many times these habits are deeply engrained in the individual's personality and cannot be changed—or the person is happy with the habit and will not change.

Dating will reveal a person's pattern of behavior. Honesty and open communication within the relationship, as well as understanding and consideration, can help to resolve some of the problems that might arise as a result of personal habits.

Family Tensions

Stories are always floating around about in-laws, especially "the mother-in-law"! Yet the majority of married people get along reasonably well with their spouse's family. There may be areas of friction, however, that can contribute to problems in a marriage.

Only through dating can you actually see the kind of family a person comes from and the nature of the relationships that exist within the family. As you view the interaction between family members, it may give you some additional insight into how your potential spouse will treat you and/or your children.

You can also tell if the other family members like you, accept you, tolerate you, or if they are hostile. You can tell if your partner-to-be is dominated by his or her family or is free to be his or her own person. By dating, you can see if the family will contribute to your marital happiness or interfere with your relationship and if living nearby would be a mistake or a blessing. As minor as these tensions may seem during dating, they can blossom into real problems and cause a strain on the marriage relationship.

Religious Differences

Religion helps shape a person's philosophy and moral behavior. Hence, it can play an important role in marital relationships. To avoid any confrontations as a result of differences in religious beliefs and practices, it is better if two persons share the same religious outlook and the same general degree of religiousness in their approach to life. For example, a marriage between two Christians, even of different denominations, would have more in common religiously than a marriage between a Christian and a Buddhist. And a marriage between two Catholics would have more in common than a marriage between a Catholic and a Baptist.

But merely belonging externally to the same religion or denomination is not the most crucial factor; it is the union of mind and heart that is important. Certainly, a marriage between a loving, open-minded Catholic, and a loving, open-minded Protestant would have much more going for it than one between an open-minded Catholic and a selfish, opinionated Catholic whose religion consists of occasional attendance at religious ceremonies.

When a couple has children, religion will also affect their relationship. When religious beliefs and practices are shared by all members of a family, a comfortable environment for love and spiritual growth will exist. In a family of little or no religious conviction, the problem of responding to questions about religion which children inevitably raise will certainly create difficulties. In a family of differing religious interpretation or denomination, a child, expecting unity in parents, may be confused by the expression of two differing outlooks on life and religious practices. Unless the parents are able to explain the reasons for their differences and demonstrate that their differences do not divide them, the children may have problems accepting religion as anything but divisive. If one parent is religious and the other is not, the children may be pulled in two directions. They may also question the purposefulness of religion if it is not valued by one parent.

The greater the religious difference between two people contemplating marriage, the greater the potential problems. It is for this reason that most religious groups do not encourage **interfaith marriages.** Yet, only the couple can decide if the difficulties are such that they cannot be reconciled. They should be discussed before marriage, and ways of resolving the problems should be decided on well in advance. One of the ways of determining whether or not religious differences will be a problem in marriage is to see if they are before marriage—that is, during the dating period. It is a mistake, however, to assume that religious differences are of only minor importance. Too many people later regret their inability to share the religious dimension of their life with their spouse.

The greater the religious difference between two people contemplating marriage, the greater the potential problems.

Interfaith marriages: Marriage between two people of different religious interpretation or denomination.

1. What role does dating without sex play?
2. Describe the six areas where differences can be discussed and issues resolved by a couple before they enter into the engagement aspect of a relationship.
3. Describe characteristics of an individual's personal habits that you would admire in your partner.
4. How important is religion in a marriage relationship? If you continue to practice your religion as you are now doing after you have children, what religious influence will you have on them?

Racial Background or Nationality

Another area in personal relationships that may provide problems for marriage partners is the racial background or nationality of the partners. This usually occurs where there are strong, conflicting customs or where there is a community prejudice against marrying someone of a particular group.

Persons contemplating an interracial, intercultural, or international, marriage need to consider the strains their marriage would be under—not from prejudices in themselves (for they love each other), but from external pressures in a prejudiced society. Social strains may result from the loss of friendships, from not being able to live in one or the other partner's society, or from the experiences their children might have as they grow up in a curious or hostile world. If the couple experiences any one or more of these problems, they might wonder if the marriage would be worth all these sacrifices and if they would be able to withstand all the pressures.

On the other hand, if their love is strong and they are confident that their children will be secure enough within the happiness of the home to withstand the external pressures, a couple could be justified in and admired for taking these risks. Certainly, a shared religious value system would be a tremendous assistance in these circumstances.

Interracial marriage: Marriage between people of different races.

All people should work toward the day when racial and national prejudices and bigotry will disappear from society.

Lifestyle Aspirations

One aspect of living together in marriage that many dating couples do not think about at all is **lifestyle.** They rarely consider how they are going to live once they have settled into married life. When two people are deep in the throes of early love, it is not unusual for them to avoid discussion of any differences they might have in their economic, educational, or cultural background—or to consider what they will have in common when their early romantic love settles into married living.

Dating enables an individual to explore his or her own tastes, desires, needs, ambitions, and priorities, as well as those of prospective partners. It also enables couples to plan—and prepare—for a particular level and style of living toward which they can build. Two major issues that can affect a couple's lifestyle are finances and the personal goals and ambitions of the partners.

Financial considerations are
always a major concern in a
marital relationship.

Financial considerations are always a major concern in a marital relationship. Indeed, they greatly influence a couple's lifestyle. A marriage that begins at too early an age can lock a couple into a continuous round of near-poverty struggles from which they rarely escape. This is especially true when one or both partners has to forego an adequate education necessary to compete in our society, or when the individuals are not capable of further education or more than routine and low-paying jobs. Financial struggles are difficult enough, but if it is not what a person is used to, it can be fatal for a marriage.

Another aspect of lifestyle which is becoming increasingly important in our society is the changing role of women in society and in marriage. In days when the patterns of family living seemed to be more simple and determined largely by economic and procreational necessities (the man was the breadwinner; the woman stayed home to raise the children), lifestyle more or less took care of itself.

Today, however, family finances may necessitate the part-time or full-time employment of a wife. In addition, women are more educated and are talented enough to pursue their own personal ambitions. Because it is more possible for them to plan the size of their families, more confidently, many women aspire to roles beyond and in addition to the home and family. A man and a woman contemplating marriage need to give serious thought to whether they can adjust to each other's lifestyle in this regard after they are married.

It might be that a couple's personalities are compatible, but their ambitions are not. (For example, if a man is insecure in his sense of masculine image or leadership, the fact that his wife may earn more money than he earns could be a serious blow to his pride and perhaps to his mistaken belief that he is "supposed to be" the breadwinner). The partners need to decide what their individual goals and ambitions are, evaluate the compatibility of these goals and ambitions, and determine how they would feel if one or both of them would have to sacrifice a specific form of dedication. It would also be wise to discuss whether such a sacrifice would cripple their personalities and lead to bitterness and resentment or would be compensated for by what they would gain from sharing life with their partner.

Especially when young people become so deeply involved in a relationship that they can only look forward to an early marriage, they need to consider how it will likely affect the prospects for a lifestyle that is in keeping with their ambitions, desires, and talents.

Maturity Level

Perhaps one of the most important issues for young people to consider when contemplating marriage is the question of maturity—the personal, psychological, social, and spiritual readiness factors that are so essential for a successful marriage.

Maturation: The act or process of maturing; growing.

In today's complex world, training for any career takes much longer than ever before. Preparation for marriage, more important than any career, should normally be expected to take longer, too. People would not think of going to a teenage doctor, or to a lawyer who had never studied law. Yet some young people commit their lives to a marriage with a partner who hardly knows himself or herself, has experienced little of

life, and knows little or nothing about the total range of possibilities in adult living which could still change their growing personalities enormously.

Maturation is an ongoing process that usually evolves with age and as a result of personal experiences. A young couple who have had limited personal experiences may tie themselves prematurely to a relationship which later on becomes stifling because it cuts off possibilities they would otherwise have naturally needed to explore. This can be especially true in the case of teenage marriages.

Of course, it is possible that two exceptionally mature teenagers might find in one another such comprehensive openness that they would have a good chance of growing into adulthood and enlarging their horizons together. Unfortunately, many people believe they are mature long before they have developed the skills for truly mature decision-making and problem-solving.

Dating gives individuals the opportunity to explore their own feelings about the kind of person they want to make a commitment to in marriage. Consideration of all of these six particular areas can help two

Dating gives individuals the opportunity to explore their own feelings about the kind of person they want to make a commitment to in marriage.

131

people know whether or not they are mature enough to marry and if they are compatible with each other. Through extended dating and open, honest communication, some of these potential problems can be resolved and success in marriage can be assured.

1. What are some of the problems that could arise from an interracial, intercultural, or international marriage?
2. Describe two major issues that can affect a couple's lifestyle in marriage.
3. What readiness factors indicate a readiness and maturity that are essential for a successful marriage?

Summary

- Dating is the process used for selecting, finally, the one person we want to live with in that exclusive lifestyle called marriage. What we do when we date is culturally conditioned. Why we date is at once a psychological and biological phenomenon.
- Dating on a more casual basis helps two people to know whether or not they are mature enough to marry and if they are compatible with each other. Certain areas where differences can be discussed and issues resolved by a couple before they enter into the engagement aspect of a relationship are personal habits, family tensions, religious differences, racial background or nationality, lifestyle aspirations, and maturity level.

Review, Discussion, Research, and Reflection

1. Talk to your parents about dating customs when they were your age. Compare their actions with the actions of a typical date today. List the pros and cons of dating in each period.
2. What attributes would you like your prospective marriage partner to have? Write them in the form of a newspaper advertisement (i.e., wanted: male, eighteen years of age, intelligent, compassionate, etc.).
3. What personal habits mentioned in this text do you believe would interfere most with a marriage relationship? Give reasons for your answer.
4. Do you personally think that religion is important in a marriage relationship? Why? Why not?
5. In an open forum, discuss the position of each individual in the following cases:
   a. Sheila, a computer analyst making a salary equal to her husband's, is offered a better paying job and a higher position with the company in a distant city. Her husband, well situated as a loan officer in a local bank, thinks Sheila should forego the job opportunity and stay where she is.
   b. Joe, a licensed electrician with the Texas Power Company, objects to his wife's wanting to work part-time as a hairdresser. "A woman's place," says Joe, "is in the home."
   c. Jed, a black athlete, and Peggy, a white cheerleader, begin dating casually. They say they do not care what others think or say. Soon they become serious and promise to wait for each other until after college.
6. What effect, do you think, would different levels of economics, education, and culture have on a marriage relationship? Discuss this question with your parents.

Projects

1. List ten personal habits a dating partner might exhibit. Conduct a survey of at least eight of your peers. Ask them to rate these personal habits on a scale of one to ten (1 = best; 10 = worst). Compile the results and report your findings.
2. Interview, if possible, three couples who are living in an interfaith marriage, and ask that they share the pros and cons of living in an interfaith marriage. Prepare a report on the results.
3. Research the failure rate of teen marriages in your area. If possible, find out the average length of time the marriages lasted and some of the reasons for failure.

Words You Should Know

Be sure that you can define the following words and can use them in meaningful sentences:

companionship
compatibility
maturation
interracial marriage
dating
interfaith marriage
lifestyle

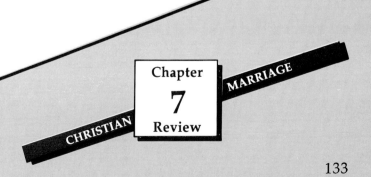

CHRISTIAN MARRIAGE

Chapter

7

Review

The Challenges of Serious Dating

ARE YOU SEEING JEFF AGAIN TONIGHT, CATHY?

I SORT OF EXPECTED I WOULD, ANDREA, BUT I DON'T KNOW...

RELATIONSHIPS BETWEEN MEN AND WOMEN ARE SO CONFUSING NOW I DON'T KNOW WHAT'S GOING ON.

HOW AM I SUPPOSED TO KNOW IF HE'S NOT CALLING ME OR I'M NOT CALLING HIM?

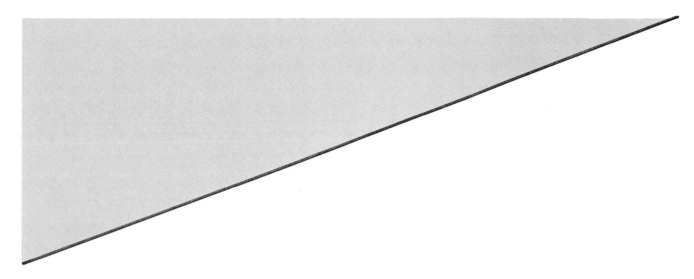

1. By this time in your life you may have faced the "going steady" question. If you have not, you most likely will soon. In any event, you know that there are pros and cons to the question of people your age going steady. On a sheet of paper, list reasons you think people your age have, or use, for going steady. On the same sheet of paper, list reasons you have, or others give, for not going steady.
2. In an open forum, or in some other way, find out what your classmates have put for their reasons and find out which ones are common for both categories. Then discuss the pros and cons of going steady.

Going Steady

As people begin to have more than a casual relationship with a person of the other sex, they face social, practical, psychological, religious, and moral challenges that require careful consideration and some well-thought-out responses. A person should know, in advance, what he or she will do under one or another circumstance.

It is not unusual, either, for young men and young women to have special questions and concerns about some aspect of steady dating. Some, for example, have found that they are apprehensive about dating seriously lest their personal value system be seriously challenged by their date or by some of their friends. Others find "going steady" a problem— they are not ready to tie themselves to a particular person or dating style. Others fear that they will feel pressured into "having sex" before they really want to, and many fear the drug and alcohol scene that is sometimes part of going steady. Some fear that if they become too serious, they might eventually become victims by being jilted or cast aside. Many feel socially inept or personally inadequate, and some feel financially embarrassed.

If dating is so "dangerous," some older teens ask, should they date? The answer, of course, is yes. It is natural and it is fun. It is good, wholesome, holy, and maturing. It becomes "dangerous" when it involves activity beyond the acceptable in terms of maturity and morality.

"Going steady," says Dr. Carlfred B. Broderick of Pennsylvania State University, "is the beginning of the end. If a couple passes from the level of light petting to heavy petting, the girl is likely to press for increased assurances that the relationship is important to the boy: that he loves her, and that they may share their futures together.

"Similarly, a boy who has committed himself to the extent of giving a girl his school ring is likely to feel that it now is appropriate for him to press for greater intimacy. . . . Once a serious relationship gets started, it takes little or no effort to get more and more involved. But it takes an act of the will to hold the line."

Teenagers who find themselves on the threshold of becoming too involved in sexual intimacies need to ask themselves, "Am I ready for this? Is this what I really want? Can I handle the demanding relationship such involvement requires? Am I psychologically, socially, intellectually, and emotionally ready to tie myself to this person when I know so little of him or her, of myself, my world, and my future? Does our proposed behavior imply a commitment we are unable to make? Do I not have some responsibility to my parents, my family, and society? Is this moral? Am I hurting myself, my partner, anyone else?"

Dating and the Problem of Intimacy

Of course, many in your **peer group** are going steady and some of them have become sexually involved. One of the biggest decisions you will make in looking ahead toward marriage is your decision to have sex or not to have sex before marriage.

Peer group: Individuals of one's own age and interests.

With all the messages you receive from the media and the various input from peers and friends, it would not be surprising if you felt confused and perplexed about the issue. Even older people experienced in sexual matters are often very confused by the conflicting signals sent out about sex and sexual behavior. Listed below are some of the reasons given for saying "no" to sexual intimacy in dating, and some of the reasons people give for saying "yes." Some of the reasons given may seem more plausible than others. The honesty and maturity behind each reason should be major consideration. The decision to wait until marriage for sexual intimacy cannot be made for you by someone else. Likewise, the decision to become sexually involved cannot be made for you by someone else.

Some people have said "no" to becoming sexually intimate because:

- They were sticking to their own moral conviction that sexual intimacy is meant to be expressed in a loving marriage.
- They were concerned about the possibility of an unplanned pregnancy.
- They were concerned about getting a sexually transmitted disease (VD).
- They realized "giving in" to sex would not truly prove their love.
- They did not really care enough about the other person.
- They were concerned about what their parents would say if they found out.
- They just were not interested in having sex at that particular time.
- They were concerned about their reputation—and what their friends would say.
- They believed the probable pleasure was not worth the risks.
- They were concerned about their own performance: Would they do "it" right?

- They would not use someone else just to meet their own physical urges.
- They were ashamed of their body.
- They were involved with other things.

On the other hand, some have said "yes" because:

- They deeply cared for, or were in love with the individual.
- They wanted to be loved.
- They wanted to make their partner love them.
- They were pressured by friends or peers to experience sex.
- They wanted to prove their love.
- They wanted to satisfy their own curiosity: What is it really like?
- They wanted to prove they were a man or a woman.
- They wanted to be cool, macho.
- They wanted to be popular.
- They wanted to be accepted.
- It was a way of holding onto their partner.
- They wanted a baby.
- They were rebelling against their parents.
- They just did not know how to say "no"!

Making the Decision

To make a decision with full knowledge of who and what you are and with full knowledge of the consequences of that decision, you must explore what sexual involvement means to you physically, emotionally, and spiritually.

Physically, if you say "no," **there are no risks.** On the other hand, if you say "yes," there are three physical concerns; the question of birth control (considered in chapter 3), the possibility of an unplanned pregnancy (and the man is just as involved as the woman in this), and the possibility of contracting a venereal disease.

The physical effects of an unwanted pregnancy vary and depend on the age and physical condition of the woman. With proper medical care, the physical effects can be dealt with. The emotional effects can often be devastating. Both the young man and the young woman face a situation that is at once extremely serious, personally embarrassing, socially upheaving, financially very difficult, and threatening to one's lifestyle. It is a condition neither young person is prepared to meet.

Another concern young men and young women need to give attention to in considering sexual intimacy outside of marriage is the high probability of contracting a venereal disease—a veritable plague, according to many medical people. A venereal disease is a sexually-transmitted disease that is highly contagious, often physically debilitating, and, in some cases, life threatening. Although there are many types of venereal disease, there are three that can cause irreparable damage: syphilis, gonorrhea, and herpes II.

The emotional effects of an unwanted pregnancy can be devastating.

138

Syphilis is a sore, or ulcerous lesion which appears at the point of contact. Although the sores may disappear in two to six weeks, the disease remains in the system travelling through the blood stream. If left untreated, syphilis can cause damage to vital organs such as the heart, lungs, kidneys, and brain. In some cases, it can cause a person to become severely incapacitated and it can even cause death. Syphilis can be cured if a person seeks treatment early.

Gonorrhea is a contagious inflammation of the urethra or vagina. Although it most often manifests itself with a pus-like discharge, it is also possible that it can be present in either the male or female but not manifest itself. If left untreated, it can cause serious damage to the reproductive organs. Gonorrhea is the principal cause of sterility in the United States. It can be cured if early treatment is sought.

Herpes II is another sexually-transmitted disease that is characterized by clusters of blister-like sores that appear on the mucous membranes of the reproductive and elimination organs. The sores are very painful, a cause of embarrassment, and highly contagious. Although the blister may disappear from time to time, the disease remains with a person and can flair up at any time. Medication can help with the pain, but at the present time there is no cure for herpes II.

In addition, multiple sexual partners increase the likelihood of cancer; and evidence that Aids may be spread by heterosexual as well as homosexual sexual relations is beginning to emerge.

While most people are aware of the physical ramifications of sexual involvement, they are not always aware that the emotional aspects of having sex can be just as devastating.

Emotionally, if you say "no," you might find yourself asking "Am I okay?" Many times labels are placed upon individuals because they choose not to have sex ("He's gay," "she's afraid," or "she's frigid," etc.). If you explore in your own mind why you elect not to have sex (for example, from moral conviction, it's important for you to be a virgin when you get married, you do not want to have to worry about pregnancy, and so forth), you will respect your own convictions, feelings, and values and will not be swayed by name-calling, emotional hurts, snubs, or innuendoes.

Another emotion-laden question you might find yourself asking if you elect not to become sexually intimate on a date is "How do I compare with others? Is everybody doing it?" The answer is, really, quite simple. No, not everyone is doing it. A lot more people your age are talking about it than are actually involved in it. In any case, that should not be an important factor. The question is whether nonmarital sex is moral.

A third emotional factor that might influence your decision is fear of losing a relationship. The other side of that coin, of course, is, "Is having sex worth the risk of pregnancy and worth going against the value system I have been raised with?" A serious question in that same area is, "Will having sex change the relationship?" An equally serious question is, "How will I feel if I have sex and how will my partner feel about me?"

Through it all, remember, there is no guarantee that a right decision will not hurt. You may, indeed, suffer snubs or hurts, teasing, or name-calling. You might lose someone you care about. But if you resist sexual involvement and act according to your convictions, you will feel better about yourself, you will gain the respect of those who count, and you will know that you have done the right thing. You may be emotionally upset for the moment, but you will ultimately have peace of mind and self-respect.

Venereal disease: Any number of sexually-transmitted diseases that are highly contagious. (Examples: Syphilis, Gonorrhea, Herpes II)

According to the American Health magazine (April, 1984) there are twenty-eight different viruses, bacteria, fungi, and parasites that are sexually transmitted.

If you say "yes" to sexual intimacy when you date, you will experience a variety of emotional responses. At first, you may feel guilty. You may worry about venereal disease or about pregnancy. You may worry about the reaction of your parents if they find out you are having sex with your boyfriend or girlfriend. You may wonder if you are being used. You may feel scared, frustrated, and helpless and even more so if pregnancy develops. If it should, you will worry about how your life will change and what your having sex has cost you. You may feel anger, even revulsion, and despair. You may consider suicide. No momentary pleasure or giving in to please someone else will then seem worth it.

In addition, you may also feel anger, hurt, or regret if a pregnancy occurs and someone other than you decides how to handle the situation. For example, if, as a man, you believe abortion is wrong, but your girlfriend does not want the responsibility of raising a child because she wants to continue with her education at this time without a child, you may be faced with her making a decision to terminate the pregnancy, to end the life of your child. After all, United States law allows a woman to make that decision on her own. It is a decision over which you have no control and one you will have to live with for the rest of your life.

Other Things to Consider

When contemplating the decision whether or not to become sexually involved, other very important questions need to be considered. You need to think about your responsibilities to yourself and to your partner. You need to think about your responsibilities to your parents, to society, and to the world. You must ask yourself whether having sex fits into your goals in life. You need to scrutinize both your own and your partner's reasons for having sex.

Spiritually, the person who says "no" may feel at peace from making a decision in keeping with his or her Christian values. In addition, religious values can give a person the impetus and the courage to make the decision to avoid sexual expression outside of marriage. If these religious values are shared by the dating couple, they will be better able to discuss their feelings for each other and to cooperate in their decision to wait.

The person who says "yes" to sexual intimacy during the dating stage rejects religious values, rationalizes them, or ignores them. None of these three automatically relieves guilt, or satisfies for all time, or insures there will be no regret. However, anyone looking back on an experience of sexual intimacy inappropriate to the situation can express sorrow, make amends, and experience the loving forgiveness of God. The Sacrament of Reconciliation is the ordinary means of celebrating this forgiveness.

Remember, saying yes or no to sexual intimacy is a decision no one makes for you. If you say "no," no matter what your reason, life may be fairly uncomplicated for some time. If, however, you say "yes," then other decisions will necessarily follow.

Think about It

The following list of questions is presented in order to illustrate how complicated the seemingly-simple decision to have sex can be. Because abortion is an "unspeakable crime," in the words of Pope John Paul II, and because abortion is objective grounds for automatic excommunication, if one has previous knowledge of that penalty, we assume the people

It is right and all right to say "no."

The Sacrament of Reconciliation is the ordinary means of celebrating God's forgiveness.

involved would not include abortion as a possible option when an unwanted pregnancy occurs.

Anyone who has had, or cooperated with, an abortion should consult with their parish priest about how to be restored to full communion with the Church.

Consequences and decisions faced by those who choose to be sexually active:

1. What is moral and what is not?
2. Should I use some form of conception control?
   - If I am going to be sexually active, is it responsible to not use some form of conception control?
   - Do I want to use a natural method (periodic abstinence) or an artificial method? Why?
   - If I choose a natural method, where do I get the best information about it?
   - If I choose an artificial method, how does it work, how effective is it, and what are the risks?
   - Can I use an artificial method of birth control in the way required?
3. What will I do if a pregnancy occurs?

The young woman:

- Will I tell my parents? How?
- Will I continue the pregnancy?
- What is the moral thing to do?
- Will I get married?
- Do I care enough for the child's father to make a life-commitment in marriage?
- Could we really make marriage work for us?
- Will I raise the child in a single-parent home?
- Can I handle the emotional and financial responsibilities of single parenting?
- Will I continue my education?
- Will I continue to live at home?
- Will I need to place the child in a foster home?
- Will I place the child for adoption?
- Can I live with this decision the rest of my life?
- Will our relationship continue after adoption and in what way?
- What would be best for me?
- What would be best for the child?
- What would be best for my relationship with the child's father?
- What services are offered by Birthright and Catholic Charities or Catholic Social Services?

The young man

- Will I tell my parents? How?
- Do I want the pregnancy to continue?
- What is the moral thing to do?
- Will I get married?
- Do I care enough for the child's mother to make a life-commitment in marriage?
- Could we really make marriage work for us?
- Will I continue my education?
- Will I pay child support if we do not marry and the mother keeps the baby?
- What is my responsibility to the child, the mother of the child, myself?
- Will I cooperate in placing the child for adoption?
- Can I live with this decision the rest of my life?
- Will our relationship continue after adoption and in what way?
- How can I assist with the pregnancy and birth?
- What would be best for me?
- What would be best for the child?
- What would be best for my relationship with the child's mother?
- What services are offered by Birthright and Catholic Charities or Catholic Social Services?

4. What will I do if I contract a sexually-transmitted disease?
   • What will I tell my partner?
   • How will I feel about my partner?
   • Where will I get help?
   • Will I tell my parents?
   • Will I continue my relationship with my partner?
   • If I do not marry this person, what, if anything, will I tell my future spouse?
5. Consequences and decisions faced by those who choose not to be sexually active:
   • none of the above!

How to Say No

After exploring the physical, emotional, and spiritual aspects of sexual involvement, many people find it easier to say "no." Here are ways that can help:

1. **Know the person you are dating.** Sometimes individuals have gained a reputation for being "easy" or "on the make." If you choose not to become involved sexually, date someone who will not try to persuade you to have sex. Date people who think as you do.
2. **Know where you are going on a date.** You can choose dating activities that are less likely to lead to sexual involvement. Making dates for the movies, dances, skating, picnics, and parties where there are other people around, make it far easier to say no than, for example, parking in some remote place.

3. **Express your feelings honestly.** You should be able to communicate your feelings to your partner. Rather than just saying "no" and chancing that the other person may feel rejected, you should be able to express why you do not want to have sexual relations. It should be a decision that is arrived at with thoughtful consideration. For example, you should be able to say "I don't think I'm ready for this," "I don't want to have to worry about pregnancy" (both men and women need to be concerned with that), "I believe sexual intimacy is for married, committed couples," or "I want to wait until I get married. It has nothing to do with my personal feelings for you or with the extent to which I care for you." When you express your feelings in those ways, the other person will not feel rejected and may even be inclined to respect your feelings and your ability to say "no."

It's up to you! The important thing to remember is that *you* must decide. People, old and young, rarely ask anyone's permission to have sex. They make that decision on their own.

It is too important a decision to be made under the influence of strong physical drives or artificial means such as alcohol or drugs. Neither do you want someone else to "force" you into something you do not want by flattery, threats, emotional manipulation, or promises.

---

1. State several good reasons why people should date.
2. What are some of the questions young adults need to ask themselves when they are on the threshold of a serious relationship?
3. State six reasons why an individual would say "no" to having sex before marriage. State six reasons why an individual would say "yes" to having sex before marriage. Which reasons appear to be most sound and valid? Why?
4. Contrast the physical, emotional, and spiritual results of saying "yes," or saying "no," to becoming sexually involved with another person before marriage.

The Catholic Church and Sexual Intimacy in Dating

Teenagers and young adults hear conflicting voices about petting and sexual intercourse for people who are dating seriously. There is no doubt that there are two schools of thought about petting and sexual intercourse in casual dating: one says it is all right; the other says it is not. Opinions vary also on petting *and* sexual intercourse for young people who date seriously, are in love, and have at least an understanding about marriage.

Many segments of society say that it is all right. Almost all parents, however, are against it (but tolerate it and often assume that it is happening). Most high school counselors advise against it, most medical doctors, psychologists, psychiatrists, and Christian Churches speak against it. The Catholic Church, in particular, considers it sinful. The question is, why do these people and groups tell teens and young adults that it is wrong?

Teenagers and young adults are not the only ones concerned with "how far to go" in expressing their sexuality in their relationships with persons of the other sex. Single people of all ages are, also.

There is no doubt that in every relationship between a man and a woman, no matter how "platonic" or "professional" it may seem, there is some degree of tension. Sexuality colors every experience—looking into the eyes of another, the impact of a tone of voice, or spending time in a person's company. It may also include entertaining imaginations and daydreams about someone special, and all those vague semiconscious longings and stirrings which are the backdrop of every human inter-sexual experience. *Since sexuality enters every experience to at least some degree, the questions of how much physical expression to give to it outside of marriage must be asked and answered by every person.*

The answer is not simple. It has societal, practical, psychological, cultural, religious, and moral overtones that must be taken into consideration. It is not anymore true to say that one's sexual life is no one else's concern but the individual's than it is to say that one's economic, or social, or recreational life is one's own. People do not live in isolation from one another. What they do affects every other human being alive—and coming generations as well.

The Reasons Explained

The societal, practical, cultural, religious, and moral reasons for cautions about sexual intercourse for young people before marriage can be summarized as follows:

Societal: From the most primitive times, society has established through laws and by custom, limitations on all forms of human behavior. It has tried to direct sexual expression to the good of society; that is, to the goals and purposes that a particular group of people have established as a social unit. Although they may vary from culture to culture and from time to time, laws and customs on sexual behavior have been established by all societies so that they may function smoothly.

Practical: Because of the very nature and meaning of human sexual expression, people have set certain practical limits on sexual expression. In such instances as the doctor-patient or parent-child relationship, for example, common sense has established behavior limits.

Cultural: The psychological and emotional aspects of human sexual expression which place limitations on human sexual behavior have already been discussed. You are also familiar with customs in various countries which limit sexual expression of one kind or another. For example, different societies have differing standards of modesty. In some countries, women must cover their faces with veils and not look men in the eye, while in other parts of the world, men and women wear little or no clothing. Just as modesty has different cultural limits, so do interpersonal relationships of a sexual nature. In many countries of the world, young people are always chaperoned when in the company of the other sex; in others, various forms of unchaperoned dating are the custom.

The reason for the laws and customs associated with human sexual expression is that people have always recognized the radical tension between the deep, sacred meaning of sex and the force of human sexual drives. Ideally, the latter can express the former; but, in various stages of growing up (and some adults are not grown up psychologically), the two are not necessarily integrated. Therefore, societies have found it neces-

The reason for the laws and customs associated with human sexual expression is that people have always recognized the radical tension between the deep, sacred meaning of sex and the force of human sexual drives.

146

sary to establish general rules relating to sexual behavior for those individuals whom experience has shown need guidance in this area.

Religious: In reflecting on the religious meaning of the human experience of sexual expression, the Catholic Church recognizes that with most people, only the marriage relationship satisfies the whole complex of cravings which make up a person's sexuality. It knows that the acts of intercourse and related acts of loveplay cannot, as mere actions, satisfy the total emotional, psychological, and spiritual needs of two persons. The Church knows, as do most thinking people, that even when physical expression has been carried to completion, there remains a sense (vague perhaps, or tragically conscious) of unfulfillment, of frustration; of "this can't be all . . ." when the physical act is not part of a total lifetime commitment of each person to the other. Outside of marriage, sexual expression cannot be completely life-giving and love-giving.

Therefore, the Church, looking upon this human experience and interpreting it with the mind of Christ reflected in the Gospels and epistles, teaches that the whole complex of sexual cravings is meant to lead to and be expressed in marriage and must not be deliberately awakened to consummation outside of marriage. The Vatican Declaration on Sexual Ethics put it this way:

> Now it is a stable union that Jesus willed, and he restored its original requirement, beginning with the sexual difference. "Have you not read that the Creator from the beginning made them male and female and that He said: This is why a man must leave father and mother, and cling to his wife, and the two become one body? They are no longer two, therefore, but one body. So then, what God has united, man must not divide."[1]
>
> Saint Paul will be even more explicit when he shows that if unmarried people or widows cannot live chastely, they have no other alternative than the stable union of marriage: " . . . it is better to marry than to be aflame with passion"[2] Through marriage, in fact, the love of married people is taken up into that love which Christ irrevocably has for the Church,[3] while dissolute sexual union[4] defiles the temple of the Holy Spirit which the Christian has become. Sexual union therefore is only legitimate if a definitive community of life has been established between the man and the woman.
>
> This is what the Church has always understood and taught, and she finds a profound agreement with her doctrine in humanity's reflection and in the lessons of history.
>
> Experience teaches us that love must find its safeguard in the stability of marriage if sexual intercourse is truly to respond to the requirements of its own finality and to those of human dignity. These requirements call for a conjugal contract sanctioned and guaranteed by society—a contract which establishes a state of life of capital importance both for the exclusive union of the man and the woman and for the good of their family and of the human community. Most often, in fact, premarital relations exclude the possibility of children, or at least the intent. What is represented to be conjugal love is not able, as it absolutely should be, to develop into paternal and maternal love. Or, if it does happen to do so, this will be to the detriment of the children, who will be deprived of the stable environment in which they ought to develop in order to find in it the way and the means of their insertion into society as a whole.
>
> The consent given by people who wish to be united in marriage must therefore be manifested externally and in a manner which makes it valid in the eyes of society. As far as the faithful are concerned, their consent to the setting up of a community of conjugal life must be expressed according to the laws of the Church. It is a consent which makes their marriage a sacrament of Christ.[5]

This norm is offered to help each generation of people, as it struggles with its own sexual identity and its sexual drives, avoid the unhappiness that comes from learning, through bitter experience, the hurt of broken hearts and shattered dreams or the injustice to an unwanted child.

1. Cf. Matthew 19:4–6.

2. Cf. 1 Corinthians 7:9.

3. Cf. Ephesians 5:25–32.

4. Sexual intercourse outside marriage is formally condemned: 1 *Corinthians* 5:1; 6:9; 7:2; 10:8; *Ephesians* 5:5; 1 *Timothy* 1:10; *Hebrews* 13:4; and with explicit reasons: 1 *Corinthians* 6:12–20.

5. The Vatican Declaration on Sexual Ethics," *ORIGINS:* p. 488, 489; NC Documentary Service; Vol 5: No. 31, January 22, 1976.

Moral: It is from this source—the human experience of people religiously interpreted by our faith community—that Catholics take their moral stance concerning sexual behavior. For them, sexual morality is not determined only by law (which is necessary), or by custom, or by humanitarian ethics, all of which are good and important in developing moral values by which to guide one's sexual life. *The Catholic moral stance is determined by what is the right thing to do in light of the Gospel to express what it means for a person to be truly human.* For Catholics, to be truly human means to live in such a way as to reflect the Divine Dimension of life—the dimension brought to people by Jesus, who, Christians believe, is the Son of God who expressed his divinity through his complete human nature. Catholics believe that they are called to express their manhood or womanhood through their actions as Christian men or women. Their values are Christ's values, their sexual values his sexual values. His sexual values are plain, simple, and clear: because people are created in God's image, they are called to express their love in a creative way—in the mutuality of lives lived in intimate love with the one, and only the one, to whom they have pledged themselves.

Catholic thinking about sex is summed up in St. Paul's letter to the Galatian Christians (who were no strangers to the sexual mores of the pagan world around them):

> As for you, my brothers, you were called to be free. But do not let this freedom become an excuse for letting your physical desires control you. Instead, let love make you serve one another.
>
> What I say is this: let the Spirit direct your lives, and you will not satisfy the desires of the human nature. For what our human nature wants is opposed to what the Spirit wants, and what the Spirit wants is opposed to what our human nature wants. These two are enemies, and this means that you cannot do what you want to do. If the Spirit leads you, then you are not subject to the law.

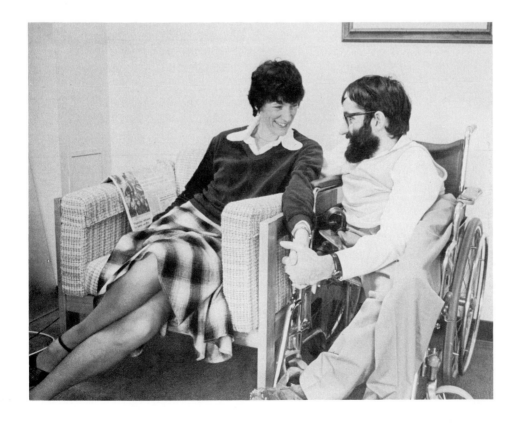

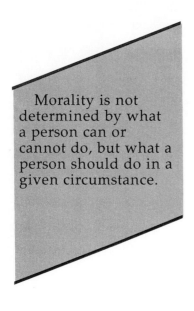

Morality is not determined by what a person can or cannot do, but what a person should do in a given circumstance.

What human nature does is quite plain. It shows itself in immoral, filthy, and indecent actions; in worship of idols and witchcraft. People become enemies and they fight; they become jealous, angry, and ambitious. They separate into parties and groups; they are envious, get drunk, have orgies, and do other things like these. I warn you now as I have before: those who do these things will not possess the Kingdom of God.

But the Spirit produces love, joy, peace, patience, kindness, goodness, faithfulness, humility, and self-control. There is no law against such things as these. And those who belong to Christ Jesus have put to death their human nature with all its passions and desires. The Spirit has given us life: he must also control our lives.[6]

It must be clearly understood that the Catholic faith community is not against sex. It is *for* sex as an expression of true love and dedication. When sex expresses true love, for Catholics it is moral; when it does not, it is immoral. For Catholics, the right use of sex in marriage is a beautiful and holy action; outside of marriage the same act cannot express the love-giving and life-giving aspects of marriage, because the same commitment is not present. Even if a couple intends to marry, they have not yet formally committed themselves to each other and are not, therefore, formally bound to each other. Sexual expression outside of a marriage which is loving and committed falls short of the ideal and norms presented by the Church which are within the capabilities of everyone.

1. Why has society established laws and customs on sexual behavior?
2. Why have there been certain practical limits set on sexual expression? Do you think they are necessary? Why?
3. Why does the Catholic Church believe that only the marriage relationship satisfies the whole complex of cravings which make up a person's sexuality?
4. What is the Catholic moral stance concerning sexual behavior?
5. How would you respond to one of your peers who says to you that no Church has a right to tell me how I'm going to behave?

Teen Marriages

After dating for a period of time, it is not unusual for a young couple to feel they are mature enough to be married. Even so, as strong as that love may seem, it may not survive the undue and unexpected strains that sometimes come from an early marriage.

What often occurs when a teen couple elects to marry is that they tie themselves prematurely to a relationship which later may prove to be stifling as it cuts off possibilities they would otherwise have naturally explored.

Of course, it is possible that two exceptionally mature teenagers might find in one another such comprehensive openness that they would have a good chance of growing into adulthood and enlarging their horizons together. Most often, however, this is not the case. Teenagers, by

6. Cf. Galatians 5:13, 16–25.

and large, just are not old enough to cope with the problems that marriage presents to a teenager. Financial problems such as housing, food, clothing, means of transportation, entertainment, and an army of hidden costs that inexperienced teens do not even dream of, are suddenly thrust upon them.

There are also social problems that can be created by their early marriage. Where, for example, does the couple fit in society? Do they become part of the "older" married set, or are they still members of their old social group? Does she still run around with her single girl friends? Does he go off with the boys and leave her at home? Can he go out until three or four in the morning as he might have done before they were married? Where does each one fit in individually? Where could the couple live—alone, or with parents? And how will they handle the unspoken criticism by people who do not approve of teen marriages?

Other concerns may arise if a pregnancy occurs, because the problem of parenting for teenagers can be overwhelming. Most teenage girls are neither physically nor psychologically ready for the responsibilities of caring for a child or managing a household. They are not ready for the twenty-four hour demands of babies—feeding, diapering, exercising, nurturing, playing—not to mention caring for them when they are sick. Neither are most teenage girls ready for the demands of caring for a house and managing a budget—especially since finances are all too often far less than needed and desired.

All of these, however, are nothing compared to the psychological problems of getting along with each other in the uncommon world of their intimate living. They just cannot escape nagging self-doubts, worries about their spouse, insecurity about their abilities to make it, and coping with the emotional strain of having to face problems they had no time to prepare for.

Other psychological problems may occur if there is a premature halt to the educational process for either partner—or both. They may feel frustration or regret, or blame the other partner because they were unable to achieve their goals in life. Take, for example, a young man who may have always dreamed of becoming an engineer. If he has to forego college in order to secure a job to support a family, the emotional results could be devastating. Or a young woman who interrupts her education because of a pregnancy may take her frustration and anger out on her child. Child abuse today is not uncommon in families with teenage parents.

Very few teenagers who get married have no regrets. They wonder what they missed, who they might eventually have married, what they could have been or could have done, and what "the next five years of their life would have been like."

Why, then, do they get married? "The dilemma of sex is not sex itself," said one teenager who wanted sex without responsibility, only to marry *because he had to.* "It's fun. Young people enjoy it, but they don't want the disadvantages—specifically, children. But they don't care. They think it can't happen to them. Then it does."

Adults who advise a teenage couple against getting married are not being spoilsports or authoritarian, nor are they rattling off statistics just to scare the young couple. They know what responsibilities are entailed in a marriage. Far from wanting to prevent the couple from being happily married, they specifically want them to be happy in marriage. That is why they advise against it at this stage of life. Very often these adults

Teens who do not finish high school earn, on the average, 50 percent less than those who do.

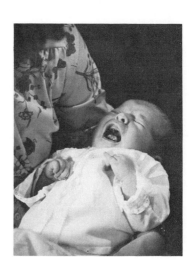

*B*elow are excerpts from an article in **Parade**, a magazine supplement found in many of the nation's Sunday papers. It appeared in the June 17, 1984 issue. It was researched and written by Ken Auletta. The article deals with the problems of teenage mothers. The reality of being pregnant and being a parent are two entirely different states of being. One is completely physical; the other entails a whole new scope of responsibilities.

Lucinda, who became pregnant when she was fifteen, had twin girls. She wants to find her own apartment but can't find one. . . . "she would like to marry the father of her children but is uncertain of him; she would like the freedom to leave the house but fears leaving the babies with a volatile grandmother, and she can't afford a babysitter; she worries about whether she can escape the beckoning welfare system, finish high school (maybe go to college), get a job and find someone to watch her children.

She is a child with responsibilites most adults don't have. "Sometimes I feel, 'What am I going to do?' " Lucinda says. . . .

There are few programs in this nation geared to the needs of children who are mothering children. Among them is the Adolescent Primary Health Care Center for teen parents who live in Houston's poverty-stricken fifth ward. Operating in an abandoned gray brick three-story school and managed by the nonprofit Urban Affairs Corp., the center offers services to young mothers who agree to remain in, or return to, one of the seven alternative schools in the district. The Houston school system provides utilities and space for counseling offices, for an alternative high school and for a day care center that serves ninety-two children.

Sharon Lovick, the dynamic, thirty-four-year-old black woman who administers the various programs run by the Urban Affairs Corp, speaks of the conflicts afflicting the young mothers she works with: "They have unrealistic expectations for their children. A lot of this is role reversal—they expect their children to give love to them and fill a void. Yet young children take."

When child-mothers fail to receive the unquestioning love they'd expected from a baby, says Lovick, some become uninterested in their children; others inflict emotional or physical abuse on them. "The physical demands of parenting—it's tiring—clash with the emotional demands of parenting." Lovick says, "It's hell to be fourteen and pregnant!"

A visit to Lovick's "Clinic," as it's called in Houston, and to the Phoenix headquarters of Via de Amistad—The Ford Foundation considers them to be two of the best models in the nation—helps one empathize with how little a fifteen- or seventeen-year-old knows about parenting.

"Frequently, when we get our kids, they may be underweight or ill," says Elisha Smith, a personable black woman who directs the staff of twenty-three that supervises the babies enrolled at the Houston Clinic's day-care center. "Some of the babies are not social. They don't smile or respond to a human face. Often, our parents are unaware of the fact that you have to talk to your child. They come here and, after a while, we see a complete change." Teen mothers come to pick up their babies after school and notice that the babies are smiling, talking or being affectionate.

Valencia, a sixteen-year-old black girl from Houston's fifth ward, is nine months pregnant and has been coming to the Clinic since she learned she was to have a baby. She is in the eleventh grade and is accompanied by Jeffrey, nineteen, the husband with whom she does not live. "Most girls think they can take one pill and they won't get pregnant," says Valencia. Jeffrey adds that, for the young man, having sex early is a way of showing "manhood." The Clinic put Valencia together with other expectant mothers. "I learned how to eat well during pregnancy," she says. "I learned you shouldn't diet when pregnant. And you had to stay away from drugs."

"They taught me about nutrition and how to brush Tommy's teeth and get him in to see a dentist," says sixteen-year-old Anita, a skinny white

girl from North Carolina who now lives in Phoenix and has the letters L-O-V-E tattooed on four fingers of her left hand.

Many of these girls must cope with peer pressures that pull them away from their babies. "In almost any population where babies have babies," says Dr. Amanda Fouther-Austin, former project manager of the Houston Clinic, "the critical issue that the adolescent deals with is self-definition: 'Who . . . am I?' And they must do this at a time when peer pressure is dominant. A baby is introduced who tells them: 'Don't deal with yourself. Deal with me.' "

The causes of out-of-wedlock teen births are multiple and often baffling.

Clearly, sex education offers no panacea. Even where birth control is available, ignorance of it is widespread. . . . Feeling the deprivations that go with poverty, many young girls believe a child will give them the love they crave. Others are lured into motherhood by the expectation of support from the welfare system or the opportunity to escape a bitter home environment. Many do not wish to marry the unemployed fathers of their children, fearful that it will mean a life of pain, or drugs, drink and violence.

The sexual revolution provides the background music. Sex is normal—studies show that 50 percent of U.S. teenage girls fifteen and over have had sex. And, increasingly, having a baby out of wedlock is "normal." "Society says that having sex is the vogue," says Sharon Lovick. "They advertise oatmeal with sex: 'Be sexy.' 'Be slim.' 'The macho man.' In all these ways, we say sex is OK. And we're dealing with a child who doesn't get love and attention at home. Our children are lonely and unloved. So they try to substitute sexual contact for intimacy."

The programs in Houston and Phoenix try to ease the pressures on these child-mothers, but they are no cure-all. There is broad agreement that the best answer is prevention.

Parade June 17, 1984 p. 6 from *Sarasota Herald Tribune.*

have known other teenagers who cherished the same illusion that *their* marriage would be the magic one that would survive, and they saw it fail. And parents who see their own son or daughter getting too deeply involved too soon face a difficult situation. Because they are deeply concerned *for* their son's or daughter's eventual happy marriage, they wind up appearing to be against marriage or against happiness when they try to inject the reasonable advice to "cool it" into the flame of infatuation which in young years is so easily mistaken for love.

The only thing worse than rushing into a young marriage on the basis of an infatuation that looks like love, is to rush into a marriage based on a previous mistake.

The only thing worse than rushing into a young marriage on the basis of an infatuation that looks like love, is to rush into a marriage based on nothing but a previous mistake. "Shotgun" marriages solve no problems and usually create worse ones. They cannot confer respectability upon a previous action. No ceremony is capable of conferring instant maturity. Experience shows that the child "on the way" is much better off adopted by a mature couple, or in a foster home, or in the home of older relatives who are settled and mature, than in the hands of a hastily married couple who have nothing in common except a responsibility neither of them wants.

When a couple, even a teenage couple, do decide that marriage is the proper step for them at this time and when the Church, through ministers and parents, agree with that decision, the Church turns its full resources of teaching, counselling, planning, and support to help the couple live out the Christian vocation of marriage. As we have underlined, the failure rate of teen marriages is shocking. And it's far worse when pregnancy is involved before marriage. Yet it is a fact that teen marriages work in some cases. The assistance of the Church and parents and reliance on God's grace can be of great help.

1. List some of the problems a teenage couple may face in marriage.
2. Why are adults most apt to advise a teenage couple against getting married?
3. Describe some of the difficulties a single, teenage mother might encounter in establishing a new life for herself and her child.

Summary

• Several important issues in the dating process that are of concern for young adults today are going steady, sexual intimacy, marriage, and children.
• Going steady may result in a situation where the couple is on the threshold of sexual intimacy before they are ready for the responsibilities of that type of relationship. For them, it is important to explore not only the physical and emotional ramifications of sexual intimacy, but to adhere to their own sound, moral values in making a decision.
• Young couples who feel they have achieved mature sexual love and want to consummate it with marriage usually find they are unprepared for the financial, social, and psychological problems that arise in a marriage for which they are not completely ready.

Review, Discussion, Research, and Reflection

1. Discuss in an open forum the pros and cons of adoption versus marriage in the case of out-of-wedlock pregnancy.
2. What are some of the laws and customs our society places on the expression of sexual behavior?
3. Explore and list the procedures individuals would go through if they suspected they had a venereal disease. Where in your community would they seek help in the diagnosis and treatment of the disease?
4. Describe the many ways you believe an individual can say "no" to sexual involvement.
5. What do you believe are some of the pros and cons of teenage marriages? List them, and explain your answers.
6. What does the Catholic Church teach about sexual intimacy?
7. What do you believe are some of the causes of out-of-wedlock teen births?

Projects

1. Write five questions about concerns you believe your peers have regarding going steady. Survey five students on their feelings about these concerns. Write a conclusion based upon their responses.
2. Research and list the various resources in your community that provide assistance for "children having children." Indicate which organizations provide assistance for the father, mother, or child. Is there an equal amount of assistance for all three? If not, what do you recommend could be done to provide an equal amount of services for all concerned?
3. Assume that one of your friends is seriously thinking about getting married before finishing school. Make a list of things you would advise your friend about. Be prepared to compare your list with those of your classmates.

Words You Should Know

Be sure that you can define the following words and can use them in meaningful sentences:

going steady

peer group

venereal disease

herpes II

syphilis

gonorrhea

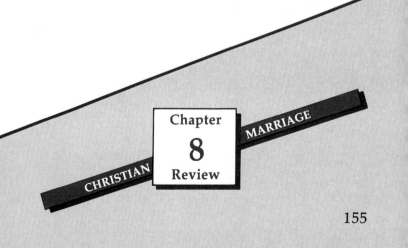

CHRISTIAN MARRIAGE

Chapter 8 Review

Part 3

Growth toward Mature Sexual Love

Man and woman constitute two modes of realizing, on the part of the human creature, a determined participation in the divine being: They are created in the "image and likeness of God" and they fully accomplish such vocation not only as single persons, but also as couples, which are communities of love.

— Educational Guidance in Human Love, no. 26, November 1, 1983

Understanding Your Reproductive System

I WONDER WHAT BEING IN LOVE IS REALLY LIKE, LAWRENCE.

MY MOM SAYS YOU KINDA GET BUTTERFLIES IN YOUR STOMACH.

AN' YOU JUST GO ALL GOOFY-LIKE INSIDE. WHY- ARE YOU IN LOVE OR SOMETHIN?

NO WAY!

I WANNA KNOW WHAT TO AVOID.

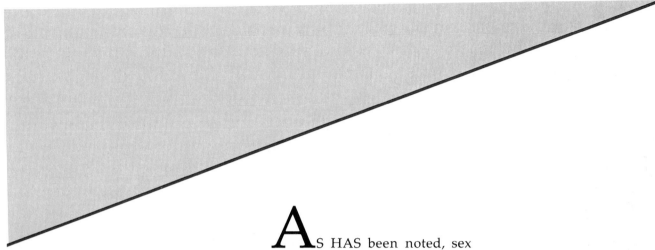

AS HAS been noted, sex and sexual matters are interesting and attention-getting for most people. Even those whom some researchers have labelled "the nonsexual" (those who have little or no interest in sex and those who are turned off by sex in any of its expressions) are concerned about sexual matters—if only in a negative way. Because sex and sexual matters are interesting for most people, and because you are at the beginning of your whole life's experience of sex, there may be some questions you would like to ask about sex but are too shy or embarrassed to ask in public. If there are, write your two most important "sex questions" on a small piece of paper and turn them in to your teacher. During the course of this part of the book, your questions will be addressed and responded to.

What Is Mature Sexual Love?

Thus far, marriage has been discussed as the way of life most people choose. Preparation for marriage has also been discussed. To make both of them viable in your life, it is important for you to understand your reproductive system, your sexual feelings, and the process of growth toward mature sexual love—an absolutely necessary ingredient in a happy marriage.

Mature sexual love is the love of a man and a woman which has grown and ripened into a total love relationship. Young persons in love and older persons in the midst of a new, loving relationship do not have mature sexual love. They have not experienced each other nor loved each other long enough or deep enough to have grown into mature sexual love. It comes only with a long-term, loving, sexual relationship.

Mature sexual love is sexual in the profoundest meaning of the word. It encompasses the whole being of the man and the woman. It includes, but is more than, sex, more than friendship, more than family, more than children, more than whatever binds them together externally. It is comfortable, warm, sure, unruffled, and it is accepting of the person with whom we have lived in love for a long time. It is what St. Paul called a deep, secret truth. He compared Christ's love for his people to this kind of love. (Ephesians 5:31–33).

In order for love to grow into mature sexual love, a person—and a couple—needs to understand that sex in its most basic meaning is only one part of a person's total life experience.

Sex: One Part of a Person's Total Life Experience

As conscious as we are of our sexual feelings under the stress of sexual stimuli, the most important question concerning our sexual response is not what sort of sexual feelings we have, but how we integrate our sexual drives into our total life pattern.

To begin with, it can be taken for granted that we do have sexual drives drawing us to sexual union and to relationships with the other sex. Such drives are a necessary part of our nature as human beings. Second, we recognize that sex, in all of its manifestations, is interesting and exciting. It arouses our curiosity, creates a chemical flow felt in our bodies, and causes physical, emotional, and psychological reactions which are directly related to the strength of the stimulus and our cultural upbringing.

Sexual needs, drives, desires, and interests vary from person to person and from circumstance to circumstance.

Third, everyone must realize, for his or her own peace of mind, that sexual needs, drives, desires, and interests vary from person to person, and from circumstance to circumstance. Sexual response is not programmed. Too many variables enter into each sexual encounter making each a unique experience in itself.

Fourth, sex, as a part of life's total experience, is not isolated from life. It is not a phenomenon unrelated to the way people experience life or express their humanity. It is part and parcel of what it means to be human. How we experience and express sex in our lives depends on who we are, what we are, what our state in life is, and how we value sex in relation to our personal sexuality.

To integrate our sex life into our total life experience and not treat it as a separate phenomenon, we need to understand our sexual nature.

Many times we are confused by the sexual feelings we experience and the things we see and hear about sex because we do not completely understand the sexual functions of our bodies. We know something is "going on" within our bodies, but we are not sure what it means or why it is happening.

Why Sexual Feelings Occur

Sexual feelings occur because your body has been preparing you for what is going on in you and to you sexually. Your pituitary gland, located at the base of your brain, has been sending growth signals in the form of chemicals called hormones to various parts of your body so that they develop to fulfill their mature adult functions. Your feet, for example, have been growing so that they will be able to support your body in its adult phase. Your muscles have been developing so that they will be able to support your adult activities. Signals have also been sent to your sex organs and glands, causing them to develop to fulfill their adult functions.

It is part of human nature to seek love and to give love.

For most people your age, the sex organs are almost fully matured and are capable of responding to sex signals which arouse sexual desires and corresponding physical reactions. This is the first reason why sexual feelings increase during the teen years.

A second reason you may be experiencing increased sexual feelings in your body is that it is part of human nature to seek love and to give love. It is also part of human nature to seek union with the one loved.

The ultimate expression of this union is sexual intercourse. What may be happening in your body sexually is that your body may be responding to an attraction you may feel toward another person. The attraction may be great or small, general or particular. Your body's sexual response corresponds to the degree of the attraction.

A third reason you may be experiencing heightened sexual interest and feelings is that it is part of your body's sexual mechanisms to seek release. Because of body chemistry, sexual tensions sometimes build up in the body, and the body seeks relief. This relief takes many forms and is accomplished in many ways. In boys, for example, it may be in a spontaneous erection and the involuntary emission of semen during sleep. This is referred to medically as a nocturnal emission. Girls, too, may experience dreams involving sexual release. Sometimes release is sought in self-stimulation and exploration, though this is a misuse of sexual powers and not the ideal of sexual expression found in a mature, loving, committed relationship. Another possible release may simply be the turning of one's attention to some other interest.

A fourth reason for the sexual feelings you may be experiencing in your body is the procreative drive of human nature. Men and women experience a strong, natural drive to perpetuate the human race—to have children—and to nurture and care for them. This drive may be stronger in some than in others, but it is a sexual drive experienced by most of the human race.

Nocturnal emission: A spontaneous erection and the involuntary emission of semen during sleep.

Procreation: The producing of offspring.

---

1. What is mature sexual love?
2. What is the most important question an individual should consider about his or her sexual response?
3. Why does an individual need to understand his or her sexual nature?
4. Why do sexual feelings occur?

Why Your Reproductive System Functions as It Does

By the late teens, many young people will have experienced sexual feelings. A young man may have experienced such physical sexual reactions as an erection of the penis, excitement in the genital area, and an ejaculation. A young woman will have settled into a more or less regular monthly cycle of discharging blood and mucosal tissue from the uterus, known as menstruation. Young women, too, may have experienced genital excitement. All of these experiences are part of nature's most awesome phenomena associated with the onset of puberty and are an important part of becoming an adult.

Puberty is the stage of development at which a young man's or a young woman's reproductive organs become functionally operative and the secondary sex characteristics that distinguish males from females develop. It is important to note here that there is tremendous variation in the ages at which individuals reach puberty. There is no proper or right age for this to occur. There is also no relationship between an individual's ability to respond sexually and the age at which they first menstruate or ejaculate. Interestingly enough, over the past century in the United States the average age for reaching puberty has decreased by slightly over three years. What happens physically to both males and females that prepares them for their adult reproductive functions is a very unique, special experience.

Ejaculation: The expulsion of semen from the penis.

Menstruation: The discharge of blood from the uterus through the vagina that usually occurs at four-week intervals in women between the ages of puberty and menopause.

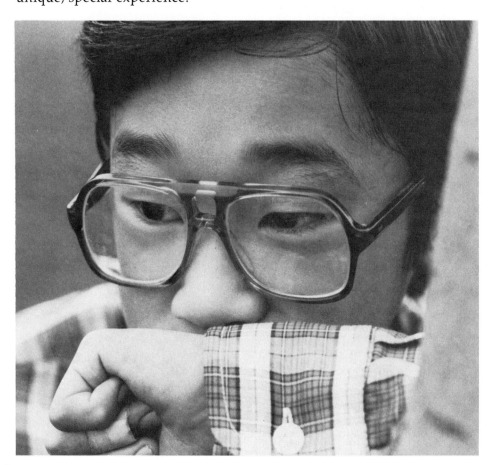

162

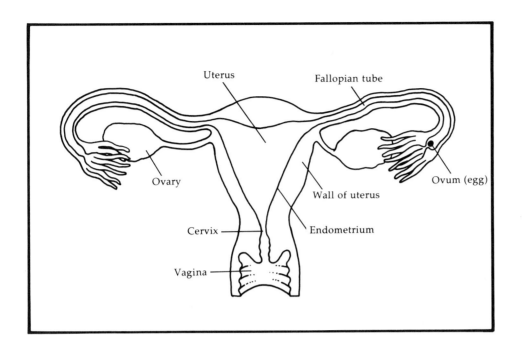

Labels in the figure:
Uterus
Fallopian tube
Ovary
Ovum (egg)
Wall of uterus
Cervix
Endometrium
Vagina

How a Woman's Reproductive System Functions

Young girls usually experience their adolescent growth spurt and enter puberty about two years before boys. A woman's body is different sexually from a man's not simply in its external sexual characteristics but also in its internal structure, function, and purpose.

A woman's sexual, or reproductive organs can be classified in three groups: (1) the external sexual parts, collectively called the "vulva" or external genitalia; (2) the "vestibule," which contains the urinary canal, the clitoris, and the vagina, a sheathlike passageway leading from the vulva to the third part; and (3) the cervix, uterus, fallopian tubes, and ovaries. Except for the outer lips, all female sex organs are within a woman's body and are located at the base of her trunk.

1. The outer lips are two fleshy folds of skin which protect the inner lips, folds of flesh surrounding the clitoris, the urinary canal outlet, and the vagina. The clitoris is a small highly sensitive piece of erectile tissue located above the urethra. It is the center of sexual pleasure in women.
2. The vagina is the receptacle for the male reproductive organ and receives the male sperm which then begin the journey in search of a female egg. The vagina is about four inches in length and extends from the inner lips to the cervix, the opening to the uterus. It is remarkable for its elasticity. It not only receives the erect male reproductive organ; it also serves as the passageway for the child in the womb struggling to make its way to the outside world.

   In most female newborns the entrance to the vagina is usually partly closed with a membrane called the hymen. The hymen may have either a single opening or a number of small or large openings

Cervix: The neck, or narrow portion, of the uterus (womb) that forms its lower end and opens into the vagina.

Ovaries: The two female sex glands found on either side of the uterus, in which the ova (egg cells) are formed. They also produce hormones which influence female body characteristics.

163

to allow for the exiting of blood during menstruation. (It is also possible for a female to be born without a hymen.) The presence of a hymen indicates that a woman has never had sexual intercourse, or is a virgin. The absence of a hymen, however, is not a sign that a woman is not a virgin. In some females (when the hymen is present), the opening in the hymen develops naturally, or it may also enlarge to some degree through the use of tampons. Medical treatment or medical intervention to prepare the woman for intercourse may break the hymen.

3. The ovaries are small almond-shaped glands about three quarters of an inch in length that are located at the end of each fallopian tube. They are responsible (1) for producing the sex hormones estrogen and progesterone that are important in the development of sexual maturity in females, (2) for the regulation of a woman's menstrual cycle, and (3) for the achievement and maintenance of a pregnancy.

In addition, the ovaries are responsible for producing the female reproductive cell (egg) called the ovum. Although women are born with all of the ova or eggs they will ever produce, it is not until they enter puberty that they begin to release a ripened egg each month on an alternating basis from the ovaries. This is called ovulation, and it is regulated by the amount of and interactions among certain hormones in the female's body. Although the release of more than one egg is possible, the majority of women release only one egg at a time. At the same time that the ovum is maturing in the ovary, the lining of the uterus, called the endometrium, begins to thicken with blood and mucosal tissue. This build-up of the endometrium is in preparation for the implantation of the fertilized egg.

When the ovum leaves the ovary, it is captured by the fringed end of the Fallopian tube and begins its journey to the uterus. If the ovum is not fertilized in the fallopian tube, it passes out of the womb along with the blood and mucosal tissue in a process known as menstruation and is an indication that the woman may now be ovulating and capable of producing a child. There is considerable variation in the age at which women reach menarche. Most women experience their first menstruation between the ages of eight and eighteen and will continue to menstruate (except during pregnancy) until they reach menopause. Menopause is the period of natural cessation of menstruation. This usually occurs between the ages of forty-five and fifty-five. (A woman is considered no longer able to become pregnant when she has gone a full year without menstruating.)

It is usually not long after the onset of menarche that a woman begins to menstruate at regular intervals. (Many women say, "have their period.") This is known as the menstrual cycle. The average length of the human menstrual cycle is twenty-eight days. However, some women's bodies adjust to a three-week, or twenty-one-day cycle, while others have their periods every five weeks, or thirty-five days. It is possible, however, that a woman may never establish a regular cycle of menstruating; then she is said to have an irregular menstrual cycle. These are all very normal for a woman.

The menstrual cycle begins with the first day of the menstrual flow. Ovulation occurs about fourteen days before a woman starts her next menstrual cycle. Some women feel a slight twinge in their pelvic region about the time this happens. This is called Mittelschmerz, German for

Ovulation: Release of the mature (ripe) ovum from the ovary to one of the fallopian tubes.

Endometrium: The mucus lining of the uterus, which thickens and fills with blood in preparation for a fertilized ovum.

Menarche: The onset of the menstrual cycle in a girl.

Menopause: The end of menstruation in women, usually between the ages of forty-five and fifty-five. Sometimes referred to as "change of life."

"middle pain." However, since this may occur as long as one day before or one day after ovulation, or may never be felt at all, it is not a reliable indicator of the moment of ovulation.

As discussed in chapter 3, a more accurate way for a woman to determine when ovulation occurs is to notice the changes in the vaginal discharge during the middle part of a typical cycle. By evaluating her vaginal discharge daily, a woman can tell not only when ovulation occurs, but can also calculate when the next menstrual cycle will begin. On a regular basis, ovulation can be calculated by a trained woman. However, she must be aware that factors such as extensive travel, considerable weight loss, or emotional trauma can cause a woman to ovulate sooner than normal or later than usual.

When a woman menstruates, or has her period, she needs to wear some type of disposable, absorbent material to collect the menstrual flow. Several brands of pads and napkins that vary in size and absorbency are available, as are tampons. Tampons are made of absorbent material shaped into a small roll that can be easily inserted into the vagina to absorb the flow.

However, in 1980, the use of certain tampons was linked to a rare disease called toxic shock syndrome (TSS). It seems that staph germs, which ordinarily are present in the body and do not cause any problems, multiply more readily when a woman inserts a tampon made of especially absorbent materials into her vagina. As the germs multiply, they produce a toxin (poisonous substance), and this poison is then absorbed into the blood stream, causing toxic shock syndrome. Some of the symptoms of TSS may include chills and fever, a red rash, aching muscles, painful joints, and perhaps vomiting or diarrhea. If a woman ever experiences any of these symptoms while using tampons, she should discontinue their use and see a doctor immediately. TSS can be fatal within

Menstrual cycle: The length of time from when a woman begins to menstruate one month to the next time she menstruates.

Toxic shock syndrome: A disease believed to be caused by the use of tampons in women. Staph germs multiply in the vagina and produce a toxin that is then absorbed into the blood stream.

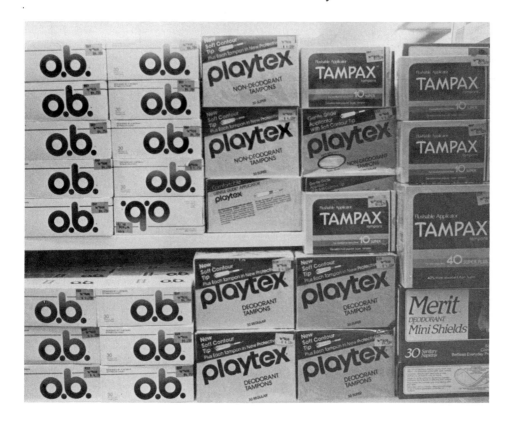

What is the purpose of pubic hair?

Like the hair under one's arms, pubic hair serves as a cushion to prevent chafing under friction.

What causes body odor?

Several different things such as bacteria, excessive perspiration, certain kinds of food, and so forth can cause body odor. Sometimes, certain secretions from the sex organs can cause odors. It is important to respect your body and care for it. Daily bathing will control body odor, and clean clothes and showering after vigorous exercise are a must.

Why are the sex organs called the genitals?

Because the sex organs are the source or the beginning of life. The word comes from the ancient Greek word meaning "to beget children."

How much blood is lost during menstruation?

It's important to understand that no blood needed by the body is lost in the normal monthly menstrual flow. The total amount of blood and tissue that leaves the body is about a half of a cup. It is extra material that serves no useful purpose until a woman is ready to have a baby.

Can a girl go swimming or take a bath during her period?

Surely she can. The menstrual flow will usually stop or decrease when a girl gets into water. A girl can wash, dry quickly and put on fresh menstrual protection before it starts again.

What is circumcision?

Circumcision is the removal of the foreskin that is at the end of the penis. It is often done when a baby is only a few days old. In the Jewish family, it is a religious ceremony.

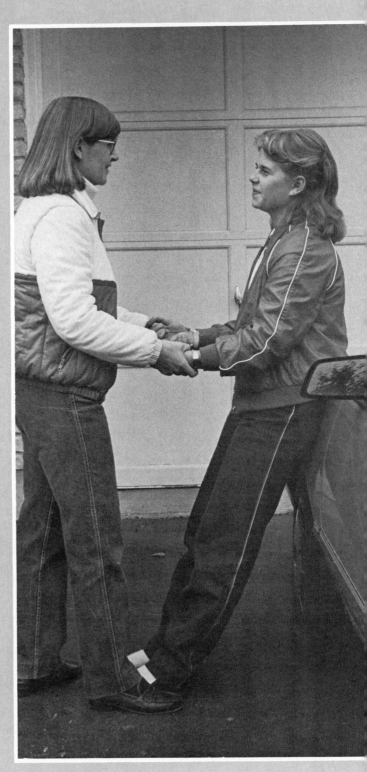

How old must a person be before he can have an erection?

Beneath the skin of the penis there are tissues made of a spongy material. When blood rushes into the spaces of this tissue the penis stiffens and becomes larger. Males of every age, even tiny babies, have erections. Some causes of erection are a full bladder, the friction of tight clothing, or stimulating thoughts and dreams.

Does a penis have to be a certain size when a boy is grown up?

No. Just as there are differences in the size of other parts of the body, so the penis and testicles may be different in size in different males. The size is unimportant, for when erect, all penises are approximately the same size.

Do more hair and a deeper voice make a person more of a man?

No. A person's manliness has nothing to do with the amount of hair on his body or with the deepness of his voice.

Do urine and semen ever pass from the body at the same time?

No. When semen passes, the body has a special way by means of valves and muscle contractions to prevent urine from passing at the same time.

At what age do most boys begin to have nocturnal emissions?

There is no definite age, but they usually begin between the ages of twelve and sixteen. It is also possible never to have nocturnal emissions.

Can a boy be a father?

Yes, it is possible for a boy to be a father as soon as his body is mature enough to produce sperm cells. But this can only happen if he has sexual intercourse with a girl whose body is producing egg cells and a sperm cell fertilizes one of them.

What is sexual intercourse?

Sexual intercourse is the sexual union of a man and a woman. During intercourse, the penis of the man is placed in the woman's vagina (opening of the body between a woman's legs.) If sperm leaves the man's body and enters the woman's body through ejaculation, a woman may become pregnant.

How often do people have sexual intercourse?

That depends on a lot of circumstances: the time, the place, the availability, the desire, the need, the effect of moral standards (e.g., in Natural Family Planning), and the purpose. The true guide for married people is love. Sexual intercourse must never be forced. It should be the final touch to physical and other acts of love leading up to total, desired union.

Do men need more sex than women?

Some men desire more sex than some women, and some women desire more sex than some men. Sexual needs vary from person to person, from time to time, and from age to age. There is no norm, standard, gauge, or measure for each and every person's sexual needs.

Does everybody have to have sex?

No. Almost all persons have sexual needs and feel sexual drives. Some people, for example, priests in the Latin Rite and other Catholic or Orthodox religious and Buddhist monks, take a vow of celibacy and never have sex. Many other people remain single and celibate all their lives or for long periods. Some married people do not have sex for long periods of time, for example, when their spouses are absent or sick, or when one or the other is unable to have sex for some reason.

two or three days. Incidence of TSS is more common among younger women than among older women. Even if there are no signs of difficulty, some health authorities recommend that tampons should be used only intermittently during a woman's period, never for a full day or full night. An important key is frequent change.

In addition to the reproductive organs in a woman, there are certain parts of the female body that have a special response to sexual stimulation. These are called secondary sex organs. Together with the primary reproductive organs mentioned above, they make up what is called the "erogenous" areas, or zones. The principal secondary sex organs in a woman are the breasts, which, in addition to responding to the hormones of pregnancy to produce milk for a newborn child, also respond to sexual stimulation and create great desire and sexual excitement when fondled or caressed during love-making. A woman's mouth, neck, ears, and thighs are also sexually responsive to stimulation.

It is not hard to see that if you are a young woman, what happens in your body as you grow to adult maturity can be puzzling and maybe even frightening from time to time. The challenge is not in what you are experiencing within yourself physically, mentally, emotionally, and psychologically, it is in how you respond to these experiences.

---

1. Describe puberty and the physical changes that occur with it. What are two important points to remember about puberty mentioned in the book?
2. Describe the menstrual cycle. When, specifically, does ovulation ordinarily occur within the menstrual cycle? What is it called when menstruation begins? When it ends?
3. Name three factors that can influence when ovulation occurs.
4. What causes toxic shock syndrome? What are its symptoms? How can it be prevented?

How a Man's Reproductive System Functions

Adolescent boys' interests and concerns about sex and their own sexual feelings are also the result of what is happening in their bodies as they grow to sexual maturity and of the cultural atmosphere in which they grow.

A young man's growth through puberty lasts from four to seven years. Progress to and through puberty varies considerably from man to man. A change or lowering of the voice; the appearance of body hair in the pubic region and under the arms and eventually on the face and chest; spontaneous penile erections from various sources of stimulation, not all necessarily sexual; and the ability to ejaculate sperm are all signs that a young man is well on his way to physical adulthood.

Like that of the female, the male reproductive system is composed of intricate, delicately balanced, and demanding structures. These structures include the penis, scrotum, testicles (or testes), and the ducts which lead to the penis.

The principal exterior sexual organ of the male is the penis, located at the base of the trunk of the body. It is made up of three columns of spongy tissue which accept and retain blood during sexual excitement and cause the penis to become erect and hard. It also has a urethra, or tube leading from the bladder, and the glans, or head of the penis.

The penis allows for the elimination of waste water from the body and serves as the means to inject sperm into the vagina of a female. When a grown man's penis is limp (or flaccid), it is about the length of a finger but somewhat thicker; when erect, it is usually about six inches in length. With the exception of rare or obvious abnormalities, penises of any size work perfectly well in performing their reproductive function.

Scrotum: The sac or pouch suspended from the groin of a male that contains the testicles and their accessory organs.

Testicle (testes): The male sex gland which produces spermatozoa (sperm).

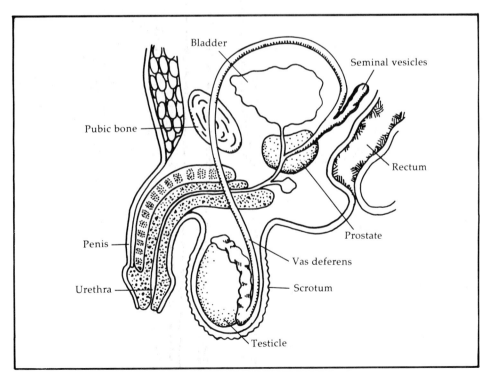

169

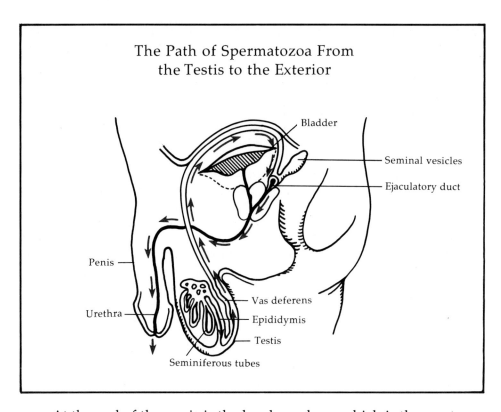

The Path of Spermatozoa From the Testis to the Exterior

Bladder

Seminal vesicles

Ejaculatory duct

Penis

Vas deferens

Urethra

Epididymis

Testis

Seminiferous tubes

Glans: The head of the penis, exposed either when the foreskin is pushed back or permanently after circumcision.

Circumcision: Surgical removal of the foreskin, or prepuce, of the penis. Originally, a Jewish rite performed as a sign of reception into their faith; now generally performed for purposes of cleanliness. No longer automatically recommended by doctors.

At the end of the penis is the head, or glans, which is the most sensitive area because it is supplied with many nerves. At birth, the glans is covered by a loose sheath of skin called the foreskin. In the United States, many male infants have this foreskin removed in the hospital or in a religious ceremony in a process known as circumcision. If a male has a foreskin, it can be pushed back from the glans, making it possible to clean underneath it. Whether you have been circumcised or not, there is no evidence that circumcised males are any more or less responsive sexually than uncircumcised ones, or that circumcision affects reproduction.

A second exterior sexual organ of the male is the scrotum, a fleshy pouch containing a double sac that hangs below the base of the penis. Each sac contains a testicle in which sperm cells (male reproductive seeds called spermatozoa) are produced. Each testicle is about the size and shape of a female ovary—about one inch wide and two inches long—and each produces millions of sperm from the time a male enters puberty until advanced age.

The sperm are shaped like tadpoles with a tail that enable them to swim. They are also invisible to the naked eye. When the sperm leave the testicles, they move through an eighteen inch tube called the vas deferens and move into the pelvic area to a kind of reservoir or storage area, called the ampulla, and the seminal vesicles. The secretion of the seminal vesicle contains a variety of nutrients which are thought to provide sperm cells with energy and motility. At the time of ejaculation, the contents of the seminal vesicles are emptied into the ejaculatory ducts, greatly increasing the volume of the fluid that is discharged from the vas deferens. The fluid, which contains sperm cells and the secretion of the seminal vesicle, is called *seminal fluid or semen.*

Between two hundred and four hundred million sperm are ejaculated with each ejaculation unless sexual release occurs very frequently. (It takes the testicles five to seven days to return to their normal count.

Intercourse more often than twice a week lowers the sperm count proportionately.) The muscular contractions that force the semen past the prostate gland located between the bladder and the base of the penis, and the resulting ejaculation, are known as an orgasm. An orgasm in a woman is also the felt reaction of muscular contractions in her pelvis, vagina and uterus in response to direct or indirect stimulation of the clitoris. In both men and women, an orgasm is the climax of sexual activity and the moment of most intense pleasure and excitement. It is a total bodily response to the most intense and intimate activity of human beings.

The prostate gland contains nerve centers which regulate the flow of blood to the penis in an erection. Recent research demonstrates the complicated relationship that exists among these nerves, the spinal cord, and the brain. All must work in harmony so that the sexual organs of a male can function properly in sexual activity. It is a well-known fact that the mind—the mental state—of a male has a very great influence on his sexual performance.

Like the female, a man's secondary sex organs—his breasts, lips, neck, ears, and thighs—are responsive to sexual stimuli. Erotic touching of these areas will trigger a response in the primary sex organs and stimulate the processes which set the male sexual response into high gear.

What happens sexually to young men as they grow to maturity is that their bodies are preparing them for their adult sexual life. It is important that they remember that their adult sexual life is their total life

Semen: The fluid made up of sperm, secretions from the seminal vesicles, prostate, and Cowper's gland and the epididymis. Ejaculated through the penis when the male reaches orgasm.

Prostate gland: Male gland which surrounds the urethra and neck of the bladder and secretes part of the seminal fluid.

as a sexual person, not simply their sexual activity. Part of that adult sexual life will be their response to sexual stimulation. When they are sexually aroused, whether it be by sight, touch, or thought, their bodies react sexually. But when they are young and unable to handle the responsibilities that follow from consummated sexual relations, they need to be cautious and careful. Their bodies will almost always respond automatically to sexual stimulation. Their self-worth and their personal moral values will determine their personal response to this stimulation.

1. Describe some of the physical changes of puberty that a young man will experience.
2. What are sperm? Where are they produced? Through what process do they leave the body?
3. What will determine a person's response to sexual stimulation?

Summary

- We need to understand our sexual nature if we are to integrate sex into our total life experience and not treat it as a separate phenomenon.
- We need to know that the physical changes that occur with the onset of puberty and throughout adolescence are the result of chemicals called hormones and that our individual progress as men and women may vary considerably.
- Most important of all, we need to know that the challenge is not in what we are experiencing within us physically, mentally, emotionally, and psychologically, but in how we respond to the challenges we face with our sexual feelings.

Review, Discussion, Research, and Reflection

1. In an open forum discuss how the media (and in particular, the movies and television) depict individuals expressing their sexual drives. Is there a consistent message being given? If so, what is it?
2. How knowledgeable are young adults today about their body's sexual functions? Where do they get most of their information on this subject? How accurate do you think this information is?
3. Ask your parents where they learned all about their bodies and their sexual functions. Do they feel their source of information was accurate? Do they wish they had had more information available to them? If so, where would they have found it?
4. Surveys today show that most young adults have very little information about their body's sexual functions. Do you agree or disagree? Support your opinion.
5. The variations in growth patterns for males and females throughout adolescent are considerable. Do you believe these variations have any effect on an individual's self-concept? On how others see him or her? Should they? Explain.

Projects

1. If you needed information on your reproductive system and your body's sexual functions, where would you go in your community? List the various resources that are available: give the name of the organization, the address, telephone number, and charge (if any). If there is a hot line in your community, list that number, also. Why are some groups, such as, Planned Parenthood opposed by the Catholic Church and other Church groups?
2. Consult your local health department on the number of cases of toxic shock syndrome that have been reported in your community during the past year. Try to determine what preventative measures are being taken to alert women to this problem. What recommendations do you have?

Words You Should Know

Be sure that you can define the following words and can use them in meaningful sentences:

pituitary gland
hormones
nocturnal emission
erection
ejaculation
penis
urethra
menstruation
vulva
clitoris
vagina
cervix
hymen
ovaries
fallopian tube
ovulation
endometrium
menarche
menopause
menstrual cycle
mittelschmerz
toxic shock syndrome
glans
circumcision
scrotum
testicle
sperm (spermatozoa)
vas deferens
seminal vesicles
semen
prostate gland

CHRISTIAN MARRIAGE

Chapter 9 Review

Chapter **10**

CHRISTIAN MARRIAGE

Understanding Your Sexual Feelings

WHEN I WAS A KID—I USED TO IMAGINE THE KIND OF MAN I'D MARRY.

I'D IMAGINE HIS FACE, HIS EYES, HIS VOICE, HIS HAIR—EVEN MINUTE DETAILS ABOUT HIS PERSONALITY!

DID YOU DO THAT TOO, JOHN? SURE. DID YOUR IMAGINARY GIRL LOOK ANYTHING LIKE ME?

I DON'T KNOW.... I NEVER GOT ABOVE THE NECK.

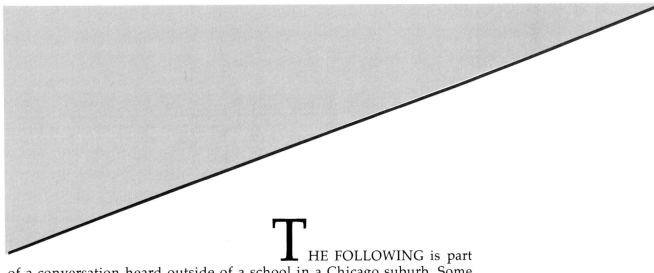

THE FOLLOWING is part of a conversation heard outside of a school in a Chicago suburb. Some students from a Life Planning Course were waiting for the school bus to take them home.

Maria: Of course I know what's going on in my body and I know why, chemically. What bothers me is why it happens. Why is it necessary and why does it happen with one particular person more than another?

Lisa: Don't you like it, Maria?

Maria: Of course. But sometimes it interferes with my life. I mean, it happens and I get all goosey, but I have other things I'd like to concentrate on. I mean, if I weren't so distracted in that class I'd learn more. Sometimes I wish it wouldn't happen at a particular time. Later, yes, now, no.

Katie: Don't you like boys, Maria?

Maria: Are you kidding? I love 'em! That's the trouble. When Jesse goes by, things happen, but I wish I weren't so involved. I've got plans—things to do, and places to see, and college, and all that. I hate being pulled in two directions. Don't you ever feel like that? Don't you wish you didn't have those feelings sometimes? Don't you wish you could go on living without sex and love, for now, anyway?

In an open forum, discuss the following:

1. What do you think Maria is really trying to say?
2. What reasons does she give for her feelings?
3. Do you think many teenagers think the way Maria does? If so, why do you believe they think that way? If not, why do you think they do not?
4. Do you think it would be better if sexual awareness were in some sense delayed, say, until after high school? If so, how do you think it can be accomplished?

Sexual Feelings Are Natural

All human beings are born with the capacity to experience sexual pleasure and to be responsive to certain sexual stimuli. A major reason for this is to insure procreation and the continuation of the human race.

Although these two systems, the sexual response system and the reproductive system, are closely related to each other, they are not the same.

Your reproductive system, which enables you to become a father or a mother, usually does not begin to function until your early teens. Your sexual response system, on the other hand, has been active to some degree since you were conceived. Since before birth, your body has been preparing you for the biological urges you may now be experiencing as a young adult.

As you become physically mature, your body reacts to sexual stimuli in a more pronounced fashion than it did before. You may find your natural biological drive moving you more and more intensely toward fulfillment of your sexual urges. It is natural for you to be interested in and curious about whatever is happening to your whole being, including your sexual being.

Not everyone, of course, has an intense interest in sex and sexual matters—or even a great interest—at the beginning of physical maturity. Some may only be mildly interested, and some may not be interested at all.

The fact that some individuals do not feel these strong sexual impulses does not mean that they are sexually retarded. Sexual drives are like all other human instincts. In some people, they are stronger than in others. In some, they manifest themselves later than they do in others.

Cultural, environmental, and social influences can also contribute either to early or late blossoming of sexual drives and opportunities. For some individuals, health factors, family conventions, moral attitudes, and religious convictions influence early or late development of sexual interests. In all, biological differences, inherited tendencies, bodily time clocks, and varying external factors create a wide variety of sexual interest, sexual development, and sexual fulfillment.

The only certain thing is that all healthy human beings are biologically impelled to sexual activity to some degree. That is all part of God's plan.

The Reality of Sexual Feelings

Every individual is born with the capacity to be sexually responsive and to experience sexual pleasure. Although people experience their sexual drives more intensely following the onset of puberty, the same individual's sex drives vary at different times and sexual drives vary from person to person. Physical well-being, psychological circumstances, and age are among the influences that affect sexual drives, sexual desires, and sexual expressions.

The sex drive in young adult males is usually greater than it is in young adult females. In many women, sex drives and sex needs tend to be periodic and vary according to their particular moods and situations. In addition, for women, there appears to be far more individual variation, not only in their sexual awakening, but in the intensity of their sexual drives as well. Whereas a man's sexual drive is more likely to peak in his late teens or early twenties, for women this is more likely to occur in her late thirties or early forties.

It is important to be aware that there can be shifts in sexual drives and patterns in both men and women as they grow older. Whereas a young male in his teens may experience a strong sex drive and be capable of experiencing four to eight orgasms a day, whether or not there is any emotional attachment, by the time he reaches the age of fifty he may be satisfied with two orgasms a week, and the focus of his sexual pleasure will normally have shifted from purely physical pleasure to a more emotional involvement.

This does not mean that men do not experience strong sexual urges after late adolescence, or that women do not experience strong sexual hungers in their adolescence. It simply says that sexual drives begin to manifest themselves early in life and continue throughout life, but also that they differ from person to person and at different times of one's life. They are part of what it means to be human.

Sexual Drives Vs. Sexual Feelings

Sexual drives are one thing; sexual feelings are another. Sexual drives are those natural forces impelling a person to sexual activity. These basic biological inclinations toward sexual responsiveness are refined through personal experimentation and experience.

Sexual feelings, on the other hand, are the emotional and bodily sensations associated with sexual activity. They are not confined to physical pleasure and physical relief. Tenderness, concern, sensitivity, restraint, and respect are just a few examples of other sexual feelings.

Sexual feelings: The emotional and bodily sensations associated with sexual activity.

When expressing sexual feelings, it is important for an individual to differentiate between a sexual expression that grows out of love based upon mutual trust, and a sexual expression that grows out of lust. In addition, one needs to learn to recognize sex pressures, not only from within oneself but from others.

What Was He Saying?

About two thousand years ago, in response to an inquiry about sexual intercourse with another person's wife, Jesus said: "You have heard the commandment, 'You shall not commit adultery.' What I say to you is: anyone who looks lustfully at a woman has already committed adultery with her in his thoughts." (*Matthew* 5:27–28)

What was Jesus saying? Was he condemning sexual feelings, sexual desires? Was he excoriating sexual fantasies, or sexual gratification—in anticipation or in actuality—with a marriage partner? Not at all. What Jesus was condemning was lust—the strong desire to have sexual intercourse with a person we do not truly love.

Jesus knew of and experienced the beauty and attraction of women. He knew of and understood the nature of human sexual love. He also knew of and witnessed the devastation of adulterous actions. He saw the effect of uncontrolled sexual desires in men who made chattels of women, who used them for personal, selfish pleasure, casting them aside when their desires were fulfilled.

What Jesus was saying was that men and women were created for a purpose. He was reminding his listeners that men and women were part of God's design for creating and developing the world. He was putting women back into their rightful position in the scheme of things, and reaffirming the sacredness of sexual intercourse.

To Jesus, lust was only one of the uncontrolled drives that people experience, and he spoke out against them all. He spoke out against anything that degraded people or made them less than they were created to be. He saw lust as dehumanizing.

Jesus knew that the true love of a man for a woman and a woman for a man was the most beautiful expression of God's love, and he reminded his listeners that whatever interfered with or destroyed that love was wrong. He knew that lust attacked the very structure of society, destroyed the trust that married men and women must have for a successful relationship, broke up families, and made it virtually impossible for children to grow up in the atmosphere of love they so desperately need.

What Jesus was saying is that lust begins in the mind. Anyone who knows and understands human nature, knows and understands the difference between love and lust, and why one is to be sought and the other avoided. Jesus certainly did, and he made no excuses for what he had to say.

As young adults begin to experience these sexual feelings, they need to be aware of the fact that physical acts of sex, whatever they are, can never be separated from their human dimensions. If it is true that every human act carries some meaning (a word of thanks, for example, or an insult), it is especially true of the actions of sex. Their very nature makes them such that they carry a message above and beyond the actions themselves.

Because this is so, to be really satisfying, sex acts must always be associated with what they mean—not simply to an individual engaged in a particular sexual activity, but also and more so to what it means to the sexual partner. If, for example, a person discovers that he or she was used for sexual exploitation, emotional responses such as dislike, hate, mistrust, and bitterness can develop and be counterproductive to the relationship.

If, on the other hand, sexual activity evolves from the mutual love and commitment that is meant to be part of marriage and a concern for one's partner's feelings, it can produce happiness and a sense of well-being. Concern for "the other" should also be a part of the early stages of learning to love and should be the first step in growing into mature sexual love.

Mature sexual love is a love that has grown and developed through the curiosity and experimental stages, and through the early feelings of tenderness and care into an unselfish commitment to another person's total welfare. It is a sexual love that has moved through the stages of maturation to a level of security; calmness; acceptance; oneness; and union of body, mind, heart, spirit, and will. It is, as St. Paul said, "patient."

Sexual exploitation: Use of another person solely for one's own sexual satisfaction.

Mature sexual love: A love that has grown and developed through the curiosity and experimental stages, and through the early feelings of tenderness and care into an unselfish commitment to another person's total welfare.

---

1. How do your reproductive system and your sexual response system differ?
2. What things affect a person's sexual responses?
3. How do sexual drives and sexual feelings differ?
4. What seem to be the differences between male and female responses to sexual drives and sexual feelings? Do you think it is important for people involved in a relationship to be aware of these differences? If so, why? If not, why not?

Looking Ahead: Exploring Your Sexual Feelings

While you are in the process of growing into mature sexual love, it might be wise to explore your feelings to discover the kind of person you would like to commit yourself to *for the rest of your life.* Have you ever considered what love means to you? Is there a difference for you between "romantic" love, in which the couple lives "happily ever after," and "unconditional" love, with no conditions, no strings attached? Do you use love as a basis for involvement? What does motivate you into a relationship? To successfully achieve mature, sexual love, it is important to answer some of these questions and look deeply within yourself to determine your level of commitment to another.

Sexual drives move people toward sexual union. Sexual feelings move them toward mature, sexual love.

Remember, however, that nobody is perfect, and if you spend your time putting everyone through a microscopic examination, you may miss the forest because of the trees. That, you may find, could be worse than finding someone who is less than the ideal. As Tennyson put it: "It is better to have loved and lost than never to have loved at all!"

On the other hand, do not just settle for *anything*—giving yourself to whoever satisfies your present physical needs. Save yourself for the one you can live with *as a person* and for a lifetime. After all, it is extremely rare that a man and a woman are not *physically* compatible (though they may become so for other reasons). But it is not at all rare for two persons, nice enough perhaps in their own right, to clash as persons. In the daily give-and-take of a total life together, personality differences may well assume a magnitude all out of proportion to the nature of the incident which started the clash. The result? They grow further and further apart until they can hardly stand each other. What started out as love, or at least had the appearance of love, changes to indifference, perhaps contempt, hurtful language, even hatred. And this is the opposite of what every person is looking for: total acceptance.

As obvious as all this seems in the dispassionate atmosphere of reading or discussion, you may find it an entirely different matter under the pressure of sexual emotions. When the sex drive takes over in a relationship, reason (conscience, if you will) retreats. It does not stand a chance! That is why it is so important to understand the difference between sexual drives and sexual nature.

Remember, your sexual drive is nonexclusive. It can be satisfied by release with any sexual partner—or none. It can be satisfied for a time, until your bodily mechanisms build up the tensions which again seek release. But your sexual nature demands total acceptance—a feeling of belonging—all the time. So even though your physical sexual appetite, because it is felt in the body, *seems* most urgent, your person requires satisfaction in a much deeper, broader way. To experience the fullness of your human person, you need to experience the satisfaction of your sexual nature in ways that are compatible with your needs as an individual human person.

For most individuals, fulfilling their sexual needs as persons is accomplished by an intimate relationship with someone of the other sex. For some, fulfilling sexual needs is seemingly accomplished through an intimate relationship with persons of their own sex. For still others, it is found in the single or celibate life. Because, however, the general thrust of human nature is toward an intimate sexual relationship with a person of the other sex, that kind of relationship is the concern of most people.

There are many options in today's society. That is why it is so important to explore your own feelings regarding the type of relationship you want to establish with another person and the kind of commitment you are willing to make in that relationship. Do not be surprised, however, if you find that what you think you value most in a relationship today changes as the years go by. For some young people, the good looks and popularity of their partner top their list of what they value most in a relationship. Then they find, as they experience life more, that good communication, honesty, trust, and other deeper values become significantly more important.

Sex Is More than Physical Pleasure

Perhaps the word "sex" is such a highly charged word for most people in our culture because it is basic to human life. Each person is a sexual being—a male or a female—and sex on the one hand and sexuality on the other get to the very heart of our existence as human beings.

Perhaps it is because sex and sexuality are so mysterious, so exciting, so secret, so personal, and so sacred to each of us that they occupy a primal place in the expression of who we are.

Perhaps it is because sex and sexuality, touching as they do the very fiber of our being, arouse the most basic instinct of what it means to be human and touch the creative instinct that lodges at the very center of our being.

Perhaps it is because God created human beings as sexual beings and established sexual drives as the means by which all living things can participate in His creative process.

Whatever the reason, or combination of reasons, there is little doubt that sex (or at least an awareness of the importance of sex in one's own life) is a major concern of almost every human being.

Concern for sex, of course, ebbs and flows. At times, sex is a force that almost overwhelms; at other times, it fades from our consciousness. When the impulse is strong, it demands that a response be considered.

"If all I wanted was sex," says a prominent bachelor, "I could have any one of a hundred girls for a wife. But I want more than that. I want someone who's fun to be with. Someone I can share my life with, not simply my bed."

When more powerful forces make it recede, it lies quietly, to be awakened when a stimulus or our own intention once again stirs us to action.

It is during the moments of physical awakening to a sexual stimulus that the challenge of personal response is tested to the greatest extent. How we react and what we do in response to sexual stimuli are among the most important decisions we are called on to make in our daily contact with other people. How we react and what we do in response to *strong* sexual stimuli demonstrates the value system we have integrated into our persons, the depth of our understanding of the nature and purpose of our sexual drives, and the concern we have for other people.

We can react in either of two ways. First, we can respond sexually to our physical urges because we feel them and act without regard to the consequences. We can ignore the responsibility we have to ourselves, to another person, to a possible pregnancy, to society, and to a whole host of things that can result from irresponsible sex.

Second, we can choose to respond to awakened sexual drives in keeping with what our human understanding of the meaning of sex in our lives is. That is to say, we can act with intelligence, responding with our human ability to think, weigh, consider, and judge what sex really is, what it is for us in our lives, and what it is for us at the moment. And we can respond in keeping with the religious values that have been part of our upbringing.

For persons who respond to their whole *human* nature, sex is more than a pleasurable physical activity. It is creative. It brings new life to those who respond to it in a truly human way, and it makes new human life possible. For them, sex is not an end in itself, a bodily activity that is somehow unrelated to who they are as human beings. It is an expression of love. It is an expression of who they are. For them, sex has deep, personal meaning.

It is during the moments of physical awakening to a sexual stimulus that the challenge of personal response is tested to the greatest extent.

God created human beings as sexual beings and established sexual drives as the means by which all living things can participate in His creative process.

---

1. What does your book mean when it says: "Your sex drive is nonexclusive, but your sexual nature demands total acceptance"?
2. What factors influence how individuals react and what they do in response to strong sexual stimuli?
3. Describe two ways individuals can respond to sexual stimuli.
4. Your book says, "As obvious as all of this seems in the dispassionate atmosphere of reading or discussion, you may find it an entirely different matter under the pressure of sexual emotions." What does this mean to you? Do you think it is true? If so, why? If not, why not?

Sexual Intimacy in Perspective

When most young men and young women are experiencing the force of their sexual appetites, they are impelled to sexual union. Outside forces, too, such as peer-group pressure, curiosity, the media, conversations, stories heard, and the urge to "see what it feels like" encourage young men and young women to "try it."

Under such forces, most young people do not really care about the philosophical aspects of sexual love, or the warnings, strictures, or advice of society. They just want to experience the tenderness, warmth, and acceptance of someone else's love, and to feel the specialness of someone else's body. This is the almost universal feeling of young persons—and of older persons, too, who are experiencing a new love.

What to do about it is the problem. One way to handle it is to put sexual intimacy into perspective.

As you go through life, you will experience many reasons for having sexual intercourse. Once a person has matured to understand and experience sexual intercourse as the ultimate physical expression of permanent love, it is unrealistic to think that he or she will not be curious, feel drawn to satisfy a physical urge, or wish to express affection for someone else. Physical sexual urges are blind. If the right stimulus is present and all systems are go, the physical response will take place.

The important personal and moral question is: How will we use our sexual abilities? If they are used in the right place, at the right time, for the right ends, they promote good. If they are used in the wrong way, they can be a source of evil. They become immoral, unethical, or sinful actions to the degree that they deviate from the love-giving and life-giving expression of human sexuality in a loving, committed marriage.

If your values are based on Christ's view of life, and if you believe that Jesus is the Son of God, your expression of who you are and your integration of sex in your life will be in tune with Jesus' view of sex and sexuality. For him, men and women were God's beloved creation worthy of the utmost respect and love. For him, sex was sacred, love-giving, and life-giving. For the Church, trying always to reflect the mind of Christ, your sexuality means your humanity raised to a God-impregnated level by baptism. You are a sacred person, "a temple of the Holy Spirit," as St. Paul said. For the Church, your sex life is a sacred life—responsibility which requires commitment, love, and procreation. The Church urges you to care for your sex life and the sex life of your sexual partner as Christ did, honoring the dignity, integrity, purity, and humanity of yourself and others.

You must remember that you are at the beginning of your sexual experiences. You are, as it were, a babe in the woods. Even teens who have had some physical sexual experience, are not experienced—that is, mature—in sexual expression, simply because they are not old enough or capable of properly interpreting their experience. You have passed through the first stage of sexual growth (you know the theory, you are familiar with both the scientific and street terms for parts of the body and actions associated with physical sex), but you are just at the very beginning of the second, or selective state.

For the next several years, if everything goes right, your sexual attitudes, interpretations, and expressions will mature. Hopefully your sexuality will become more meaningful so that it will be part of the cause for personal growth and satisfaction. It will take on this meaning if it expresses, for you, the totality of your human nature—the nature that is moving you to express true love, exclusive love, committed to a particular person.

That is why the question of how you will use your sexual capabilities is so important. Your capacity for expressing yourself in sexual intercourse must be put into the perspective of your entire life. You need to determine what *you* want from life and what sexual intercourse (or any other form of sexual intimacy) means for you as part of your total life and the expression of your personal values.

> The absence of spiritual values is a contributing factor in deteriorating male/female relationships. People without spiritual values cannot transcend the physical limitations of any sexual relationship.
>
> —*Viktor Frankl*

Beyond Sexual Intimacy

When you are in the curiosity or the physical-urge phase of your growth to sexual maturity, the desire to satisfy your curiosity and/or to relieve your physical tensions may be uppermost in your mind. The physical aspects of another person's body or the experience of sexual intercourse may be the goal or end toward which you are moving. To the uninitiated or inexperienced, these seem to be the zenith or highpoint of interpersonal relationships. This phase of sexual growth usually lasts three or four years and is the cause for many teen marriages. When this phase is over, most young adults move into a plateau phase where they are much calmer about things, and seek fulfillment in other ways. They become more selective about who would make a good marriage partner and are willing to wait, and set other priorities before making a total commitment.

As you become more mature, you will learn that sexual intercourse, as highly charged as it is, is not the goal of interpersonal relationships. It is only one of the many expressions of such relationships. Of far more importance, you will learn, is your total attitude toward another person—the way you treat him or her, and the kind of loving person you are. If sexual intercourse were the secret to total happiness and security and the only end to which interpersonal relationships were directed, there would be no unhappy married people, no prostitutes, no gigolos, and no cohabiting singles!

As your curiosity and the physical phase of your growth to sexual maturity becomes less urgent (though you will, if you truly love someone, continue to be curious and experience strong physical feelings), you will

As you become more mature, you will realize that sexual intercourse is not the goal of interpersonal relationships.

184

move into the friendship stage of interpersonal relationships. Sexual curiosity and physical drives alone can last only so long. If they are the only basis for your relationship with another person, the relationship will fade when the curiosity or satisfaction is alleviated. Indeed, romantic love can not only fade but disappear if it is not complemented by friendship and moving toward unconditional love and acceptance of the other person. What really counts in developing a sexual relationship is your ability to be friends with the person toward whom you are moving selectively.

What makes a person human is not his or her body, but the expression of the person through the body. It is the personality, or spirit, or soul of the person that is attractive and desirable. So to have a truly meaningful sexual relationship (that is, past a simple act of copulation), it is necessary to like the person—to be friends with him or her because of the kind of person he or she is. There must be common interests, common concerns, a consistent philosophy of living, compatibility of life-style, feelings of admiration, and a desire to be with that person beyond the physical attraction he or she may have for us.

To put sexual intercourse into its proper perspective as you begin to move into the more serious aspects of selectivity, you must see the person beyond his or her physical magnetism or desirability as much as you possibly can. For this reason, among others, it is not wise to become physically involved with a person of the other sex too soon. Physical intimacy puts you on a different level of relationship and signals too exclusive a claim from which it is much more difficult to withdraw. It says more to each party than either may wish to say. Of course, a "one-night stand" affair is an entirely different story. This poses a whole other set of personal, psychological, and moral questions which are not the subject under discussion at the moment.

You must judge your attraction for a person in much the same way you judge any other person: by his or her qualities as a person. You must determine why you want to be with that person—whether it is because you genuinely like the person, or whether it is because you can get from him or her what you want. In the one case, it is friendship. In the other, it is exploitation, whether the motive be sex, money, position, prestige, security, or pleasure. The second set of motives is immoral, no matter what rationalization takes place.

At the same time, you must be friendly yourself, developing those human qualities that you expect in your friends. If you expect others to be honest, sincere, trustworthy, capable, secure, and accepting, you must be so yourself. If you want others to be courteous, polite, thoughtful, forebearing, controlled, understanding, generous, and caring, you must be also.

To keep sexual intercourse in its proper perspective, you need to remember that sexual intercourse is momentary and fleeting; friendship is lasting and solid. Philia is more complete than eros. Agape, or unconditional love, goes beyond both. Friendship is what you have with a person; sexual intercourse is what you do with a person. Friendship encompasses the totality of your relationship; sexual intercourse is only one expression of a relationship.

Sexual intercourse can be personal or impersonal, generous or selfish. It can be an expression of love or an empty imitation of one of love's most profound acts. At its best, sexual intercourse is a special message for a uniquely important person in our life. At its worst, it is an act of violence, attacking the very dignity and worth of another person.

What makes a person human is not his or her body, but the expression of the person through the body.

Catholics mean by the word "sin," an action that is a freely chosen attack on or a violation of another person's human rights.

Sexual intercourse is not the whole of a person's sexual life or sexual relationship with another person. It is a singular, unique, sacred, and special expression of a particular love for a particular person. If it has these qualities sexual intercourse says it all; if it does not, sexual intercourse is less than it should be, can be, and is for those who truly love one another.

Sexual Intimacy for Catholics

Catholics believe that sexual intercourse is a holy, grace-bestowing act when it takes place in marriage. They believe this because they believe that marriage is the God-ordained mode of existence best suited for a man and a woman to experience the totality of their commitment and to raise whatever children may result from their mutual love. In marriage, Catholics believe, God operates most freely to bring a man and a woman in love to their mutually creative potential. They can not only bring a child into existence, they can raise it to its greatest potential as a human being in the context of a stable family relationship.

For this reason, Catholics (and most other people) consider sexual intimacy sinful outside of the bond of love called marriage. Sexual intimacy outside of marriage not only lacks the fullness of the human dimension of sexual intimacy, and as regards the formal sacramental nature of Catholic marriage, it also lacks and goes against the divine dimension inherent in such sacramental marriage. Catholics believe sexual intimacy outside of marriage is a desecration of a holy action. As in all matters of evil, the degree of moral responsibility in a particular situation depends on the degree of knowledge, free will, and commitment to the evil involved, the distance one has strayed from the ideal and norm, and the amount of harm done to the individuals and society involved or affected.

---

1. Name some forces that are encouraging young adults to be sexually active today. Do these forces put sexual intimacy in proper perspective? Why? Why not?
2. Why is it important to put sexual intimacy into perspective?
3. Why is it unwise to become physically involved with a person of the other sex too soon?
4. Take some time to discuss with your parent(s) and/or some adult you have confidence in the place sexual intimacy has in a relationship.

Summary

- Every human being is born with the capacity to be sexually responsive and to experience sexual pleasure.
- Sexual drives begin to manifest themselves early in life and continue throughout life. They are a part of what it means to be human. For persons who respond holistically to their human nature, sex is more than a pleasurable, physical activity. It is creative and an expression of love.
- For Catholics, sexual intercourse is a holy, grace-bestowing act when it takes place in a loving, committed marriage.

Catholics believe marriage is a sacrament. That is, it is a sign and realization of the reality of God's saving acts in the life of the husband and the wife. That is why sexual intercourse is called "grace-bestowing." Catholics believe grace is the action of God in the life of an individual. Therefore, in a sacramental marriage, all the good acts of a loving husband and wife are grace-bestowing: God is bringing the married couple to their creative fulfillment through their marriage.

Grace: The action of God in the life of an individual.

186

Review, Discussion, Research, and Reflection

1. Name several influences that contribute to early or late development of sexual interests for individuals.
2. What is the difference between "romantic" love and "unconditional" love? Which is most important for a couple contemplating marriage?
3. Your book stresses that sexual intercourse should be put into its proper perspective in any male/female relationship. Explain what is meant by that.
4. What makes a person human according to your book? Do you agree or disagree? Explain your answer.
5. How does your book describe sexual intercourse? How does it differentiate between sexual intercourse and friendship? Do you agree or disagree? Explain.
6. How do Catholics view sexual intercourse? Do individuals with different religious backgrounds view it the same way? How do some other religious groups feel about sexual intercourse outside of marriage? nonreligious groups?
7. Your book states that there is a difference between the expression of sexual feelings that grows out of love based on mutual trust and the expression of sexual feelings that grows out of one or both partner's lust. Do you agree? How are the relationships of the partners different in the two cases?

Project

Your book states that your capacity for expressing yourself in sexual intimacy must be put into the perspective of your entire life. Survey five married couples and ask them to outline what they believe to be criteria for young people to use to determine where the expression of sexual feelings fits into their life.

Words You Should Know

Be sure that you can define the following words and can use them in meaningful sentences:

sexual drives
sexual feelings
copulation
unconditional love
grace
sexual exploitation
mature sexual love

CHRISTIAN MARRIAGE

Chapter
10
Review

Growth toward Mature Sexual Love

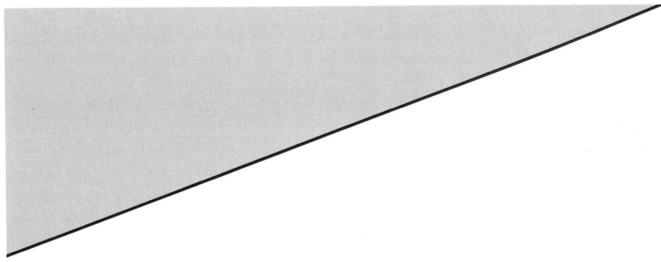

They sat with their faces turned up to the benign sun, its warmth so eagerly anticipated through the raw Vienna winter. . . . He stretched out an arm, put his hand palm up on the center of the table. She laid her hand in his, lightly. It was cool to his touch, quiet, waiting, her skin fresh and moist in his grasp. Martha looked at him closely, head on, for the first time. . . .

Eli put his head out the back door of the house and called, "The sun is setting. Time to gather ourselves together and walk to the train."

They collected their belongings. By the stoop, Martha reached up to break off a sprig of lime to take home. They were standing very close, with Martha's arms in the air. Sigmund glanced toward the door to make sure they were alone. He thought, "Now is the time. But carefully, carefully. If she is not ready, if she has not begun to love me, I may offend her."

Though only a few inches separated them, it seemed to him an interminable time before he covered the distance of all the world, of all his life. Martha had already plucked the small branch but she had not yet lowered her arms. Her eyes were still enormous from the import of what he had revealed; she was breathing deeply, her lips slightly parted. Would she welcome him? He could not be sure. But she seemed so vital, so lovely and warm and happy.

Slowly, so that he could stop at any instant without embarrassment or revelation of his intent, he put out his arms, placed them about her slender waist, drew her to him. With his lips only a breath away she lowered her arms as gently about his neck as the falling lime blossoms; and his lips met hers, alive and palpitant with the sweetness of life.[1]

One day you, in all probability, will experience the tender, sweet, tentative uncertainty, and the infinity of real love's first bloom (if you have not already experienced it). When you do, your whole life will change. You will have begun one of life's most exciting and rewarding experiences.

- *What brings people to this kind of love?*
- *How different is it from the love we have for other things?*
- *How different is it from the love we have for other people?*
- *In an open forum, discuss what is "different" about this kind of love.*

1. Excerpt from *The Passions of the Mind* by Irving Stone. Copyright © 1971 by Irving Stone. Published by Doubleday & Company, Inc.

Mature Sexual Love Is Special

Mature sexual love does not develop overnight. As in all other things, people grow into mature sexual love. It must be cultivated.

True love between a man and a woman is a beautiful thing that encompasses feelings not usually experienced in other loving relationships. Objectively speaking, true love is only one of many kinds of relationships which can exist between people. Other relationships, for example, a parent-child, sibling, close relative, or friend relationship, include certain kinds of love as do the relationships of acquaintance or camaraderie.

Humanly speaking, however, true love between a man and a woman is not simply one kind of relationship. It is special, unique, and uncommonly total. It penetrates to the very depth of being, impelling toward intimate union and lasting commitment. It convinces each person who experiences it that no one has ever felt exactly *that* way before.

The loved one in this kind of relationship becomes so special, so dear in the mind and the heart of the lover, that only poetry, it seems, describes that relationship. In this kind of relationship, the whole being—body, mind, heart, and soul—are given over to the loved one.

Maturation: The act or process of maturing; growing.

Elizabeth Barret Browning, an English poet, perhaps said it best:

The first time he kissed me, he but only kissed
The fingers of this hand wherewith I write;
And ever since it grew more clean and white,
Slow to world greetings—quick with its "Oh, list"
When the angels speak. A ring of amethyst
I could not wear here, plainer to my sight,
Than that first kiss. The second passed in height
The first, and sought my forehead, and half missed,
Half falling on the hair. O beyond meed!
That was the chrism of love, which love's own crown,
With sanctifying sweetness, did precede.
The third upon my lips was folded down
In perfect, purple state; since when, indeed,
I have been proud and said, "My love, my own."[2]

When this kind of love comes into a person's life, he or she experiences a warmth, a compelling drive, and a need to express his or her love. The entire being is flooded with joy. When this kind of love is felt, a person becomes certain that now, at last, life has begun.

> *True love between a man and a woman is a beautiful thing that encompasses feelings not usually experienced in other loving relationships.*

First Stage of Growth toward Mature Sexual Love

Growth to mature sexual love is gradual. It is prepared for from birth in the experience of love that a baby has with its mother and father. The preparation continues during childhood in the love a child experiences within the family, in the neighborhood, and among relatives and friends. The preparation peaks with the onset of puberty and the emergence of adolescence when a changed relationship with persons of the other sex emerges. This changed relationship signals the beginning of growth toward mature, sexual love.

> *Growth to mature sexual love is gradual.*

The First Stage in Males

If you are a young man, you may remember one day, sometime ago, when you "discovered" girls. Remember the day? All of a sudden those objects of at least mild disdain or loving tolerance took on a new look in your mind. You lost your consuming interest in whatever you were caught up in and became interested in girls. Not fully, not completely, of course, but definitely interested.

Once this had happened, you began the first phase of your movement toward mature sexual love. Now there was no turning back. You were beginning the process of becoming a man.

As time went on, and your personal interest in girls increased, you began to investigate this new experience, this new interest. You knew that something was happening to you, but you were not quite sure yet what it was. You made a passing remark to one or two of your friends to find out if they were interested too. It was a remark that would not get

2. Browning, Elizabeth Barrett, *Sonnets from the Portuguese* (Mount Vernon, New York: The Peter Pauper Press), sonnet 38.

191

you laughed at if they were not, yet it was a lead to find out if they were going through the same thing you were. If they were, you were off and running. You tried to analyze why girls were suddenly more interesting than they had been, and you exchanged "expert" advice with your friends. You noticed the physical makeup of girls (especially *some* girls), and you wondered.

You knew about girls' anatomy, of course, from a sex education course or a biology class you might have had. Watching television or reading magazines had made you aware of the physical differences between boys and girls. But now, because of what was happening inside you, your interest became more personal, more compelling, more physical, and more exciting.

The First Stage Develops

What had been a vague stirring of interest now became more impelling. You began to *feel* different. Your body was aroused (vaguely at first), and you felt good—giddy, perhaps, but good. You began to fantasize about girls, and imagined what they really looked like. The words you heard began to take on real meaning, and you went (perhaps secretly) to the dictionary, the encyclopedia, more advanced biology books, and, perhaps, to magazines to find out more. As your interest intensified, you talked more, sought more information, daydreamed, perhaps, and felt strong desires to know, to see, and to experience. Soon your general interest in girls began to narrow down to a few girls, then, perhaps, to one.

While all this was going on, your body, mind, and emotions were undergoing subtle changes. Your body was growing and developing and feeling the effects of the physical attraction of girls. Your mind was searching, sorting out, analyzing, probing, and questioning in a new and more certain way. And your emotions were being stirred and aroused as they had never been aroused before. You felt good, but you also felt a bit uneasy, maybe worried, unsure, uncertain of your response. You felt pulled in one direction, but fear and uncertainty held you back. Physical, intellectual, emotional, and moral tensions were, more or less, the order of the day for you as far as girls were concerned.

So, to respond to your natural drives and to resolve your tensions, you worked out a compromise you were probably not even aware of. You began to single out a particular girl, and you began your campaign to meet her (if you did not know her) and to ask her to go out with you. You rehearsed your approach, being careful, of course, to leave yourself an escape route if you were refused. If you were successful, you planned your next move. You got ready for your first encounter with a girl since you began to feel different about them. You began to date in earnest.

The End of Stage One

From then on, it became increasingly easier to be with girls. (Though adventures in dating other girls posed their own problems of acceptance or rejection, of acting, and of worrying about how you did.) Even though you were more at ease with girls, your new relationship with them did not solve the problem of your interest in them. If anything, it increased. As you grew older, your interest intensified, your bodily experience became more disturbing, and your curiosity increased. Then one day, per-

haps even as a surprise to you, you felt a particular physical stirring. You felt a reaction in your genital area. You experienced your first erection directly related to your interest in girls. It bothered you, perhaps, and surprised you. It also created new physical, intellectual, and emotional reactions. Somehow you knew that you were a man. Your childhood was definitely behind you.

You may not have been aware of each of these phases as they developed in you, but they took place. In some of you, they occurred earlier than they did in others. For some of you, each phase occurred rapidly; for others, they occurred more slowly. Circumstances of biological timing, cultural and social conditions, and mental and emotional factors all affected the development of *your* sexual growth.

Timing, after all, is not important. Being fast or slow, or early or late, in experiencing sexual development has nothing to do with your masculinity. Nor does sexual experimentation. *Masculinity is a way of existing as a human being.* Being masculine is manifested in everything you do, not simply in the way you experience your sexual drives. You are a human being who is male. You express yourself humanly, and you experience the world around you as a particular kind of human being (a male). How you express yourself as a male is the important thing.

When you experienced your first conscious erection, you completed the first stage in the development of your growth toward true sexual love. You were then ready to begin the second stage—the stage that would lead you to mature sexual love, committed love, the love we call "married" love.

> *Being masculine is manifested in everything you do, not simply in the way you experience your sexual drives.*

193

The First Stage in Females

The first stage of growth toward mature, sexual love for you as a woman began some time ago when one day, you noticed a change in your growth. Your body was beginning to become more shapely as your breasts began to change in size and sensitivity. The contour of your body gradually rounded out and your pelvic area broadened.

Other changes began to manifest themselves, and then, one day blood appeared on your underclothing. It may not have been a surprise to you since you knew it would happen sooner or later, because either your hygiene classes, your mother's advice, or your sex education classes had alerted you to the facts—but it was a surprise *when it occurred to you.*

It may have been a minor thing at first that did not occur again for some time. So you said nothing, perhaps, and treated it like an unexpected phenomenon that would go away. It also could have been that you were unprepared for the experience and frightened by the whole process or were not ready for *that* yet! On the other hand, you may have been fascinated by the process and found it an exciting experience you could finally share with your friends. Whatever your response, it did not go away; you knew that it was for real.

You became conscious of your body in a new way, for now you knew what was happening. You watched your breasts develop and bought a bra that would fit you. (Did you hope, as many girls do, that your breasts would develop more rapidly so that others, boys especially, would notice that you were no longer a little girl but a woman?)

You were not yet a woman, of course, but you knew that you were on the far side of childhood and that as day followed day, you were becoming a woman. You felt, perhaps, like Anne Frank, the young Jewish girl who went into hiding with her family during the Nazi roundup of Jewish people during the Second World War. She wrote eloquently of her experiences—her feelings about herself as she grew up under such stressful circumstances. In one part of her diary, she described her own feelings when she discovered the secret of her body which made her a woman:

Anne Frank

> *A girl in the years of puberty becomes quiet within and begins to think about wonders that are happening to her body. . . .*
>
> *I think what is happening to me is so wonderful, and not only what can be seen on my body, but all that is taking place inside. I never discuss myself or any of these things with anybody; that is why I have to talk to myself about them.*
>
> *Each time I have a period—and that has only been three times—I have the feeling that in spite of all the pain, unpleasantness, and nastiness, I have a sweet secret, and that is why, although it is nothing but a nuisance to me in a way, I always long for the time that I shall feel that secret within me again. . . .[3]*

At this point in the first stage of your physical growth toward mature sexual love, your interest in boys changed subtly from involvement *among* boys to involvement *with* boys of a new and different sort. You began to feel a desire to be with them, to watch what they did, you tried to attract their attention and to be noticed by them. As you moved slowly into the second stage of your sexual interest in boys, you became concerned about them as persons—as human beings who were exciting, fun to be with, and definitely interesting. Your vague physical and emotional reactions were triggered by boys as boys. Your interest may not have been as physical as boys' interest in girls, but you were interested in them as persons, and definitely interested in particular persons who held a charm and mystery that you wanted to explore. You knew (or hoped, at least) that they were interested in you, and you suspected what the reason was, but regardless of that, you enjoyed boys because you were a girl.

The First Stage Develops

Almost without realizing it, your interest changed from boys in general to a particular boy. You were physically excited by him (whether he showed any special interest in you or not). When you were approached by a particular boy (unless for some reason he was not your type), you became excited, worried, maybe even a bit fearful. Your heart began to pound, your knees became a bit weak, and you searched frantically for the right response, the right mood, the right actions. You wanted to impress him, to make him like you—and you worried that you might not carry it off. And you thought afterwards, of course, of all the things you might have said and done!

After your first real date with a special boy, you were ready to begin your journey toward mature sexual love.

3. Excerpt from *Anne Frank: The Diary of a Young Girl*, by Anne Frank. Copyright 1952 by Otto H. Frank. Reprinted by permission of Doubleday & Company, Inc.

Your Sexual Feelings Are Special to You

Your move from childhood to middle adolescent relationships with boys may have been slow or fast. It matters not. Speed of physical development and of relationships mean nothing in growth toward mature sexual love. Every girl develops physically, intellectually, and emotionally at different rates from every other girl.

Each woman experiences peaks and valleys of growth that may be long or short, depending on many physical, intellectual, cultural, environmental, and social factors. Whatever the rate of development or progress in your sexual growth, however different your experiences and feelings are from what you are told they are supposed to be, *they are yours!* They are normal for you. You know how you feel at a particular time. You know what your stage of development is. You should be comfortable with it, and look on yourself as a special, unique, human person who expresses what she is as a woman. *Being a woman is a way of existing as a human being.* Being the woman you are is different from being a woman the way any other girl is. You have your own special feminine way of existing. For you, it is right. Being the woman you are is not only what you are, it is who you are.

Each woman experiences peaks and valleys of growth that may be long or short, depending on many physical, intellectual, cultural, environmental, and social factors.

1. How does your book describe true love?
2. When does the first stage of mature, sexual love begin?
3. What happens to males in the first phase of their move toward mature, sexual love? to women?
4. What factors affect the development of sexual growth in males and females?

Second Stage of Growth toward Mature Sexual Love

At this time in your life, you have, in all probability, passed through the first stage of growth toward mature sexual love. As a matter of fact, you may be well on your way through the second stage. This stage is sometimes called "the selective stage," in contrast to the first, often called the general or exploratory stage.

During the first stage, you were learning how to relate to persons of the other sex in a general way. While you were experiencing the first physical, mental, emotional, and social aspects of sexual attraction, so, too, were your sexual opposites. Even though you may have become interested in one particular person as you approached the end of phase one, you were still preparing yourself for the more serious sexual encounters that were to come.

During the second, or selective, stage of growth toward mature sexual love, you will be learning how to relate to a *particular* person of the other sex. You will be learning how to handle *your* sexual feelings and drives in preparation for your more serious involvement with a particular person later in life. You will be learning how to cope with the challenges involved in living out your life in total union with another person.

The Importance of Stage Two

This selective stage is, perhaps, the most important stage in your psychosexual development. It will play a major role in how you will relate to others physically, mentally, emotionally, morally, and sexually in your life as an adult. During the first stage, you were exploring sexuality in a general way. Now you are establishing patterns of sexual behavior. During this period, some questions you need to ask yourself about sex are:

- What is sex for me?
- What is its purpose in my life?
- How will I relate to others sexually?
- What does it mean to be a man or a woman?

Your personal responses to these questions will enable you to relate to others in a mature, personally satisfying and integrated way.

As soon as you begin to relate to a person of the other sex in a particular or selective way, your relationship with that person changes. It becomes more physical, more personal, more emotional, and more spiritual. Something happens. You feel it. You sense it. Once you get beyond the physical attraction, that special relationship carries with it more meaning, more depth, and more commitment than a purely physical or exploratory relationship.

Teenage girls, even more than boys, are concerned [or obsessed] with their physical appearance and development. Long before they reach adolescence, they have come to believe that their physical attributes are their greatest assets.

Every young girl "knows" that the ideal woman is small and slender, and has a well-endowed bust. These qualities are somewhat in conflict with the equally strong desire to have long, slender legs—but ambivalence and conflict are natural at this age.

Girls concentrate their anxieties on the quest for this ideal for several reasons. One, of course, is the desire for popularity which, in turn, implies future success in finding a marriage partner. Despite women's lib, most adolescent girls still consider this to be a woman's prime goal in life. Girls also tend to equate their looks with their essential nature or personality. So when a girl says she hates everything about her looks, she is very likely saying she dislikes herself or has problems in her social adjustment. If, for example, you say to a male, "You look awful today," he is likely to assume he needs a haircut or his pants pressed; say this to a female and she's likely to interpret your remark as, "You are awful."

What's more, girls are much less realistic in their ideas of what is normal and attractive. Any deviation from the ideal is considered a disaster. They tend to think they are too fat, whether they are or not, and can become fanatic about dieting. This is a real hazard to health and should be closely watched by a concerned parent. If a child is truly obese, then she should certainly diet—but under the careful supervision of a physician.

Dieting or not, she should be helped to maintain good nutrition. In particular, adolescent girls need to watch out for their iron supplies.

What traits do the girls object to in themselves? A partial list would include large hands or feet, thick ankles, heavy thighs, breasts that are too large or too small [virtually no girl is ever satisfied on this score], extreme thinness or fatness, a heavy jaw, large mouth or nose, oily skin, braces, freckles, and the "wrong" kind of hair.

Then there's the problem of how fast a girl matures. Girls who grow up fast are even worse off than their male counterparts. They usually are two years ahead of boys in development, so the early-maturing girl is even farther ahead and, in addition, is far more grown-up than most of her friends.

There are further risks if a girl grows up fast and beautiful. She may be hurt (especially in today's sexual climate) if she discovers that older boys are only interested in her physically. She may get used to the special treatment she receives but hasn't really earned and wouldn't get it if it were not for her looks. Her parents may easily encourage her social success while neglecting to praise her other qualities.

What does this add up to for the parents of teenage girls? Even though youngsters at this stage tend to ignore direct advice, they will listen to objective information on such topics as the wide variations in normal growth. They can be encouraged to develop and appreciate nonphysical assets. Parents can give attention to and rewards for attributes such as scholarship, artistic or musical talent or contributing to community life, which, unlike physical growth, are under an individual's control. We can work to ensure that schools discuss adolescent growth patterns and the complexities of emotional growth so that maturing young people understand themselves better and can avoid needless worry and embarrassment.

—Dr. Jean Mayer

Reprinted by permission of the *Chicago Tribune*—New York News Syndicate, Inc.

A selective sexual relationship is a complex thing. It begins with attraction and acceptance. From there, it proceeds through acquaintance, mutual interest, unspoken commitment, more or less going steady, and spoken or unspoken agreements about exclusivity. If things go right, the next steps include tentative arrangements for the future, preengagement activities, real commitment, marriage plans, and finally, marriage.

Stage Two Can Be Interrupted

This does not mean that every sexual relationship will move toward that particular end. It simply means that if each phase of stage two progresses as it usually does, stage three of mature sexual relationships—marriage—will follow. During stage two, however, either party may, at any time and for any reason, delay the development, postpone it, or cut it off completely. ("Sure, I like physically attractive boys," said Theresa, a high school junior in Miami, Florida, "but if that's all he is, if he's stuck on himself, if he's trying to attract other girls while I'm with him, and if he doesn't have any other interests than himself and my body, he's had it.")

During each phase of stage two, the relationship is affected by personal experiences, cultural, environmental, and social influences, and moral and religious teachings.

No two persons experience stage two of growth toward mature sexual love in exactly the same way. Some move rapidly through one phase or another; some move slowly. Some are more emotional than others at particular times. Some experience strong physical forces, while others are less physical. Whatever the experience and however long it takes, stage two is moving inexorably toward the fulfillment of nature's design: the union of two people who love each other so much that they desire to share whatever they have and whatever they are with each other alone.

Even when persons are cohabitating or "living together" or are involved in a homosexual relationship, they go through versions of these phases in their relationship.

No two persons experience stage two of growth toward mature sexual love in exactly the same way.

Becoming Other-Centered

During the exploratory period of stage one, sexual development is *self*-centered in individuals. During stage two, people learn how to become *other*-centered. They learn how to share and give of themselves without anticipation of receiving something in return. In addition, they receive satisfaction not only in the giving but in the expressed pleasure of the receiver. They demonstrate consideration of another's feelings and show signs of appreciation. Most importantly, they learn to become trustworthy and to trust another while learning not to be jealous or possessive, not to expect perfection in their partner, or not to try to control another.

As soon as a person begins to become other-centered, meaning becomes important. At each step of the way through stage two, signals are passed back and forth which reveal a person's intent and purpose. Because of these signals and their meaning, the relationship of two people going through this stage has a profound effect on each person, and as each step moves to the next, joy becomes more intense and sorrow more heartfelt if anything happens to the relationship.

Sexual growth during phase two is like a young plant: it must be nurtured with care. It can be one of the most exhilarating periods of a person's life if it follows the steps nature has provided. It can be frustrating and terribly disappointing if it is only a game.

What you do with your life—how ultimately successful it is—will depend, in large part, on how you handle your sexual relationships. How you handle them will, to a great extent, depend on the sexual values you develop and the sexual decisions you make during stage two.

During stage two, one learns how to become other-centered.

---

1. Why is the second stage of growth toward mature, sexual love sometimes called "the selective stage"?
2. What does an individual learn during "the selective stage"? Why is it so important?
3. Why can a selective, sexual relationship be a complex thing?

The Catholic Church's Guidance toward Mature Sexual Love

The Catholic community offers its members the biblical ideal as a standard against which to measure their own growth toward mature sexual love.

But the Church realizes that the goal of mature sexual love is not achieved automatically. Human beings, after all, are, by nature, limited. They have blind, selfish tendencies and feel strong physical sexual drives. They are also exposed to many conflicting signals about sex, love, and marriage. For these reasons, the Catholic community offers its members its experience and its guidance in working toward the goal of mature sexual love.

The Catholic community offers its members its experience and its guidance in working toward the goal of mature sexual love.

The Church's Spiritual Guidance

The guidance of the Church in human sexual relationships is three-fold. It is, first, spiritual. It reminds its members that they are not simply physical bodies responding to physical drives. They are spiritual beings destined for union with God forever in the community of the faithful.

It reminds them that sexuality, sex, and marriage are parts of the totality of personhood; they cannot be separated from what it means to be human. It reminds them that their sexual drives must be directed toward the fulfillment of their spiritual as well as their physical nature. Finally, it reminds them that they are new beings in Christ. They are baptized in his name and joined with him in a special relationship to give witness to others concerning the spiritual values in sexuality, sex, and marriage.

This spiritual view of humanity has been part of the Church's tradition from the beginning. In A.D. 57, for example, St. Paul, in his letter to Christians living in Rome, wrote:

> For surely you know that when we were baptized into union with Christ Jesus, we were baptized into union with his death. By our baptism, then, we were buried with him and shared his death, in order that, just as Christ was raised from death by the glorious power of the Father, so also we might live a new life. . . .
>
> —Romans 6:3–4

A woman's body is beautiful and exciting to a normal, healthy man. A man's body is beautiful and exciting to a normal, healthy woman. God gave them this attraction for each other for a reason—to enable them to participate in His creative act, His act of love.

This is what love means: creating, giving life to another. In this are we most like God—made in His image and after His likeness—creating life through love.

All the wonder, mystery, power, and meaning of creation are wrapped up in one word: *love.*

So the Church, conscious at all times of people's spiritual nature, asks its members to live not only in response to the demands of their physical drives, but also in response to the demands of their spiritual nature as well.

The Church's Sacramental Guidance

The second area in which the Catholic Church offers its experience and guidance to its members in their sexual relationships is in its sacramental life.

In the Catholic Church, marriage is a sacrament. It is a sign of God's action in a couple's married life. It is not a sacrament in the wedding ceremony alone, however. The ceremony is only one of the signs of sacramental marriage. It is a sacrament *lived out in the loving harmony which joins persons in an intimate union we call a family.* In the eyes of the Church, sexual union in marriage is sacred and holy—it is an avenue of God's grace and a source of spiritual growth.

> *Christian married couples, then . . . must remember that their Christian vocation, which began at baptism, is further specified and reinforced by the Sacrament of Matrimony. By it husband and wife are strengthened and as it were consecrated for the faithful accomplishment of their proper duties, for the carrying out of their proper vocation even to perfection, and the Christian witness which is proper to them before the whole world.*[4]

4. Excerpted from *Humane Vitae,* Encyclical Letter of Pope Paul VI, July 25, 1968. Reprinted with permission of the United States Catholic Conference Publications Office, Washington, D.C. The document in its entirety can be purchased from the Publications Office of the USCC.

Further, the Church offers the Eucharist as spiritual food to provide the spiritual energy Catholics need in their daily lives. It offers its blessing, sympathy, and understanding in the challenge each member faces as he or she grows to the maturity a well-developed sexual nature demands. The Church offers the Sacrament of Confirmation as part of the person's movement to adult Christian responsibility. It offers the Sacrament of Reconciliation as a sign of forgiveness and reconciliation and as a means of seeking God's help to direct sexual appetites to worthy ends. Finally, the Church itself is a sacrament—a sign and a means whereby its members, in mutual effort and support, try to achieve the goal of happy sexual relationships in marriage.

Married couples must remember that their Christian vocation, which began at baptism, is further specified and reinforced by the Sacrament of Matrimony.

The Church's Moral Guidance

The third area in which the Catholic Church offers its experience and guidance to its members in sexual relationships is in its moral guidance.

Experience has taught people that there are certain things that promote good sexual relationships in marriage and some things which do not. The Catholic Church tries to reflect this experience and to interpret it in the light of the Gospels.

Take the Church's law forbidding adultery among its members. Civilizations throughout history have had laws restricting sexual relations with someone other than one's spouse. Adultery is not only an offense against the psychological and social meanings of intimate sexual union; it is also socially offensive. It can destroy a family, produce hatred, revenge, and recrimination usually leading to divorce. It tears at the trust that people put in each other.

Adultery: Sexual intercourse by a person who is legally married with someone other than one's spouse.

When the Church puts its moral weight against adultery, it is not against sex. It is against an act which signifies the rejection of the ideal and norm in human sexual relationships. For the Church, adultery is not simply a human and social offense, however. It is a sin against the divine decree which makes marriage holy and sacred: the special union created by God for the development of each sexual person and the transmission of life.

The Church is not a harsh judge or a restrictive force in sexual matters. It is a careful, concerned guide advising its members on how to achieve truly happy sexual relationships. The Church is not "against sex." It is opposed to the misuse of sex which militates against the physical, emotional, psychological, and social good of the individual and society.

1. In what ways does the Catholic Church offer its experience and guidance to its members in their sexual relationships?
2. How can adultery affect members of a family? Why does the Catholic Church view it as morally wrong? Do you agree with its viewpoint? If so, why? If not, why not?
3. Why does the Catholic Church set up norms and guidelines for sexual conduct?

Other Lifestyles

Although the customary direction of human sexual drives is toward the intimate union of a single man and a single woman in the lifestyle we call marriage, there are some who choose to adopt another lifestyle.

Among the more common living arrangements other than the nuclear family (mother, father, and children), there are at the present time more than seven million single-parent families. There are over twelve million widows and widowers, about half of whom live with relatives. There are over thirty-three million single men and women living alone who have never married (including priests and religious). There are an unknown number of people living in common-law marriages, trial marriages, and contract marriages. There are also people living in communes of adults, communes of adults with children, and single-sex communes.

A variety of sexual lifestyles have evolved as a result of these living arrangements. One of them is *celibacy*, which occurs when an individual abstains from sexual activity. People who choose celibacy do so for a variety of reasons. Priests of the Western Rite of the Catholic Church, for example, forego marriage for spiritual, cultural, and pragmatic reasons.

Certain men and women forego marriage and the sexual intimacies associated with marriage to dedicate themselves to God and to a way of life whose main orientation is to prayer and/or some special activity dictated by the needs of society. They not only forego marriage, but they also promise to devote the results of their efforts to the common needs of their community (promising poverty), and to work in the common interests of their own community's goal (promising obedience). In addition, they promise to live a community life, sharing and supporting each other in a family style.

Many persons choose to remain single and uninvolved in total sexual commitment for a shorter or longer time depending on their philosophy of life and/or the circumstances of their life. They live happy, fulfilled lives as single men or single women. They voluntarily choose not to engage in sexual intimacies for their own reasons, believing that sexual intimacies are just not for them. Or they have found no partner for marriage.

Many widows and widowers choose not to remarry and not to become intimately involved with any person of the other sex. They find their happiness and fulfillment in their personal relationships with people.

There are over thirty-three million single men and women living alone who have never married (including priests and religious).

Nuclear family: Mother, father, and children.

Celibacy: Voluntary abstention from sexual intercourse.

The Question of Homosexuality

Although the traditional sexual lifestyle of most individuals today is heterosexual, an alternative lifestyle chosen by a small percentage of men and women is that of homosexual.

Homosexuals are persons who try to fulfill their sexual drives and needs through an intimate relationship with persons of their own sex. They may be either men or women. Male homosexuals are called homosexuals; females are called lesbians. Some find their sexual needs fulfilled through promiscuous relationships, while others adopt a lifestyle that imitates, to a greater or lesser degree, the permanence and exclusiveness of marriage.

In popular language, both homosexuals and lesbians are called and refer to themselves as "gay." A person who has sexual encounters with both sexes is called "bi-sexual."

There are many misconceptions about homosexuals and homosexuality. Psychologists studying human behavior and psychiatrists counseling people with sexual concerns generally agree that there are two modes of homosexual orientation and/or behavior; an inclination that may be a temporary phase and an orientation that is permanent.

Some adolescents, when young and curious, may explore one another's bodies and sexual reactions. This does not mean they are homosexuals. It just means they are expressing their curiosity inappropriately. As they get older and learn the true meaning of that mysterious and sacred aspect of themselves which is sexuality, they lose the need for such uninformed curiosity.

During young adolescence, there is often a stage of having an emotional "crush" on someone of the same sex, such as, a friend or teacher. This is nothing more than a very close friendship with strong emotional overtones and little or no physical expression. It is not an indication that one has a permanent homosexual orientation. It is a common phase of growing up, in which one's freshly emerging sexual longing has not yet recognized itself and has not yet found its proper object in a person of the other sex.

A homosexual orientation may occur if a person does not grow out of these early phases. This can happen when an experience in a young child's relationship with a trusted adult results in a strong subconscious prejudice against the other sex. Later on in life, he or she may be able to relate to a member of the other sex normally on the surface, but there is that lurking subconscious prejudice which fears the moment of truth in real intimacy with them. A person with this conditioning then satisfies the longing for acceptance and physical intimacy with someone of the same sex—with someone with whom he or she feels "safe."

Correction of such an unconscious psychological block may or may not require extensive therapy. The key to cure is the real *desire* on the person's part to face up to the condition and take the risk of overcoming a deep-seated personality pattern. Many do not have this desire but prefer to spend their entire life in homosexual relationships.

A third form of homosexual orientation that is usually a passing or pseudo-homosexual orientation is that which arises out of a cultural or an environmental circumstance. In some societies, young persons are encouraged into homosexual relationships as part of their growing to maturity. In ancient Greek, Roman, and Egyptian societies, for example, homosexual relations were considered by many to be the true expression of human relationships—heterosexual relationships were for the purpose of producing offspring. In other situations, such as during forced confinement with persons of one's own sex, homosexual relationships are a substitute for heterosexual relationships and are used as an outlet for pent-up sexual desires.

A True Homosexual Orientation

In contrast to these forms of homosexuality, the "true" or real homosexual orientation is a person who is biologically and psychologically impelled to sexual fulfillment with a person of his or her own sex. A homosexual relationship appears to the homosexual to be as normal as a heterosexual relationship is for others. Under ordinary circumstances (that is, without unjust discrimination), the homosexual can be a rela-

Heterosexual: One who is sexually attracted to or sexually active with a person of the other sex.

Homosexual: One who is sexually attracted to or sexually active with a person of the same sex.

A subconscious prejudice against the other sex may be caused by sexual abuse during childhood.

tively happy, functioning individual, holding a good job, pursuing individual interests, and attempting to do his or her part in developing society.

To the casual observer, homosexuals are not easily identifiable because only a very small percentage of them can be identified by their outward appearance.

The primary difference between the true homosexual and the true heterosexual is in sexual orientation. The homosexual may attempt to attain a total, committed, loving relationship with a person of the same sex, including genital acts.

Traditionally, psychiatry and psychology have classified these acts and the condition itself as perversion and deviance. Lately, the question has become politicized in the social sciences so it is difficult to know what to make of their conflicting testimony, votes, and studies. But the Church and society, in general, do not consider the homosexual orientation to be psychologically, socially, or morally normal. (Thus "gay rights" is not an exact parallel with women's rights or rights for blacks and Hispanics.)

In addition, even many homosexuals who value permanence and exclusivity in their relationships criticize the high incidence of promiscuity and multiple partners among homosexuals. It is also true that some heterosexuals are promiscuous or do not achieve permanence and exclusivity. It is true that cultural and social conditions may increase its incidence among homosexuals and create other maladjustments. But the

should be one's claim to acceptance or human rights or to being loved by us all; it is the fact we are all brothers and sisters under the Fatherhood of God. Our community must explore ways to secure the legitimate rights of all our citizens, regardless of sexual orientation, while being sensitive to the understanding and hopes of all involved.

On a more personal level, we wish to express our concern and compassion for those men and women who experience pain and confusion due to a true homosexual orientation. We pray that through all the spiritual and pastoral means available they will recognize Christ's and the Church's love for them and our hope that they will come to live in His peace.

Excerpted from a pastoral letter of Bishop Francis Mugavero of Brooklyn, New York.

Whatever the cause of the homosexual orientation, both to those who share that orientation and to society in general, there are certain cautions we wish to put forward.

We urge homosexual men and women to avoid identifying their personhood with their sexual orientation. They are so much more as persons than this single aspect of their personality. That richness must not be lost.

Being subject to misunderstanding and at times unjust discrimination has resulted in an overreaction on the part of some persons at homosexual orientation. It is not homosexuality which statistics are morally instructive and important and may point to something about the homosexual relationship itself. It is not unimportant that the percentage of lifelong relationships of an exclusive nature is very small among practicing homosexuals.

It should not go unmentioned that while there are venereal diseases among heterosexuals, indeed in alarming proportions, the same is true of homosexuals. The fatal disease, AIDS, shows up particularly among homosexual men, and the danger of contamination of our blood banks is probably related to homosexual activity.

Homosexuality and the Catholic Church

Even though studies into the causes for homosexuality are continuing, and the data on the biological, emotional, psychological, and social aspects are incomplete, something must be said about the moral aspects of homosexual behavior.

Catholics believe homosexual genital acts are morally wrong not only because they deviate from the normally accepted mode of human sexual behavior, but also because they have no way of achieving the natural creative purpose of male/female sexual relationships.

Catholics believe homosexual genital acts are morally wrong not only because they deviate from the normally accepted mode of human sexual behavior, but also because they have no way of achieving the natural creative purpose of male/female sexual relationships.

The fact that the body of a male and the body of a female are complementary to one another gives heterosexual relations an insurmountable advantage in this regard. Intimate sexual acts are not *only* ways of expressing a degree of relationship, and of giving and receiving emotional, intellectual, social, and personal fulfillment. But intimate sex acts are also ways of expressing a relationship that is open to and directed toward the possibility of procreation. This is another reason for the differences in male/female reproductive systems. Any homosexual relationship excludes this procreative possibility; it is, therefore, incomplete.

Those who are homosexual due to arrested sexual development have an obligation to do something about their condition. Just as a person who is suffering from some serious medical problem has an obligation to seek medical help, so does a person who experiences some form of arrested sexual development. If the person does not, he or she is morally responsible for individual actions insofar as he or she is able to overcome the problem. The individual is morally bound to try to overcome the difficulty by seeking help and by making a personal commitment to avoid the causes of such actions. Arrested sexual development may be the cause of homosexual actions and may be the cause of occasional lapses into homosexual actions, but it is no excuse for not striving to grow into mature heterosexual relationships or, at least, away from homosexual actions.

Arrested sexual development may be the cause of occasional lapses into homosexual actions, but it is no excuse for not striving to grow into mature heterosexual relationships.

Persons who are "true" homosexuals have a unique problem. They may feel impelled to seek total acceptance by living in loving concern for another human being of the same sex. This does not mean, however, that they have to engage in genital sexual acts or that they are totally without moral obligation.

The Catholic Church passes no moral judgment on persons who feel they have a homosexual orientation; the homosexual orientation, as such, is not sinful. But the Church does apply the same rules of sexual behavior to homosexuals as it does to heterosexuals. Genital sexual acts outside of the heterosexual married state are considered sinful. Because marriage is not a possibility for homosexuals, this principle has the effect of demanding that the homosexual remain celibate and refrain from all genital sexual behavior. The Catholic Church believes it is not the homosexual orientation that is sinful; it is the sexual activity which violates the human moral norms.

It is important to stress that the causes for a person's homosexual orientation are not fully understood. Why a particular person is homosexual cannot yet be explained in any definite way. Genetics, hormones, parental upbringing, cultural factors, and individual experiences are factors that may be significant in particular cases.

Hatred of homosexuals and denial of common civil rights are not morally justified.

All people were saved from a nondivine existence through the coming of the Divine into creation in the person of Jesus, who is the Son of God who expressed himself humanly. Christians believe that Jesus has called all people to share in the Kingdom of God. As St. Paul said in his letter to the Galatian Christians:

> It is through faith that all of you are God's sons in union with Christ Jesus. You were baptized into union with Christ, and now you are clothed, so to speak, with the life of Christ himself. So there is no difference between Jews and Gentiles, between slaves and free men, between men and women; you are all one in union with Christ Jesus.
>
> —Galatians 3:26–28

1. State some reasons why an individual may experience celibacy as a sexual lifestyle.
2. Give two modes of homosexual orientation described in your book.
3. Why does the Catholic Church consider homosexual activity to be morally wrong? Why is a homosexual relationship incomplete?

Summary

- Growth toward mature sexual love is a gradual process that no two persons experience in exactly the same way.
- Circumstances of biological timing, cultural and social conditions, and mental and emotional factors all affect the development of an individual's sexual growth. Speed of physical development and of relationships means nothing in the final analysis of the true sexual relationship called marriage.
- Although the customary direction of human sexual drive is toward the intimate union of a man and a woman in marriage, there are some who choose to adopt another kind of lifestyle.
- Catholics look to the Bible for a religious understanding of human sexuality. They know that the Catholic Church offers its experience and its guidance to help its members grow into mature, sexual love relationships.

Review, Discussion, Research, and Reflection

1. What are the differences between stages one and two in growing into mature, sexual love? Why do these steps seem to be necessary?
2. What do you understand by mature, sexual love?
3. Did you find the descriptions of stage one to be fairly accurate of your own experience? If not, how did your experience differ?
4. What is the purpose of stage two in growth to mature, sexual love? What do you think will probably happen to young men and women who skip or drastically shorten stage two?
5. Can you give three reasons why some young people in certain relationships should interrupt stage two? Give reasons for your answers.
6. What does the Catholic Church offer its members to assist them in their goal of mature sexual love?
7. How does the Catholic Church view the Sacrament of Marriage?
8. In an open forum, discuss whether or not the Catholic Church has an obligation to offer its guidance to its members on all moral questions.
9. Are you aware of any examples of mature, sexual love? If so, describe them.
10. Can mature sexual love be experienced by teenagers? Why? Why not?
11. What is the difference between true homosexuality and other expressions of homosexuality?
12. Do you think homosexuals are discriminated against? Why? Why not? Should they be?

Projects

1. Outline in stages what you would like to experience in your own personal growth towards mature, sexual love. Have you completed any stages? What remains? Do you have any personal criteria that must be met before you move on to another stage? Be specific in describing a scenario that is right for you.
2. Select five television shows depicting married relationships. Do they portray mature, sexual love as it is described in this book? If not, how is it portrayed. Compare the way mature, sexual love is depicted in the shows. Are there any comparisons? Contradictions? Why do you think mature, sexual love is portrayed the way it is?

Words You Should Know

Be sure that you can define the following words and can use them in meaningful sentences:

maturation

celibacy

heterosexual

homosexual

lesbian

adultery

nuclear family

CHRISTIAN MARRIAGE
Chapter 11 Review

Chapter 12

CHRISTIAN MARRIAGE

Complementarity: The Ultimate Expression of Mature Sexual Love

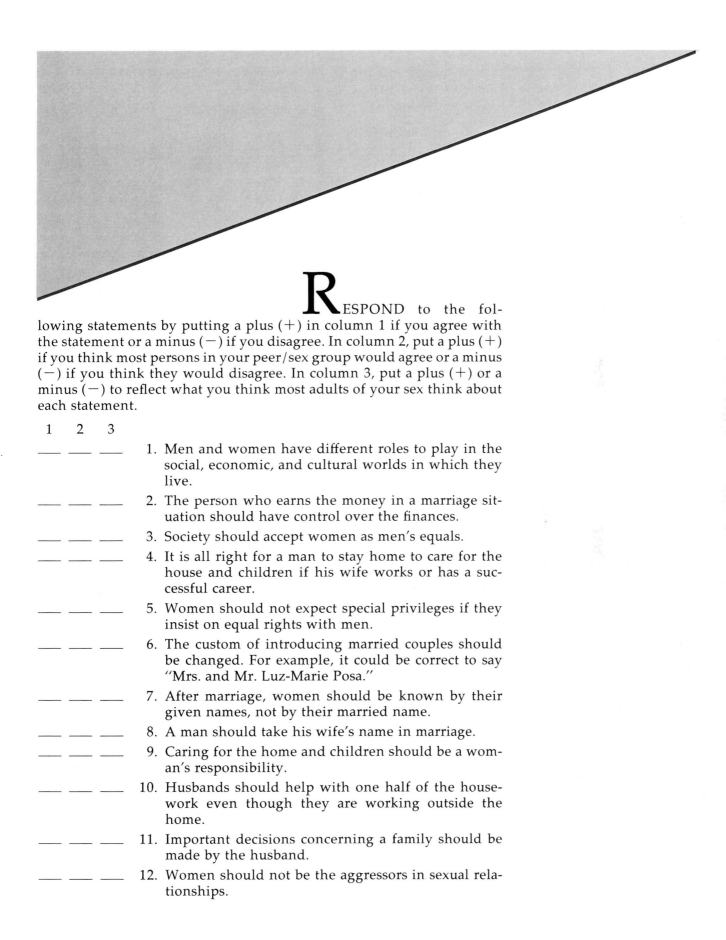

RESPOND to the following statements by putting a plus (+) in column 1 if you agree with the statement or a minus (−) if you disagree. In column 2, put a plus (+) if you think most persons in your peer/sex group would agree or a minus (−) if you think they would disagree. In column 3, put a plus (+) or a minus (−) to reflect what you think most adults of your sex think about each statement.

1 2 3

__ __ __ 1. Men and women have different roles to play in the social, economic, and cultural worlds in which they live.

__ __ __ 2. The person who earns the money in a marriage situation should have control over the finances.

__ __ __ 3. Society should accept women as men's equals.

__ __ __ 4. It is all right for a man to stay home to care for the house and children if his wife works or has a successful career.

__ __ __ 5. Women should not expect special privileges if they insist on equal rights with men.

__ __ __ 6. The custom of introducing married couples should be changed. For example, it could be correct to say "Mrs. and Mr. Luz-Marie Posa."

__ __ __ 7. After marriage, women should be known by their given names, not by their married name.

__ __ __ 8. A man should take his wife's name in marriage.

__ __ __ 9. Caring for the home and children should be a woman's responsibility.

__ __ __ 10. Husbands should help with one half of the housework even though they are working outside the home.

__ __ __ 11. Important decisions concerning a family should be made by the husband.

__ __ __ 12. Women should not be the aggressors in sexual relationships.

___ ___ ___ 13. Women who dress imprudently have no one but themselves to blame if they are raped.

___ ___ ___ 14. Society should be protected from homosexuals.

___ ___ ___ 15. Political office should be held by qualified people regardless of their sex.

___ ___ ___ 16. Girls should pay their own way on a date.

___ ___ ___ 17. It is a woman's responsibility to avoid pregnancy if having a child would pose a severe problem.

___ ___ ___ 18. To develop a truly happy sexual relationship, the partners should do everything together.

___ ___ ___ 19. People who remain single are not sexually fulfilled.

___ ___ ___ 20. Neither men nor women should belong to associations which exclude one or the other from membership.

What Is Complementarity?

Growth toward mature sexual love brings a man and a woman closer to each other as *persons*. When a man and a woman share their deepest emotions, their ideas, and their lives in marriage, each gives to the other something neither one could have alone. They "complete" each other. They complement each other in a way no other kind of human relationship does.

Complementarity in that kind of male/female relationship means that a man and a woman in love have a special kind of relationship. They get along together as persons. They like to be together as persons. They are good friends. Each feels special to and about the other.

True male/female complementarity means not conflict or opposition, not domination and subjugation, not stereotypical roles for either the male or the female, but loving cooperation in whatever tasks face the man and the woman in whatever role best suits the individual in a particular situation. Each adds his or her strengths to the common strengths of both. Together, they promote the true good of the society in which they live.

Sexual Intimacy in Complementarity

The complementarity of men and women is expressed and experienced in all aspects of human living. Nowhere, however, is it so perfectly exemplified as in the acts of love of a man and a woman who truly love each other. Because their bodies, bodily experiences, and emotional responses are different by their gender, a male and female bring somewhat different gifts to one another on a physical basis alone.

But complementarity between the sexes does not consist only in their ability to have a sexual union. It consists in the mutuality of their persons. If the sexual acts are not acts of love but only a means to physical stimulation, sexual union may take place—but they do not express full complementarity. They only express the ability to have sex, physical complementarity.

People who are truly sexually liberated are those who have integrated sex into their total lives. For them, sex is an expression of a special relationship—one part of their total, committed relationship. For them, sex is one expression of their mutual complementarity. For them, a male/female relationship is not based or dependent primarily on sex. It is based primarily on liking/loving each other and on mutual respect for each other as human beings. Even though nonphysical differences between a male and a female may be, in part, socially conditioned and even difficult to name, it is still a reality that a man and a woman tend to be different from one another (usually more than two members of the same sex are). When a man and a woman love each other, especially in marital love, they are loving what is different from themselves, in this sense. They affirm and accept what is "other." They approach agape or unconditional love by this very fact.

Their sex acts are a giving of self to the other. They arise out of the love, respect, friendship, and desire for union that each has for the other. They express their mutuality and their complementarity. They go beyond *self*-satisfying; they are *other*-satisfying.

Complementarity, however, does not mean that two persons must think and act completely alike, or that each loses himself or herself in the totality of the other. It simply means that the more they complement each other, the better their relationship will be.

Complementarity in sexual intercourse is expressed in the acts of love between persons who truly love each other and are committed to each other in marriage.

> Mature sexual love means more than a union of bodies. It means a union of persons. That is why complementarity is the ultimate expression of mature, sexual love.

Complementarity: Completing; existing together so as to complete or make whole.

Married love: The special feeling that exists between a man and a woman who have learned in marriage to really love each other.

1. Describe complementarity in a male/female relationship.
2. What should a true understanding of male/female complementarity include? What should it not include?
3. How does your book say people who are truly sexually liberated treat sex?

Complementarity reaches its highest point and most satisfying expression in the sexual union of a man and a woman committed solely to each other in married love. This is so because human beings have human minds that look for meaning in the actions of people with whom they come in contact.

All of us are alert to signs given by others which tell us whether people are friendly or hostile, respectful or indifferent, reserved or open toward us as individuals. Known as "body language," these signs tell us people's attitudes even when no overt signs are given. We are even more conscious of meaning when the signs are obvious. Words, gestures, facial expressions, and the like tell us of our relationship, and we respond appropriately.

In addition, because we are human, we require signs from people intimating the nature of our relationship with them. The closer the relationship, and the greater the emotional involvement, the more necessary the signs. Someone who purchases a new car, for example, will find a best friend's response and acceptance of it far more important than the response of a neighbor who lives down the street.

Body language: A nonverbal message given with a facial expression or by some movement of an individual's body.

In relationships between men and women, the closer the relationship, the greater the meaning contained in the interpersonal actions. As a male-female relationship moves from friendship to intimacy, the signs of a deepening relationship appear. A handshake changes into a meaningful touch, a kiss changes from a greeting to a message of deepening physical desire, "being with" changes to "being together," and companionship changes to exclusiveness. It is all part of the growth toward mature, sexual love.

For most human beings, the sign of total commitment, of total giving, of total sharing, is sexual intercourse. In the giving of one's body, through which the *whole person* is expressed in nature's most intimate action, a person is giving himself or herself completely. More than that cannot be given.

It is exactly because human beings are human that the physical act of sexual intercourse has more meaning for them. (Sexual intercourse can, of course, also be exploitative, or it can be an expression of something less than its totality. But that is not what is under discussion at the moment.) Sexual intercourse not only makes reproduction possible. It also makes possible the giving and receiving of emotional, intellectual, social, and personal fulfillment that is not possible for one person alone. *In other words, sexual intercourse can be the means whereby sexuality expresses itself in its most profound way.*

Complementarity in Marriage Fulfills Love's Expectations

It is because sexual intercourse has such profound meaning for human beings that it finds its fullest meaning in the totality of committed love which marriage implies. In this way of being and living, the complementarity of married love best fulfills the expectations of human love.

In married love the characteristics and qualities of human love which people long for are present. There is complete trust, total commitment,

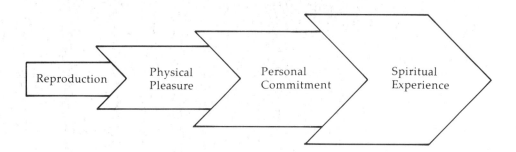

Reproduction → Physical Pleasure → Personal Commitment → Spiritual Experience

perfect fidelity, and the assurance of permanence—qualities that provide a comfort and strength to encourage not only personal growth but a mutual growth of both partners that best fulfills the expectations of human love.

If married love is supposed to fulfill the human expectations for love, why is it that so many people are only moderately happy in their marriages, some are unhappy, and some so unhappy that they seek a divorce? Why is it that some marriages which are supposed to have the potential for extended human happiness produce unhappiness?

The answer lies not in marriage, as such, but in the normal human limitations that are present in any human experience. It also lies in the differing developmental levels of individuals in marriage and in the nature of the relationships of some people who get married.

Some people are unhappy in marriage because they should not have been married in the first place. Some are unhappy because they married before they were ready, while others who get married are "high risk" people—they cannot cope with the marriage experience. Some come from backgrounds which militate against successful marital relationships, and some marry the wrong persons. (In the last instance, it is significant that many persons who fail in the first marriage are "successful" in their second. On the other hand some other people tend to repeat their mistake, again marrying someone unsuitable and incompatible.)

Some people are unhappy in marriage because, as partners, they do not grow together—socially, psychologically, religiously, or educationally. Their marriage becomes strained to the breaking point because of developing differences in outlook, goals, ambitions, desires, and tastes. These differences often result in neglect, indifference, and hostility and turn a potentially creative experience into an endured existence or a very unhappy situation.

Some people are unhappy in marriage because they are success oriented and spend significantly more time and energy on their work than with their partner. They put their careers before their marriage and take their marriage for granted. Some marriages are unhappy because one or the other partner becomes sexually involved with another person, while others simply let their relationship erode.

Because some people are unhappy in a particular marriage experience does not mean that marriage destroys love, as it is sometimes claimed. To have a good marriage—or to be good in anything—takes considerable time and energy. Whether it is being an Olympic gymnast, a football star, or a gourmet cook, a person has to care about it, be committed to it, and **work hard at it** so that he or she can be all that he or she wants to be. This is also true of a good marriage. Marriage by itself does not produce

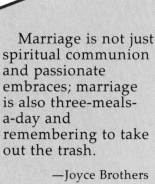

Marriage is not just spiritual communion and passionate embraces; marriage is also three-meals-a-day and remembering to take out the trash.

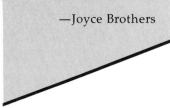

—Joyce Brothers

happiness. It only provides the circumstances for maximizing happiness for those who choose it. And when complementarity exists within the marriage—when there is complete trust, total commitment, perfect fidelity, and the assurance of permanence—it enhances the partners' relationship and fulfills their expectations of human love.

Complementarity in sexual intercourse is expressed in the acts of love between persons who truly love each other and are committed to each other in marriage.

A Christian Understanding of Male/Female Complementarity

Christians understand that God did not create simply to create, like a person idly whittling on a stick that he throws away when something better comes along. *He created to share.*

The whole process of creative evolution was moving to a point brought about by God. Each step in the process led to and produced the next, until people evolved to a point at which creation was ready to be able to share the Divine Life fully. Humanity was the vehicle for the Divine Impregnation of creation, for the Son of God took a human nature, and in so doing, made creation a full sharer in the Divine. For this reason, men and women as sharers of a common humanity, are offered the opportunity to be sharers in the Divine Life according to their limited capacities. Christians understand this to be the ultimate dignity of a human being: each person possesses the offer and potential for Divine Life and each person is called to share the Divine Life forever. As Saint Paul says in his first Epistle to the Corinthians:

"You know that your bodies are parts of the body of Christ. . . . Don't you know that your body is the temple of the Holy Spirit, who lives in you and was given to you by God? You do not belong to yourself but to God; he bought you for a price. So use your bodies for God's glory."
—1 Corinthians 6:15,19–20

In his second Epistle to the Corinthians St. Paul says:

"For we know that when this tent we live in—our body here on earth— is torn down, God will have a house in heaven for us to live in, a home He Himself has made, which will last forever."
—2 Corinthians 5:1

For this reason, Christians believe that each person is sacred.

Christians also believe that love is sacred, for in it and through it each person best expresses what it means to be human. Just as God's love is creative, so is His image of love, the love people have for each other. Through it, they grow to become what they were created to become. The signs that express their special love in marriage are sacred because, like God's love, it produces new life in the environment best suited for life: the married love of a man and a woman who grow together in love. In this love, a man and a woman who are committed in love to each other are most complementary, most nearly suited to become what God ordained. Together they are the image of God.

Christians hope and pray that people will understand that men and women were created by God to be complementary—to learn from each other, to need each other, to be one in mind and heart. They know that if they do, they will cease being in conflict, cease exploitation, cease using bodily gifts and beauties for selfish ends, and use their talents as men and women to create a world in which both can live unafraid of and unembarrassed by their unique sexual natures.

Complementarity's Goal

Complementarity is the goal toward which the sexual nature, sexual drives, and sexual feelings of every human being are impelling them. They are driving them to mutual, respectful cooperation as human beings in promoting the social and spiritual ends of creation.

Whether a particular man or a particular woman expresses his or her sexual nature and sexual drives in married love, in the single state, in the religious life, or in the priesthood, each is complementing all the others in achieving the end God had in mind by creating human beings: sharing His life in love forever. Human beings begin to experience this love when they complement each other in any of several relationships they may experience in their lives.

When they learn to live in love, they will, as the first Epistle of John says:

> ". . . come to know and to believe in the love God has for us. God is love, and he who abides in love abides in God and God in him. Our love is brought to perfection in this, that we should have confidence on the day of judgment; for our relation to this world is just like His."
>
> —1 John 4:16

1. When does complementarity reach its highest point and most satisfying expression?
2. What does your book say sexual intimacy is a sign of for most human beings? What does it make possible?
3. What are the characteristics and qualities of human love in married love? What do they provide?
4. Why are some people unhappy in marriage? Can you think of any other reasons? If so, be prepared to say what they are.
5. What do Christians understand to be the ultimate dignity of a human being?

Summary

- When a man and a woman share emotions, ideas, and their lives, each gives to the other something which neither could have alone. Complementarity in a relationship encompasses all this and more and is essential to achieving mature, sexual love.
- The complementarity of a man and a woman is expressed and experienced in all aspects of human living. Nowhere, however, is it so perfectly exemplified as in the acts of love of a man and a woman who truly love each other.
- When complementarity exists within a marriage, when there is complete trust, total commitment, perfect fidelity, and the assurance of permanence, it enhances the partners' relationship and fulfills their expectations.

Review, Discussion, Research, and Reflection

1. What do you think is the main thrust of the chapter on male/female complementarity? Do you agree or disagree with this thrust? Do your friends agree or disagree?
2. Why does your book claim that sexual intercourse is the ultimate expression of complementarity?
3. In what ways does the treatment of male/female relationships, and especially the treatment of the meaning of sexual intercourse, differ from the treatment of these in the media?
4. Do you believe a couple has to be a certain age to attain complementarity in their relationship? If so, explain your answer. If not, describe what you believe is a good age and explain why.
5. What does your book mean when it says "sexuality is operating in human living even when sex is not"? Do you agree or disagree? Explain your answer.
6. Describe what your book means by "complementarity between the sexes consists in the mutuality of their persons."
7. What does your book mean when it talks about complementarity in sexual intercourse?
8. What does your book mean when it says "sexual intercourse can be the means whereby sexuality expresses itself in its most profound way."

Projects

1. Look up the following passages in your Bible. Keeping in mind the cultural and environmental conditions of the time these were written, discuss what each is saying about male/female complementarity and whether or not what each is saying has any validity in today's cultural situation:

Proverbs 6:20–35	*Ephesians 5:3–7*
Proverbs 31:10–31	*Colossians 3:1–21*
Sirach 26:1–18	*Titus 2:1–7*
Ephesians 4:22–33	*Proverbs 5:20–23*

2. Take some time in the next few days to go off by yourself to think through your own philosophy of sexual behavior for yourself. Pray over your decision, asking the Holy Spirit to guide you. A good place to do this would be in your parish or local church.
3. Some time in the next few days, have a serious discussion with either or both of your parents on a philosophy of sex for yourself.
4. With two or three others, compose a statement of sexual philosophy on which you can generally agree. State any areas of strong disagreement in the final copy. Then, with other groups, compose a statement of sexual philosophy that reflects the feelings of the entire group, again presenting strong minority views.

Words You Should Know

Be sure that you can define the following words and can use them in meaningful sentences:

complementarity
body language
married love

CHRISTIAN MARRIAGE

Chapter
12
Review

Word List

Abortion   The ending, or termination, of a pregnancy before the fetus ordinarily is capable of living on its own. It usually causes or is followed by the death of the fetus.

There are three types: (the third type is a form of the second):

1. **Spontaneous** (miscarriage)   A termination done by nature usually due to some abnormal development of the fetus.

2. **Voluntary**   Pregnancy termination performed by human interference in the pregnancy process.

3. **Therapeutic**   An abortion to save the life of the pregnant woman. Sometimes this term is also used to mean abortion of a genetically defective fetus or an abortion performed because the pregnancy is considered a threat to the health, not the life, of the pregnant woman.

Abstinence   To voluntarily avoid: In sexual connotation, to refrain from sexual intercourse.

Adolescence   The period of life between puberty and adulthood in human development, extending mainly over the teen years.

Adultery   Sexual intercourse by a person who is legally married with someone other than one's mate. The term is sometimes used to describe any sexual intercourse outside marriage.

Agape   The brotherly or spiritual love of one Christian for another, corresponding to the love of God for people. Unconditional love; love not seeking any return.

Aggressive   Imposing either physical or emotional harm upon another human being.

Annulment   A Catholic Church decree that a previous marriage was not a valid marriage in the eyes of the Church. Therefore that person is free to marry with the approval and blessing of the Church.

Artificial insemination   The medical procedure of injecting semen—from the husband, from a sperm bank, or from another donor—into the vagina close to the cervix by artificial means; can enable pregnancy in spite of fertility problems.

Assertive   Expressing what you believe to be right in a positive and respectful manner.

Bisexual   Term commonly used to describe a sexual interest in both sexes.

Body language   A nonverbal message given with a facial expression or some movement of an individual's body.

Celibacy   Voluntarily choosing not to be married nor to engage in sexual intercourse.

Cervix   The neck, or narrow portion, of the uterus or the womb that forms the lower end of the womb and opens into the vagina.

Chastity   Abstention from illicit sexual intercourse; the virtue of living one's sexuality in a manner which is moral according to one's state in life, by which a person chooses to express and/or stay in control of one's sexual desires according to one's vocation.

Circumcision   Surgical removal of the foreskin or prepuce of the penis. Originally, a Jewish rite performed as a sign of reception into their faith; now generally performed for purposes of cleanliness. It is no longer automatically recommended by doctors.

Clitoris   The small, highly sensitive female organ located just above the urethra; the center of sexual pleasure in women.

Coitus   Sexual intercourse between male and female, in which the penis is inserted into the vagina.

Companionship   A fellowship; individuals being frequently in the company of one another.

Compatibility   The ability to exist together in harmony.

Complementarity   Completing a union of persons; as applied to sex, the ultimate expression of mature sexual love; when a man and a woman complement each other in a way no other kind of human relationship can.

Complementary   Completing; existing together so as to complete or make whole.

Complimentary   That which praises, admires, or compliments.

Conception (impregnation)   Penetration of the ovum (female egg cell) by a sperm, resulting in the beginning of a new human life.

Contraception (birth control)   The prevention of conception by use of devices, drugs, or other means before, during, or after sexual intercourse; often called *artificial birth control* or conception control.

Copulate   To connect; to join in sexual union.

Covenant Relationship   When a married couple promise and publicly declare total commitment to each other alone and adopt a way of life which expresses this special relationship.

Dating   A step in the acceptance process leading to the type of relationship that desires intimate union.

Divorce   A judicial declaration dissolving a marriage.

Ejaculation   The expulsion of semen from the penis.

Embryo   The unborn in its earliest stages of development. In humans, the fertilized ovum during the first eight weeks of its growth.

Endometrium   The mucus lining of the uterus, which thickens and fills with blood in preparation for a fertilized ovum.

Erection   The stiffening and enlargement of the penis as a result of blood engorgement in the spongy tissue of the penis, usually during sexual excitement.

Erogenous zone   Any area of the body that is sexually sensitive or stimulating such as mouth, neck, ears, breasts, nipples, and genitals.

Eros   A physical, sexual kind of love.

Erotic   Capable of arousing sexual feeling.

Existentialism   The philosophical doctrine of beliefs that people have absolute freedom of choice.

Extended family   Any relative outside of the immediate family unit; i.e., grandparent, aunt, uncle, cousin, etc.

Fallopian tube   The oviduct that extends from each ovary to the uterus in the female; the place where the sperm and the egg unite (where fertilization takes place).

Fertilization   Conception; when an ovum and a sperm unite in the fallopian tube, resulting in the formation of a new life.

Fetus   In humans, the unborn child from the third month after conception until birth.

Fidelity   In marriage, faithfulness to one's spouse.

Foreplay   The beginning stage of sexual intercourse, during which partners may kiss, caress, and touch each other in ways ordinarily intended to achieve full sexual arousal and lead to sexual intercourse.

Foreskin   Loose skin covering the tip of the penis, removed during circumcision; also called the *prepuce*.

Fornication   Sexual intercourse between an unmarried man and woman.

Genital area   The area of the body where the reproductive or sex glands are located.

Genitalia (genitals; genital organs)   Visible reproductive or sex organs. Usually denotes vagina, vulva, and clitoris in females and the penis and testicles in males.

Glans   The head of the penis, exposed either when the foreskin is pushed back or permanently after circumcision.

Gonorrhea   A contagious, sexually-transmitted disease that may or may not have an inflammation of the genital mucous membrane.

Grace   The action of God in the life of an individual.

Hedonism   The philosophy or doctrine that pleasure or happiness is the highest good.

Herpes II   A contagious, sexually-transmitted disease with symptoms of clustered blisters on the genital organs. There are several kinds of herpes viruses; not all are sexually-transmitted (chicken pox, shingles).

Heterosexual   One who is sexually attracted to or sexually active with persons of the other sex.

Homosexual   One who is sexually attracted to or sexually active with persons of the same sex.

Hormone   A chemical substance produced by an endocrine gland that has a specific effect on the activities of other organs in the body.

Humanism   Any system of thought in which human interests and values are taken to be of primary or even ultimate importance.

Hymen   The membranous tissue that usually partly covers the opening of the vagina in most virgin females.

Immaturity   Not mature; childish or silly.

Impotence   A type of male sexual dysfunction; inability to achieve or maintain erection of the penis during sexual intercourse.

Incorporeal   Nonmaterial.

Infatuation   Attachment by a foolish, unrealistic, idealized, or unreasoning passion, many times mistaken for love.

Infidelity   Being unfaithful to one's spouse.

Interracial   For, between, or among people of different races.

In vitro fertilization   The uniting of the ovum and the sperm outside of the woman's body.

Labor   In childbirth, the contractions of the muscles of the uterus that first dilate the cervix, then, with the help of the abdominal muscles, push the baby through the cervix and on through the birth canal into the world.

Lesbian   A female homosexual.

Libido   Sex drive.

Married love   That special feeling that exists between a man and a woman who have learned, in marriage, to truly love each other.

Masturbation   Self-stimulation of one's sex organs, often to the point of orgasm.

Materialism   A philosophical theory where there is excessive emphasis on material objects and needs and a disinterest in spiritual values.

Maturation   The act or process of maturing; growing.

Mature sexual love   Love that has grown and developed through the curiosity and experimental stages, and through the early stages of tenderness and care into an unselfish commitment to another person's total welfare.

Menarche   The beginning of the menstrual cycle in a girl.

Menopause (change of life; climacteric)   The end of menstruation in women, usually between the ages of forty-five and fifty-five.

Menstrual cycle   The whole process of menstruation for one complete time; the length of time from when a woman begins to menstruate one month to the next time she menstruates.

Menstruation   The discharge of blood from the uterus through the vagina that usually occurs at four-week intervals in women between the ages of puberty and menopause. Sometimes called "having a period."

Miscarriage (spontaneous abortion)   The early, but natural, expulsion of the embryo or fetus from the pregnant woman before it is mature enough to survive, often due to some abnormal development of the embryo or fetus.

Mittelschmerz   The slight twinge or pain a woman may experience in her pelvic region when she ovulates.

Moral conviction   The belief that one's values are right.

Morality   Ethical decisions about the best way to be fully human; choosing one's values in life and living by them or violating them.

Natural family planning   Methods of birth control based on the avoidance of intercourse during a woman's fertile time.

Nocturnal emission (wet dream)   Involuntary male erection and ejaculation during sleep.

Orgasm   The peak, or climax, of excitement during sexual activity.

Ovaries   The two female sex glands found on either side of the uterus, in which the ova (egg cells) are formed. They also produce hormones which influence female body characteristics.

Ovulation   Release of the mature (ripe) ovum from the ovary to one of the fallopian tubes.

Ovum (plural: ova)   Female reproductive cell (egg) found in the ovary. After fertilization by a male sperm, the human zygote or fertilized egg develops into an embryo and then a fetus.

Peer group   Individuals of one's own age and interests.

Penis   The male organ for urination and copulation, including ejaculation.

Personality   The physical, mental, emotional, and social characteristics of an individual.

Philia   A special kind of love, affection, and attachment that is found in good friends.

Philosophy   A set of principles by which a person guides his or her life.

Pituitary gland   A gland located at the base of the brain that is responsible for the proper functioning of all other glands, especially the sex glands.

Placenta   A thick disk-shaped collection of blood vessels and tissues growing on the inner walls of the uterus, which provides for the nourishment of the fetus and for the elimination of waste products; expelled from the uterus after the birth of a child (afterbirth).

Pornography   Literature, motion pictures, art, or other means of expression which, without any concern for personal or moral values, intend simply to cause sexual stimulation.

Pregnancy   The period from conception to birth; the condition of having a developing embryo or fetus within the female body.

Procreation   The producing of offspring.

Promiscuous   Engaging in sexual intercourse with multiple persons and without commitment; engaging in casual sexual relationships.

Prophylactic   A device or drug used to prevent disease, often specifically venereal disease, and to prevent conception. Common term for the condom.

Prostate   Male gland which surrounds the urethra and neck of the bladder and secretes part of the seminal fluid.

Puberty   The stage of life at which a young man's or a young woman's reproductive organs become functionally operative and the secondary sex characteristics develop.

Pubic   Regarding the lower part of the abdominal area, where hair grows in a triangular patch.

Rape   Forcible sexual intercourse with a person who does not consent. *Statutory rape* means having intercourse with a consenting minor who is under the legal age for intercourse in that state.

Religious self   The part of a person that is spirit; which makes one aware of God's divine presence in one's life and enables one to relate to God directly.

Romantic love   Idealized love or infatuation.

Sacrament   Official act of the Church which signifies God's special action in the life of the person or persons receiving the sacrament.

Safe period   The interval in the menstrual cycle when the female is presumably not ovulating and therefore unable to become pregnant.

Scrotum   The sac or pouch suspended from the groin of a male that contains the testicles and their accessory organs.

Secondary sexual characteristics   The physical characteristics—other than the external sex organs—that distinguish a male from a female.

Selective state   The second stage of growth toward mature sexual love when an individual learns how to relate to a *particular* person of the opposite sex.

Self-direction   Setting goals for one's life.

Self-discipline   Living each day in a way that will get one to his or her goals.

Semen (seminal fluid: seminal emission)   The fluid made up of sperm, secretions from the seminal vesicles, prostate and Cowper's glands, and the epididymis. Ejaculated through the penis when the male reaches orgasm.

Seminal vesicles   Two storage pouches for sperm (which is produced in the testicles). Located on either side of the prostate, they are attached to and open into the sperm ducts.

Sex   Either the male or female gender of a species; also sexual intercourse, sexual activity, sexual attractiveness, and its appeal.

Sexual drives   Natural forces impelling a person to sexual activity.

Sexual dysfunction   Term used to describe problems in sexual performance.

Sexual feelings   The emotional and bodily sensations associated with sexual activity.

Sexual identity   One's gender or else the way an individual identifies with a particular sex.

Sexuality   The way individuals express themselves in their role as a male or female.

Sperm   The male reproductive cell that is capable of fertilizing the female egg and causing impregnation of the egg.

Sterility   The inability to reproduce.

Sterilization   A procedure (usually surgical) by which a male or female is rendered unable to produce children, but can still engage in sexual intercourse.

Storge   A strong, natural affection found among family members who love and respect each other. A Greek word.

Syphilis   One of the most serious sexually transmitted diseases.

Testicle (testes)   The male sex gland which produces sperm.

Toxic shock syndrome   A disease sometimes caused by the use of tampons in women. Staph germs multiply in the vagina and produce a toxin that is then absorbed into the blood stream.

Transgenderist   A person who identifies very strongly with the other sex and may dress in clothing of that sex.

Transsexual   One who feels psychologically like a member of the other sex, and perhaps even undergos "sex change" surgery to achieve the outward appearance of the other sex.

Transvestite   One who has a compulsion to dress in clothing of the other sex; "cross vest."

Umbilical cord   A flexible structure connecting the fetus and the placenta; naval cord.

Unconditional love   Love without conditions; agape; God-like love.

Urethra   The duct through which urine passes from the bladder and is excreted from the body.

Uterus   The small, muscular, pear-shaped female organ in which the fetus develops; it has the ability to expand and accommodate the growing child/children.

Vagina   The canal in the female, extending from the vulva to the cervix, that receives the penis during sexual intercourse and through which a baby passes at birth.

Values   What one considers important.

Vas deferens   The ducts in males leading from the epididymis to the seminal vesicles and the urethra.

Venereal disease (VD)   Any number of sexually-transmitted diseases that are highly contagious.

Virgin   A person who has never had sexual intercourse.

Vocation   A call from God to follow a particular way of life.

Vulva   The female's external sex organs, including the labia majora and labia minora, the outer and inner folds of skin (lips) surrounding the vagina.

Zygote   The fertilized egg.

Index

225